CW01425645

BEFORE

THE AREA MANAGER'S DIARY

THE PREQUEL

By John Heaton

To the railway staff who helped me during my railway career.

To my wife Linda for her encouragement and my daughter Amy for being there.

To the following photographers for their generous donations of photographs used in this volume and in the other 'Diaries'.

David Hunt
Colin Marsden
Peter Medley
David Mitchell
Roger Penny

All the photographs in this volume are from the author's collection unless otherwise attributed. As you will see, my photos have been chosen on the grounds of quantity rather than quality but they have been chosen to illustrate the geography and railway business of their time.

No. 40085 passes Picton signalbox, between Yarm and Northallerton, with the 17.05 Tees Yard to Healey Mills Class 7 freight on May 17, 1982

Credit:

C.J. Marsden

PREFACE

This volume of recollections is what modern television producers would term a 'prequel'. After a discreet length of time, which some might call 'undue delay', I converted the diaries I wrote as Area Manager with British Rail at Exeter into a narrative running to four volumes. A number of readers (more than one!) suggested that they might be at least vaguely interested in what I had been up to before I came to Exeter and, indeed, even in the couple of years there when a diary had not been produced.

Initially, I declined the idea, later shelved it, and ultimately decided it would not be appropriate but the Great Coronavirus

Lockdown of 2020 changed my mind. After completing a dozen or so tasks that had been waiting, even in retirement, for some spare time, I thought I might have a go at recording the earlier days. The four diary books had been numbered 1-4 so, in the modern fashion of numbering extra platforms built at railway stations, without renumbering all the pre-existing ones, I guess this volume should be numbered 0 but I will resist the temptation, as the intended humour might not be fully understood. 'Volume 5' would imply a time order and that is not the case. I feel it probably reads better after the 'proper diaries' so 'Prequel' it is.

The reluctance to marshal it in line with the others is based chiefly on the fact that it relies on memory and not on documents written at the time, which I tried hard to faithfully reproduce without editing or airbrushing in the other books. I realised that my memory had not been as accurate as I thought it was when writing up those notes. There were even forgotten incidents recorded that I enjoyed, it seemed, for the first time. Oh yes, please forgive the shorthand of referring to locos by class numbers before the new numbering system had been devised.

In this volume I have tried to recall incidents during which I learnt lessons that I subsequently tried to avoid repeating - ones which amount to experience to apply to new problems. As such I have not written the book in strictly chronological order which might have risked losing readers' attention in many years of routine before gaining real responsibility. That is not to say there were no lessons learnt in those formative years though. I apologise for the normal use of male version of nouns and pronouns in most of the book. It does not presuppose any bias on my part, as it grates with me to do it, but that is how it usually was back then.

The episodes will come mainly from memory but I filed away some documents on which I intend to draw freely, mostly projects and inquiries with which I was involved, including the opening chapter.

To assist the reader in placing the events in the correct career timescale, I shall start with a synopsis of 'where and when'.

BACKGROUND

I left school aged 18 in 1968 with 9 "O" Levels and 4 "A" Levels with a Bachelor of Education course place at the College of the Venerable Bede, Durham.

Chose instead to join the 'Railway Studentship Scheme' on the Leeds Division of British Rail's Eastern Region from 1968 to 1970, based on learning the industry by spending time actually doing some of the jobs, not just watching. Some might say teaching's gain was the railways' loss.

1970 Project team in Chief Operating Manager's Office Eastern Region H.Q. at York.
1971 Route availability for 8ft 6in container clearances and heavy axle-weight vehicles. Writing briefs for senior operating officers to use at investment meetings. Married Linda that May. I was 21, she was 18½. Took on a mortgage.
1972 Operational Finance projects. Reviewing depot establishments etc.
1973 Investment Appraisal work in Regional Finance Manager's Office, York.
1974 Post-Graduate Traffic Management accelerated promotion scheme based on the Doncaster Division.
1976 Traffic Manager, assistant to Area Manager Bradford responsible for Skipton (exclusive) to Apperley Jct, Ilkley and Bradford Forster Square.
1978 Senior Operating Supervisor, Neville Hill Depot, Leeds. 3 shifts.
1979 Area Freight Assistant, Tees Yard. 3-shifts, responsible for all aspects of freight operation on the Middlesbrough Area Manager's patch.
1980 Area Operations Manager, Middlesbrough (2nd in command to A.M.)
1982 Passenger Operations Manager Newcastle Division. Assistant to the Divisional Operating Manager. On call for serious incidents Saltburn/Boulby to Wetheral (nr. Carlisle) and Northallerton to Berwick-on-Tweed.

1983 Area Manager Exeter St. David's, responsible for Ivybridge/Paignton-Castle Cary (exclusive)-Dorchester West. Sherborne to Barnstaple and branches. 965 staff on appointment.

In the meantime I used part time day release (with a lot of evening classes!) and correspondence courses to gain a distinction in Higher National Certificate in Business Studies, Corporate Membership of the Chartered Institute of Transport (subsequently Fellowship), Yorkshire Section prize winner. I also did railway courses in Train Signalling (preliminary, intermediate, advanced) 'Inspectors' Block', Movements Planning & Operation, Passenger Station Work & Accounts and Parcel Station Work & Accounts.

1. NIGHT CALL AT NEWCASTLE

It was about 03.00 on Sunday morning, 6th February 1983, when the persistent beckoning of the telephone awoke me from the deep sleep I used to experience in those days. This could only be bad news. The area inspectors took the routine calls, the area on call manager helped out the inspectors for more serious incidents and, as the divisional on call officer, I would be summoned only to major mishaps.

I was probably not the only one who used to feel disoriented after running downstairs in these pre-mobile or even 'portable' days and trying to take in the information being supplied by the divisional control shift manager, confusingly to outsiders, termed the 'deputy chief controller'. Deputy Dawg, as the on call team sometimes termed the occasional one who woke you to let you know something that could have waited until morning, had of course been on duty all night and was probably on a caffeine high. He, as it was in Newcastle in 1983, would gabble a 'fileful' of information at you in a few seconds and then pause to await your reaction. He no doubt had a bank of phones all ringing at once demanding his attention and you would be testing his patience by asking him to repeat himself, perhaps even twice.

This time it was neither a false alarm nor over caution. In the early hours planned engineering work had required a midnight Sunday morning crew to run train 9T18 Tyne Yard to a work site at How Mill on the Carlisle line. It was formed of four vehicles including a permanent way department railway 10-tonne crane No. DRG 81312, one that outwardly looked similar to what many readers might associate with re-railing operations after a mishap. The formation was Class 31 loco, mess van, crane-jib under-runner, crane, brake van, 104 trailing tonnes.

The train was just over a mile west of Hexham at mileage 22m 15ch when the leading wheels of the crane jumped the down line track towards the 'six-foot', the gap between up and down lines. Before the train crew had identified the problem and taken appropriate action to protect movements on the opposite line from the derailment, a diverted sleeping car train passed on the up line, within a hairsbreadth of the derailed crane's jib taking the off side out of the train.

The difference in response between the incident that could have occurred and what actually happened was immeasurable; we could easily have been looking at many deaths. But the way of the railway accident investigation is that such incidents must be treated in just the same fashion as ones with more injuries because, there but for the grace of God and a few extra inches of metal, go human lives. The watchwords of an Inquiry must be 'Define the Cause' and 'Prevent a Repetition'. You might not be so lucky if there is a next time. Issues such as blame and disciplinary action might follow on but both are no higher than secondary considerations to the Inquiry Panel.

It was only a couple of minutes from my house to the A1(M) outside Durham, then taking the A69 to Hexham. I remember little of the drive which was probably spent running through everything I needed to check. The last time I had been called by Deputy Dawg it was to say a sleeping car had been detached from a down overnight train at Belford and it was 'nearly off the road'. I think I told him to call me back if and when it was actually off the road. This had not been one such call though.

The derailment site was about a quarter-mile west of the location where the former Border Counties' Railway to Riccarton Jct had left the Newcastle-Carlisle route. I probably reached there about 04.00, the scene still in darkness that February morning. The Newcastle area supervisor on call was in charge of protection but assurances, or personal checks, that this had been done were my first priority. He was in the process of introducing single line working over the up line from 04.45 until 10.55 when normal working was resumed. Site management and recovery were area responsibilities, in view of there being no casualties, so I concentrated on determination of the cause. The first job was to identify who was in charge on behalf of the civil engineer, and his mechanical engineering colleague, which is less easy for a divisional on call manager than area staff who know everyone locally.

There were many factors to determine but most would have to wait for daylight when detailed evidence such as a detailed geometric track survey (or 'plot') could be taken. There were no obvious causes, for instance a broken rail or axle. The same went for a loco speedometer check and corroboration of signal box running times to determine the speed. Much emphasis has historically been placed on this kind of information but I have always been more than sceptical. Difference of signal box clocks, train register times booked from memory and short distances between time readings militate against accuracy. If longer distances are taken an average speed is unlikely to prove what speed was being done at a given point. 10 miles in 10min is 60mph of course. If it was actually 8 or 12min by each signal box being 1min out either way the speed becomes 50-75mph. If the limit was actually 60mph then most trains could have easily accelerated from 50 to 75mph in 10 miles and indeed some to 100mph. Anyway, the maximum permissible speed for 9T18's crane was 45mph and there was no evidence to suggest it had been doing any more than that.

The Inquiry took place in the Newcastle Divisional Offices, sited above the portico of Central Station, on the following Wednesday. I was in the chair assisted by two engineers. The first was Derek Reeves, an ex-premium apprentice at Darlington, I believe. One could not have asked for better support both technically and in his approach. I sometimes travelled to work with him, if he chose not to drive the dmu. He was one of those people from whom you can learn so much just by listening to what he has to say. The second was Newcastle area civil engineer Peter Rafter whom I knew far less well. One of the two trade union observers was W. H.

Ronkersley of the drivers' union ASLEF, who usually had strong opinions.

It had been 02.23 on that dark Sunday morning in torrential rain interrupted only by sleet showers. This was the weather that must have thoroughly depressed the Roman soldiers on nearby Hadrian's wall nearly two millennia earlier. As 9T18 passed over Spital occupation crossing its guard heard a loud bang, applied the hand brake and exhibited a red danger signal to the driver from his handlamp. The double-manned crew on the Class 31 loco felt a 'retarding motion', looked back, saw sparks from the brake van and halted the train. As the driver and guard examined the up line the up sleeping car express approached but attempts to stop it failed. Fortunately, it passed clear.

The loco was detached and taken forward 1½ miles to Warden signal box to report the derailment while the guard went back to afford full detonator protection. The area traffic manager was called at 02.40, meeting the driver at Warden and proceeding on the loco to the derailment. The rolling stock engineer was summoned by Control, undertaking an examination of the derailed crane and then in daylight after it had been rerailed and moved cautiously to Hexham. The permanent way section supervisor had been at Brampton Fell, having taken possession of both lines there after the passage of the up sleeper. Hearing of the derailment he went directly to its site. Over the next two days a permanent way senior technical officer then carried out a detailed survey of track conditions.

Problems had been experienced starting the crane when its driver checked it at Tyne Yard, resulting in an hour's delay while it was fixed by the duty fitter. The unusual step was taken of proceeding to the engineering work with the crane engine running, albeit in neutral gear. A few signal checks had been experienced en route including a short stop at Prudhoe. The late running might have suggested a reason for making up time but this was not an express passenger train and no need for urgency had been discussed. The loco speedometer was reading accurately although the driver, perhaps somewhat strangely, remarked that there was a dark patch on the dial above 45mph.

Examination of the crane revealed that it had been the lightest loaded wheel that had derailed first, crossing the rail top towards the up line. We can all be thankful that the crane jib remained secure. It was leading, so disaster would have ensued had it fouled the up line. However, the coupling between the crane and its 'runner' vehicle (below the jib) became severed during the accident. All axle-boxes had been cold when inspected about an hour after the derailment.

The track condition plot showed that any irregularities were within official tolerances. For instance, the greatest deficiency was a 1-in-239 underload 17metres in rear of the derailment whereas the figure of 1-in-180 is normally accepted as being likely to initiate a derailment. However, 1-in-240 would normally receive corrective action. The gauge was 4mm wide at the point of derailment which was within tolerance.

So here we had a situation where a derailment had occurred to a vehicle without defects, on track within tolerances, at a speed apparently no higher than authorised. Who would accept responsibility? With two exceptions I have never experienced reticence within British Rail for the appropriate department to shoulder blame. As the operator, I looked to my engineers. We reviewed the evidence for factors we might have missed.

Was the fact the crane's engine was running in neutral gear an issue? Was it coincidence the process seemed to start at the user-worked crossing? Was it significant that the screw couplings used between the wagons were slack - not wound tightly? Hmmm. The rolling stock engineer believed that the slack coupling would have meant a lack of restraint against any tendency of the crane to 'hunt' (shake from side to side) following a build up of oscillation. The guard had said the permanent way staff form up the trains and prepare them like that but they prefer tight screw couplings only for twin-jib cranes. The loco to mess van coupling was quite tight but the runner to the crane was very slack. The others were tightened by just two or three turns. The rolling stock engineer's opinion was that the wheel unloading was caused by a mixture of vertical and lateral forces combining at a critical speed. It was pointed out that the two bogies of the crane had a centre-to centre distance of only 10ft, in fact a very short wheel base for a bogie vehicle.

My mind turned to the 1967 Thirsk derailment of the cement tanks into the path of experimental loco DP2 working a down express. The causes of plain line derailments had been exercising minds for years, without entirely satisfactory answers, but it was thought that tight couplings were preferable – a sort of fixed formation with buffer-to-buffer contact to stop the rear of the train 'wagging' to a state of derailment. I did not refer to the Thirsk Inquiry at the time but a preference for tight couplings formed part of the recommendations and the figures concerning cross levels were also in line with my advice on the crane derailment. Anecdotal evidence suggested that the tightly coupled afternoon fish empties from King's Cross sometimes managed to find itself checked by the preceding 'Talisman' express. We were into the territory of Derby Research scientists. Although this crane was not a common type of vehicle speeding up and down main lines amongst express passenger trains we had been very lucky in avoiding tragedy and action was imperative.

Just one track measurement at a single location had been on the borderline of needing attention. The crane was in good condition. The speed was accepted as being within the maximum allowed – the loco driver said 43mph (although cynics might say that 'he would say that'!). Should I suggest a change to track standards throughout the network? Should we scrap all similar cranes? In terms of pure logic the answer seemed simple. The somewhat arbitrary speed set for the crane was too high. If this and all other similar cranes had to be reduced in speed it was not a significant problem. I was reminded only when writing this account that the speed of loaded 'Cemflo' wagons of the type derailed at Thirsk had been reduced from 45mph to 35mph after the Inquiry.

As ever with Inquiries, a number of other irregularities emerged which had no bearing on the accident but could have been pivotal if the consequences had been more serious. The Tyne Yard driver had started his footplate career four years before I had been born. Nevertheless, it was my job to ask questions.

Question: Did you attempt to stop the oncoming passenger train by using your Bardic handlamp?
Answer: I was carrying a private lamp. I did not have my Bardic with me.
Question: Did you provide detonator protection for your train?
Answer: I should have left detonators in front of my train when I took the loco to Warden box.
Question: Did you place a track circuit clip on the opposite line?
Answer: No but I found it was clear.

The first reaction should be to put a track circuit clip on the opposite line, not to spend even a moment deciding whether the opposite line is track circuited and whether the clip will do any good or not. Regarding detonator protection in advance of the derailed train, admittedly the driver knew where his train was but it was a dark, sleety night and sillier things have happened than getting its location wrong when assisting. As for the Bardic hand lamp with its multi-coloured lenses not being used....if the side of the sleepers had been torn asunder by the crane jib because its driver had not seen a red handsignal....even if the speed had simply not been reduced as much as possible on impact...who knows what the consequences would have been, including the driver's mental health, job security and even legal repercussions. The driver acting as secondman was even more experienced and did even less. He was still on the loco when the sleeper passed instead of making his way towards it with a red light, doing little for the arguments for retention of double manning. In contrast, second man Smith on DP2 had grabbed emergency detonators and wedged himself in the loco doorway he had opened to prevent it being wedged closed by the inevitable collision and enabling him to dive out to protect the opposite line, should he survive the impact.

Back at the site of the crane derailment, the guard went back to protect his train but did not place the most distant detonators at the right place. He should have kept walking back towards Newcastle until he could make contact with the signalman at the protecting box. He unsuccessfully tried to phone from Tyne Green crossing but the guard realised Hexham box was switched out, meaning he might need to walk an extra 2½miles from Hexham to Dilston taking perhaps another hour even after reaching his full protection distance. Was the rule a reasonable expectation? Even if the sleeper train had been wrecked, the instruction would have been the same.

The template for Joint (i.e. inter-departmental) Inquiry reports was strict. The conclusion should be clear and concise. Recommendations should be in a covering letter. With a heavy heart I wrote that *the derailment occurred as a result of the interaction of the factors of speed/track on crane DRF 81312, running with slack screw couplings. The precise nature of the interaction cannot be ascertained with the knowledge currently available.*

I am not sure I would have signed off to this if I had been my boss. It was concise enough but imprecise. The accompanying recommendation was that the crane should be tested with a view to reducing its permitted speed.

In that mercurial way British Rail worked, on good days, off the crane went to Derby Research and back came a comprehensive response from the well-respected Ian Duncan,

Head of Field Trials, saying that investigations had confirmed that the riding characteristics of this type of crane were unsatisfactory at speeds above 35mph, recommending a limit of 30mph should be applied forthwith. By this time I was working at Exeter but an uncharacteristically complimentary letter from the normally gruff Derek Jenkinson arrived in the post. A cynical, unkind voice in my head suggested perhaps Derby Research were not that sure either but had no more satisfactory answer than this. But, as we will see later, they always had my confidence.

2. THE DRUNK and THE DISORDERLY?

High-pitched children's voices punctuated street games in the cul-de-sac of our home on the outskirts of Middlesbrough. Yes, the town does have some leafy suburbs even if they are populated at weekends by energetic kids. My wife Linda and I were preparing to enjoy a leisurely Saturday evening in the summer of 1981 when the phone rang. It was the on call supervisor George McVay. If I had to select someone with whom I worked as having the most knowledge of fundamental railway operating – signalling, booking offices, rostering, you name it, it would be George. He was an ex-station master of the 1950s, now approaching retirement.

Tees Yard guard Calman (alias) had been booked on duty at 17.11 to work the 17.52 dmu from Middlesbrough to Newcastle. Station supervisor Teasdale had been alerted to the guard's behaviour by a passenger and told supervisor Wood, who was just taking over from him, about the problem. British Transport police constable Bird had been called and both he and the supervisor had concluded Calman was unfit for duty owing to alcohol or drugs. P.C. Bird had decided to recommend prosecution under the Regulation of Railways Act 1842, Section 17.

I do not really understand why George needed to phone the area operations manager but he would have had his reasons. He had probably seen incidents like this escalate in the past and wanted someone of management grade to support the supervisors. No problem.

On reaching the supervisor's office I was reassured to hear the train working had been covered. Supervisor Wood said that when he encountered Calman the guard was waving his arms around directing passengers. Calman admitted to having drunk four pints of beer at lunchtime but nothing since then (!). He said that if his competence was being challenged he did not want to work his train (!!). I took him into an unoccupied office and concluded that his speech was voluble, rapid and

17

emotional. His eyes were red and glazed, shedding tears at one point. He said he could not be bothered with the formalities and he would just resign and re-apply to the London Midland Region. Presumably he thought references would not be sought. He again admitted to consuming his four pint lunch but said he had only agreed not to work his train because other people had doubted his capability. I suggested that part of his condition was over-estimating his own abilities and that a supervisor and police officer believed he was drunk.

This was before the days of independent drink and drugs tests so I told him I considered him unfit for duty owing to intoxication. He should take the weekend to reflect on his position and attend the area manager's office at 09.30 on his next turn of duty which was Tuesday. His rostered work - chiefly the 6K97 Lackenby to Hartlepool steel train - would be covered.

By now he was much calmer than he had originally been. I explained it was now my duty to take him safely home. In an apparently genuine way, he thanked me but asked that instead of taking him to his house in Whinney Banks, would I mind dropping him at a certain pub in Thornaby? Whinney Banks it was.

Life in Middlesbrough had too many such episodes, not necessarily the result of drink. When I was shift manager for the Middlesbrough area, located in the TOPS office on the first floor of an administrative block in Tees Yard, one Saturday morning, I leaned back in my chair for a few minutes' reflection. The shift was nearly over and all we needed was a few wagons on an inbound freight from Tyne Yard to be shunted into formation for weekend engineering work. In my eye corner I registered some movement on the up main line which separated the office first from the main road, and then the horse racing track. Did my eyes deceive me or was that a youth riding a motor scooter between the rails and along the sleepers of the main line track? Not only was he riding an entirely unauthorised vehicle, he was performing a move in the wrong direction in breach of signalling regulations. By now the whole office was hooting derision but I was the senior person on duty. I phoned Tees Yard box with the Message 'Obstruction Danger up and down main lines between Middlesbrough and Thornaby stations'. The signalman was clearly taken aback as he had no trains on his display at the time. "There's an idiot on a scooter heading towards Middlesbrough on the up main line," I hurriedly explained, grabbing my car keys, running down the stairs and then driving the half mile or so in the opposite direction from the scooter to the yard exit. The road ran parallel to the line for a long way. The scooter driver was making slow progress because of the rough ride so I managed to overtake him before the road and railway diverged before Newport East Junction. Trying my best imitation of a traffic cop I stood in his way with 'stop' handsignals in the traditions of police point duty rather than Section C of the then Rule Book . He drew up looking more annoyed than alarmed. When I asked what he thought he was doing riding on the railway line and lectured him on how dangerous it was he calmly replied, "The bike's not taxed so I can't ride it on the road."

I cannot remember whether the telecommunications of the time enabled me to have him arrested or I was just too astonished.

Even the most routine tasks could have their complication. I appointed the best of a bunch of promising teenagers to a booking boy job at Billingham signal box. He had shown up well in written tests and at interview. He was a quiet lad but confident enough to do the job. But as soon as he started work he caused nothing but trouble, being late, failing for duty altogether, disobeying the signalman. The final straw was when he came to work one day with green hair and refused to change the colour to one which might not mislead drivers of approaching trains. His probationary period came quickly if jerkily to an end despite the pleas of concerned but obviously desperate parents. Had they encountered an older and more sympathetic manager with teenage children of his own they might have had a more sympathetic hearing.

3. SIGNAL BOXES

In this chapter I intend to cherry-pick a few issues involving signalmen and signalboxes, taken out of their chronological order.

As I was saying, Middlesbrough, all Teesside really, had too many incidents like 'scooter boy'. When I was area operations manager I still made a few signal box visits. Keeping the standard of two visits a week, independent of payday deliveries, some of which had to be 'out-of-hours', was the routine job of the supervisors (traffic managers) and area signalling inspectors. I think it was once a week to crossing keeper locations. My job involved taking an overview that standards were being maintained but it also meant I could actually communicate directly with the often remote signalling staff. The trouble was that a handful of visits on the Whitby line would take all day. Once you had done one visit you were unlikely to find any irregularities at neighbouring boxes because there was an unofficial bell signal sent when a signaller saw a supervisory uniform, black mackintosh or management suit approaching.

It was never my way to try to creep up on signalling staff. If approach visibility was limited I would scuff the ballast and tread heavily on the stairs. I expected signalling to be 100% correct when I was there because I knew standards would fall when no one was watching. If they fell from 100% it would probably still be safe but if signalling staff could not do it right when I was there, what would happen afterwards? Sometimes I would see the signaller reach towards the block instrument shelf to 'bell' my presence on to his or her colleagues. Sometimes, if I was feeling mischievous, and usually only if I knew the member of staff could take a joke I would peruse the train register book. I would say something to the effect of, "That bell signal you sent just now, there is no entry for it in the book."

I sometimes paused to wonder if my opinion of potentially slack working was justified? The context was set by my training placements, sometimes for a full shift. The resident signaller would ring up his signalling neighbours and say, "We're working 'straight up' today". 'Regular irregularities' included failing to send the one beat 'call attention' before sending '2 pause 1' - train out of section. This was called 'knocking out' which meant your colleague did not have to rise from his reading (be it picking a winner at Sandown Park or a Tolstoy novel). I did not mind doing it so why should they? Although the answer is obvious, events could provide the reasons I was seeking.

It was a routine day in the office so I took the opportunity to jump into a spare railway car and make a couple of signal box visits. Nunthorpe looked like a decent trip and I could probably have half an hour at home for lunch. The signalbox was located on a busy road through a village that had become an outer suburb of Middlesbrough. It was served by the basic Whitby line timetable with a few peak extras turning back there, just under five miles from Middlesbrough, the line joining the Saltburn-Darlington route at Guisborough Jct just under half a mile out of town. A new station had been opened at Gypsy Lane adjacent to Marton Lane open level crossing in 1976. The signalling was absolute block on the double line from Guisborough Jct then electric token on the single line forward to Battersby.

I parked the car close to the box, and visible from it, and trod heavily on the steps. Entering the box there was no one there. The block indicator was at train' on line' and the train register confirmed a train was in section. The home signal was at danger and the train had not been signalled forward. Now what should I do? Assuming that in broad daylight on the busy street of a village there was no likelihood of alien abduction I had to decide what to do when the train arrived. Should I assume that normal conditions applied and signal it myself or might her absence might have been caused by some unforeseen safety factor about which I was unaware. As the train approached, a car drew up, the signaller opened the door and came up the steps, registering her surprise to see me standing there. She dealt with the train and I asked for an explanation. She did not seem unduly concerned as she said she had just been to fill up her car at the local petrol station. I was flabbergasted and rang the area inspector to come to Nunthorpe and arrange for someone to work the box until 14.00. I sent the signaller home and told her to report to my office at 09.00 the following morning.

A B.R. Merrymaker railtour hauled by Deltic No. 55002 'King's Own Yorkshire Light Infantry' passes Gypsy Lane station on the Middlesbrough-Whitby branch in August 1980.

The Signalmen's General Instructions P.112 'Signalman Leaving His Box' had not been applied. If there had been an incident at the level crossing there would have been no one to answer an emergency call. If 'Obstruction Danger' had been sent there would have been no one to respond. If anyone had chosen to enter the box, tampering with the equipment could have occurred. Looked at from a more lenient angle, there were plenty of opportunities at a box like Nunthorpe to go for some petrol without a train on the block.

The outcome of the disciplinary hearing was that the signaller was taken out of her post and accommodated in a vacancy on Redcar station platform, close to her home. I believed this was appropriate on the merits of the case but it also served to show other staff where the line had been drawn. My area manager, to whom I was deputy, had known the person involved for many years. "Will she be out of the box for long?" he asked. "As long as I am operations manager at least," I replied, more than a little affronted by what I took to be scarcely veiled criticism.

My Middlesbrough days were afflicted by similar incidents. I found a higher proportion of irregularities in my spot-check area operations management box visits than I had done as a supervisor at Bradford. In retrospect I should have had the supervisors in and told them in no uncertain terms that if I was finding problems at this rate they must be missing or condoning slack working.

I went to Stockton North Shore one morning, a large and busy box with a booking boy on duty. A trip freight had been accepted from Bowesfield Jct and offered on to Norton-on-Tees South as an unfitted Class 9 freight (1-4 bell signal). This would be a control order's trip to Haverton Hill, I thought, as I signed the train register. I turned to see it approaching. If it was what I had thought then it was a very short freight, hardly worth the engine power. As it approached it was obvious it was a light Class 31 loco. The signalman did not think twice. He sent train entering section, looked for the tail lamp and rang Norton South. "That 1-4 I sent you was a 2-3" he said, immediately assuming he and Bowesfield Jct had misheard the bell signals and that the light loco had not left its train behind somewhere. This was a clear example of standards being too low when I was there. Where would they go if no-one was watching? The bell signal should have been queried with Bowesfield and an alteration noted in the train register. With regard to Norton, Signalling Regulation 2 (b) was precise. "Should a signalman have sent an incorrect 'Is line clear' signal which has been acknowledged by the

24

signalman in advance, he must send the 'Last train signalled incorrectly described' (5-3) bell signal to the box in advance, and after this signal had been acknowledged, he must send the correct 'Is line clear' signal. The position of the block indicator must not be altered."

The management response to this is difficult. You cannot go around sending everyone home for every infringement but the signalman needed to be told to apply the correct regulation even if this might confuse the poor old Norton South box occupant. Should you ask for a report and then issue a disciplinary form? Should you tell the signalman he will be getting a letter of warning or just send one later? Definitely not the latter. Should you take the booking boy on one side and tell him not to copy his elder? All this springs from one relatively small incident but it is all part of the indivisibility of the signalling regulations and their application. Clearly though, enforcement was an uphill battle and not everyone on the supervisory team was participating. As an aside, the official walking route to Norton South signal box, after parking the van on a road in an adjacent estate, was to walk down the garden path of a house owned by a Thornaby driver, climb the back garden fence and scramble down an embankment. The driver received a small annuity for his cooperation.

Another day, another box visit, this time South Bank, 2 miles east of Middlesbrough. The main lines were worked by absolute block and the goods lines were permissive block. Freight trains were allowed to run on this level track between Tees Yard and Grangetown without a brake van with, instead, a tail lamp slung over the drawhook of the rear wagon. Sometimes a piece of white paper was judged sufficient. The absence of a brake van often drew criticism from passers-by, visiting railwaymen (on and off duty) and newcomers. We used to take great delight in referring anyone who mentioned the perceived problem to Table H1 of the Sectional Appendix, page 244, giving the authority to work in this fashion between Bowesfield Jct and Grangetown. Not with the white paper tail lamp substitute though.

I suspect that slackness with regard to tail lamp observation had been allowed to set in partly through such exemptions. South Bank saw a lot of light locomotive working between Thornaby depot and the block train terminals in the Grangetown area. Here was the first one, on the down goods. No tail lamp alight. The signalman showed no inclination to send 'Train Passed Without Tail Lamp' (9 bells) so I told him to do it. The next move up the goods line did not have its lamp lit either. 9 bells again. Then the next one, down the goods. The same. It was clear that this requirement was being universally ignored. I hung around for the next two moves both of which had their rear light lit. Word had obviously got round but this was one matter on which I did have a purge.

Much as I believed in the indivisibility of signal box discipline, even I had to admit there were different categories of irregularity. If we are grading them A to E with the most serious as grade A then an A* incident occurred on the Whitby branch one winter's morning. It was the normal procedure to consult the commercially produced weather forecast which gave specific details on individual locations to see if there was a threat of snow on the North Yorkshire Moors. If it was cold weather and rain was expected in the Tees Valley it was a fair bet there would be a snow warning for the Whitby line. The boxes were opened an hour or two early and a snow plough fitted loco, or a plough itself, would be sent Whitby before the first passenger train. The other variable concerned the domestic coal train to Whitby which was booked to run once a week but in winter used to run additionally on one or even two extra occasions in a week.

After snow had fallen on the coastal plain that morning it was no surprise that the Whitby line and boxes had been opened early, or that the line was consequently clear of snow. It escaped notice in the area office that there had been exceptional delay to the first up passenger train from Whitby and, when it was realised, it was simply ascribed to the weather. There was plenty of work to be done keeping the company freight trains running out of the Grangetown area and ensuring Tees Yard could continue to accept trains.

We had two young trainee signalmen on a course at Newcastle, who were late reaching signalling school, where one happened to mention that strange things had happened on his way to work this morning and he wondered how it all fitted with the regulations he had been learning. The signalling inspector doing the tuition became alarmed, told the divisional officers and they phoned me. By a hairsbreadth I had just learnt what had happened and I could relate what action had been taken. The rumour machine had reached top gear just in time and we had discovered what had caused the exceptional delay.

When the up passenger train had reached Castleton Moor signal box, just over 16 miles from Whitby and seven miles from the next signal box at Battersby, where trains had to reverse to reach Middlesbrough, it had to cross the down coal train which was approaching from Battersby. The authority to travel over the single line came in the form of a token which was issued from a machine in the signal box. Not more than one token for each section could be 'out' of the machine at any one time to ensure two trains could not be authorised onto the single line at the same time. When a train arrived, the signalman had to take the token from the driver and put it into his machine. Another one for that section could then be issued for a train to go the other way or for a train to follow from the box in rear. When a cross was to be made the opposite procedure had to be done and new tokens for the section ahead issued to each of the drivers. The drivers had to read the inscription on the token to satisfy themselves it was for the section they were about to enter.

A token was duly issued to the up passenger train driver who was by now late so he set off for Battersby with alacrity. The signalman then went to give the Castleton to Glaisdale token to the coal train driver who was in less of a hurry. He duly read the token given to him. It clearly said 'Castleton to Battersby' and waved for the signalman to come back to the loco. Clearly the two tokens had been inadvertently switched.. What could be done? And could the error be disguised? The coal train driver was asked to go through to Glaisdale without a token. After all, he was persuaded, there was only one token out of the machine and that must be in the possession of the up passenger train driver. But that was not the half of it. When the passenger train reached Battersby the Glasdale-Castleton token was obviously not going to fit in the Battersby machine.

I am not sure whether the signalman's next actions showed blind panic or remarkable clarity of thought. He sent the coal train on its way and jumped in his car to drive to Battersby to retrieve the wrong token, taking with him the Castleton-Battersby token to put in the machine on his arrival there. His decision was indefensible but the moves seemed to come automatically and might just escape detection. Perhaps this had been done before?

But the plans were to be scuppered by the up passenger train driver who, during a station stop at Kildale, bethought himself to read his token. One can scarcely imagine the dread he experienced when he read 'Glaisdale to Castleton' I imagine he re-read it a few times in sheer disbelief. Here he was on a single line with a trainload of passengers without authority. For all he knew a Castleton-Battersby token might be in the process of being issued at that very moment. If it was at Battersby he might meet another train headlong, if it was from Castleton it might be approaching behind him. He applied the logic that the only motive power behind him was the coal train on its way to shunt at Whitby, plus stock on the North Yorkshire Moors, but anything could be coming from the Middlesbrough direction via Battersby. Perhaps he might have been better to have remained at Kildale and evacuated his passengers onto a cold, exposed moorland halt. He chose to return in the hope of rectifying the matter as soon as possible.

When the up passenger train driver reached Castleton on his return he must have been in a state of despair to find there

28

was no signalman present. He phoned Battersby who had fortunately been told what was happening. When the Castleton signalman eventually returned he was able to issue the correct token, insert the 'wrong one' into the Castleton-Glaisdale machine and all was once more right with the world.

Compared with such shenanigans, the standard of the signalmen for whom I was responsible at Bradford on the former Midland main line to Scotland was extremely high. I think that recruitment on Teesside had been difficult in the full employment years of the 1950s and early/mid 1960s and we were still paying the price. Most of the Bradford signalmen would have been to university in the modern age and a good proportion of them even in the 1960s when university was by far from being an expectation even from grammar schools. A high proportion of the Bradford area signalman had been employed on the railway during the 1950s when the Leeds-Carlisle line was busy and when there were four lines throughout from Leeds to Shipley. Many had been recruited in the 1930s when the railways could take their pick of recruits during the Depression. The Mid-1970s railway was child's play to them and they tolerated what they considered over-supervision by a youngster, in fact young enough to be their offspring.

The complexities of the post-war years were described in an article I wrote for The Railway Magazine about working Wortley Jct signalbox during the early 1950s, using material provided by Noel Proudlock, who had done some time as a booking boy there prior to being able to transfer to the salaried staff ranks. The account included some serious irregularities to expedite traffic that I felt the station masters of the time should have spotted and eliminated. Perhaps they had indeed spotted them and chosen not to eliminate them. I too was slowly learning discretion but I believed the mantra that had been preached to me. The price of safety was eternal vigilance.

Perhaps the first example where I decided to exercise discretion was one summer's evening around 20.30 when I paid an out-of-hours visit to Thackley Jct signalbox. In the 1970s this was the box where the four tracks from Shipley became two through the 1,518yds Thackley tunnel to Apperley Jct, where the Ilkley line joined the Carlisle main line, some three miles away. The 1960s rationalisation had also left just two tracks for another six miles to the outskirts of Leeds. Thackley Jct was closed on nights and was there mainly to regulate the parcel train peaks and consequential light loco movements. Access was via a derelict industrial site, the canal bank, a copse, a climb over a dry-stone wall and by crossing four tracks. It was not somewhere you chose to visit in darkness. This bright summer's evening I completed the assault course, crunched the ballast and stomped on the wooden stairs. The signalman on duty was a conscientious and friendly signalman but there was a lady sitting in the signalman's arm chair. Most signal boxes had an unofficial but comfortable second-hand arm chair oozing its stuffing from one or two holes in the upholstery. As a young supervisor I had to think quickly. If this had been a young signalman with some floozy sitting in the chair some form of immediate action would have been necessary but I guessed this was Mrs Signalman and surmised there might be a medical reason for her being there, for instance not wanting to be alone in her house. Perhaps the signalman had been considering not coming to work and chosen this compromise as a way of being dutiful? I took my time signing the train register while I gave the situation some thought and then talked to Mr Signalman as if no one was there. After a couple of train moves I went on my way.

I made a visit to the same signalman in normal office hours as soon as possible and deliberately said nothing about the Thackley visit intending to put his mind at rest that what might have seemed rude ignoring his wife was actually turning a blind eye. I was aware that it was normal for wives of country signalmen to bring their lunch down from the village and stop for a cup of tea. Mrs Signalman might have had to do something of a more difficult journey to reach her husband at Thackley but the principle was not really any different. I had needed to decide whether the circumstances might lead to a distraction and of course if there had been an incident I had put my job on the line. On reflection I could have handled the situation with far more maturity, asking if there was a family problem or if any help in having preferential rostering might help. If the age difference between us had been reversed, or even something near to equal, I know I would have managed to broach the subject.

A Class 31 passes Thackley Jct's home signal with an empty parcel van train for Bradford Forster Square.

Keeping signalboxes private could be a touchy subject. The only major challenge I had was at Bowesfield Jct where the Eaglescliffe and Stockton lines converge approaching Thornaby. There were two young shift signalmen and their booking boys here who needed watching. The signal box was close to a major road and not in a good area. They decided they would ensure the privacy rules were obeyed by keeping the box door locked. This could of course be an excuse for giving time to cover a few aspects of mischief but they insisted they were just keeping the box private in accordance with the signalling regulations. The traffic assistants, ex management trainee Peter Fazackerly and former signalman Norrie Gregg, had their measure but we chose to compromise by saying any delay in opening the box when a supervisor arrived would be deemed a potential breach of discipline.

Signalmen listening to the radio was another difficult subject back in the 1970s. Occasionally someone would be too unaware of what was happening to turn it off and hide it. One such character once told me he was just mending it. The rule specifically forbade the use of radio, telephonic and other similar devices except where specially authorised. That created a problem when you wanted to talk to a signalman about the cricket. This could involve a conversation on the lines of my saying that I had not heard the score today and the signalman replying he 'had heard' England were 121 for 3 at lunch.

When I was on holiday in Dawlish shortly before moving to Exeter I had my ticket inspected at the station entrance by someone listening to the radio in their ticket booth. I stopped that when I moved there. The shunters had a battered old television in their messroom that had to go on two grounds. It was not subject to regular inspection and therefore a fire hazard. It was a losing battle though as tales came down the line that Waterloo drivers had a brand new officially sanctioned television in their messroom and even an unforgivable gambling machine. I can only presume there is no such rule nowadays with access to phones and tablets as it must be completely unenforceable.

Fairly typical of characters with whom the Bradford signalboxes were staffed was Signalman Milner at Kildwick crossing. He was unpopular with his colleagues but never caused me any problems. The kettle was always boiling when I arrived and I was invited to sit in his armchair while a couple of trains passed. His peculiarity was that he insisted on absolute right time shift changeovers. His fellow signalmen would tell tales of his riding down the main road to the signalbox at around 21.55 for the night shift but then circling the pumps at the adjacent petrol station for a couple of minutes before carefully stowing his bike, mounting the box steps, taking off his coat, getting out his pen and signing the train register with precision 'On duty 22.00'.

This was a man who told me about moving house for an extra 2/6d a week in the 1930s (£9 in 2020) and who had been a relief signalman on the Settle & Carlisle line. People who had worked with him would relate how they would see him walking across a field, from the road to the box, in a blizzard, shirt neck wide open. Then, as they left the box, they would see him wedging the box windows with folded paper to keep out the draughts.

I put his insistence on precisely right time hand-overs to criticism of the unofficial exchange of duty between the signalmen at Quintinshill in 1915 which contributed to the confusion that resulted in the wreck of a troop train and 225 deaths. Some of the staff involved were from Carlisle so the memory would have been fresh in the minds of staff on the Settle & Carlisle line when he had joined the railway some fifteen years later.

An up Class 8 freight train hauled by a Class 40 locomotive approaches Kildwick level crossing.

On the other hand it could have been that he had once been entangled in the kind of arrangement being applied at Keighley in 1976 where there was a semi-permanent vacancy. The two resident signalmen used to work permanent 12hr shifts with 06.00/18.00 changeovers, letting relief men through the door only to enable their rotation from 'days' to 'nights' and back. Their courtesy to each other amounted to making sure they arrived earlier than their colleague had relieved them twelve hours beforehand and the times often approached 05.15 and 17.15 before being corrected by events such as annual leave. That was another quirk. By a strict interpretation, the Sunday turns between two weeks of annual leave were counted as additional duties outside the annual leave pattern so the resident signalmen had prior call to be rostered for the 'time and three quarters' Sunday pay rate than the relief man who had been there all week. When I asked if they did not prefer to have unbroken time off I was given a withering answer that if they came for 12hrs pay on a Monday why would they not come for 21hrs pay on a quieter Sunday?

The potentially most serious signalling irregularity I experienced while at Bradford occurred between Cononley and Skipton Station South signal boxes one clear and bright morning. Cononley was the last box on my area but I had frequently to visit Skipton as responsible officer for planned single line working so I was familiar with the layout and its working. Cononley was a small hen-hut of a structure that had replaced the original fire-damaged one. It worked track circuit block from the Keighley direction but absolute block to Skipton which was about three miles distant.

On the morning in question two Class 40-hauled class 8 partially fitted freight trains were heading towards Cononley from Healey Mills, up the Aire Valley (but in railway parlance running 'away from London') so they were actually on the down line. One was for Carlisle and the other going to Barrow. A good distance behind them was the morning Leeds-Morecambe express, only a dmu but a more important train than most on the route in those days. There were no unusual circumstances. The signalman at Cononley was Alan Tranter a promising young man, new to both signalling and the railway, and someone in whom I saw the makings of an area inspector in due course. He was dead keen and knew his rules well. In good time he offered the first Class 8 to Skipton South and had it accepted. He cleared his signals and in due course received 'train out of section'. By now the second Class 8 was approaching so it was offered, accepted and proceeded on its way. After a while Alan started to watch the clock. The Morecambe express would be leaving Keighley now. As the seconds ticked by he considered what he should do. He could ring up Skipton and ask when he would be giving train out of section for the second freight but that might risk incurring the wrath of a more experienced colleague. He remembered his training. He decided to send the 1-5-5 bell signal 'Shunt train for following train to pass' drafted especially for such occasions but rarely, if ever, used. I bet the Skipton South signalman thought it was 2-5-5 'Train Running Away in Wrong Direction' or at least had to look up 1-5-5. Indeed the unusual nature of the bell signal might have contributed to what happened next.

The regulation says that the Skipton South signalman, on receiving the bell signal, 'must take all the necessary measures to clear the line to prevent delay to the second train.' He looked around and saw the first Class 8 sitting in his down goods loop and concluded he must have forgotten to send 'train out of section' so promptly did so, placing his block indicator to normal. Alan Tranter at Cononley immediately offered the Morecambe Express which was accepted, the block indicator went to 'line clear', Alan cleared his signals and the Morecambe Express accelerated away towards its full 70mph capability.

Only seconds after placing his block indicator to train on line for the Morecambe Express the Skipton South signalman was horrified to see the second freight train hove into sight, he cleared his home signal and ran to attract the attention of the driver waving to him to get a move on to get in clear of the home signal. His waves were acknowledged, the signalman returned to his box and replaced the home signal behind the second freight before the Morecambe dmu struck in at his berth track circuit. It had been too close to disaster for comfort.

This incident left a huge impression on me. If the admirable absolute block system that had been devised over more than a century could be overcome by just one signalman being derelict in his duty then it was my job to try to prevent such traps being laid. Alan Tranter had done nothing wrong. A few less wise members of the older generation suggested that he should not have sent such an unusual bell signal anyway. Obviously your 'mate' would be confused by it. However, a passenger train collision could easily have occurred without the usual requirement for at least two people to have made serious mistakes. Had the Class 40 failed, or hit a sheep, the Morecambe dmu would have been upon it. The line is mostly straight so it is possible it would have seen the freight early enough but no one wants to be working around such margins.

Most incidents encountered in signal box visiting were relatively minor. The most frequent was receiving 'train out of section' for the first train in a visit without 'call attention' having been sent first. So far as I was concerned the requirement was set in stone but signalmen with greater experience remembered earlier systems when it was not required. Noel Proudlock feels that sending 'call attention' before 'train entering section' was more important than before 'train out of section' but this requirement had been dropped.

A loaded MGR test run for a new Class 56 approaches Shipley Guiseley Jct.

One afternoon I visited Guiseley Jct at Shipley (now Dockfield Jct) to carry out a routine visit. A Bradford Forster Square to Ilkley train had just entered the section to Esholt Jct where the line met the Leeds-Ilkley route. The entrance to the box was at the back and from a noisy road so it seemed that I surprised the young signalman. Almost as expected the 'train out of section' bell signal came from Esholt Jct for the Ilkley train without 'call attention'. I picked up the box-to-box intercom phone. It was a senior relief signalman, Ernie Mayes, on the other end. He and I got on well but he always seemed to be trying to steal a march. If he was being facetious he would address me as Mr. Heaton. "I am sorry Mr Heaton," he started, "but I have been working at Forster Square so much lately where the railway cannot afford two block bells that I was confused for a moment." "Alright Ernie but call attention first at Esholt," He promised he would. Ernie was referring to the fact that the Midland railway formerly busy station of Bradford Forster Square had four tracks to Manningham Jct but there was only one block bell to serve both lines. Over one pair of tracks the signalmen had to comply with the normal signalling regulations but, on the other, the 'call attention' rules were reversed so trains were offered without 'call attention', were sent 'call attention' for 'train on line' and not sent it for 'train out of section'. Then the management would come pestering a poor fellow to remember to always send it from some country signalbox with four trains an hour!

I shall digress for a moment to further problems with Ernie. He once complained that when he was working Guiseley Jct he had been shot at from the opposite side of the line and the bullet had broken the window. When I attended he had gone home but I found a clean round hole in the window extruded outwards. I had no idea about what bullets might do when they hit a window but logically it seemed the bullet had gone from inside to outside. Watching detective programmes had led me to believe I should be able to find an inbound bullet, or damage from it, but there was none. Area inspector Horace Egginton, who was older and even more experienced than Ernie said the relief man held a gun licence. I did not manage to make any further progress on that one other than to ask for a couple of B.T. police patrols around the time of day the incident was alleged to have happened.

Being on call for the area was a responsibility that had a number of facets. You had to be prepared to jump into a van and head for whatever trouble was in the offing and deal with it as a first responder but very often you simply had to answer the phone and take appropriate action. On my on call weeks I used to be given the signalling rosters each evening. Sometimes the roster clerk would say he had nobody if anything went wrong. Another day he would point out a tip about who was available to work a rest day or in training somewhere and could be moved to cover a job. Occasionally I would find a job uncovered or down for someone who had said he was unavailable. These were usually balanced by the days when two signalmen had been booked in error to cover the same job.

Most days passed without a 06.10 phone call to say someone had not turned in. In fact an 06.10 phone call would be a benefit compared with the Signalmen's General instructions which specifically said, "In the event of a signal box not being opened within fifteen minutes of the appointed time, the signalmen on each side must arrange for the Station Master who has supervision of the box to be advised of the circumstances." 15min was generous and could result in substantial delay but in those days the Station Master would have been on hand to open the box. Not so in 1976. So when I was awoken one morning to be told Burley in Wharfedale signal box had not opened I had to find someone to cover, and quickly. Burley was 'straight up and down' in 1976, no junctions. Its sole function was to break an otherwise 7 mile block section into two sections of, conveniently, 3½ miles. The morning peak needed it to be open to run the extra commuter trains to time. I looked at my sheets and found Ernie Mayes, who lived at Shipley I think, was booked off on his rest day. Most signalmen who had elected to join the 'relief' did so to earn money and being booked off on their rest day was a lost opportunity. I rang Ernie and he responded quickly. I explained the units would be stacking up soon and he said he was on his way. Two hours later when I drove the van down the station approach at Bradford Exchange I was collared and asked what had happened at Burley this morning as it was still not open and heavy delay had been incurred. I explained that Ernie Mayes had said he was on his way, certainly before 06.30. By the time I phoned Burley box he was there. Why had he taken so long?. Ernie replied that it was because he had travelled from Shipley to Burley by train and it had been heavily delayed. I was almost speechless. "But a good relief man has his bag on a peg behind the door and his car keys in his coat pocket." I expostulated. "Ah, Mr Heaton, I do agree, but, you see, I am not a good relief man," he replied. Discussing these recollections with Noel Proudlock, he reassured me that Ernie had his moments even back in the early 1950s.

The nearest I came to the line being closed by my failing to cover rostering problems came one Saturday night when the line was due to close overnight until Sunday morning with no engineering work planned to cause it to remain open. There was a late charter special due back from Morecambe at about 21.30 but it had made a very late start and was not expected to be at Skipton until around 23.00. At Steeton (a level crossing and the first box west of Keighley) the signalman point blank refused to stay later than 22.00 no matter what the consequences.

Covering any railway job on a Saturday evening is difficult and every option seemed to fail. Every minute I spent trying to cover the job was a minute that would delay the train if the only option turned out being for me to drive from my home, then to the east of Huddersfield, over the moors from Brighouse to reach the Aire valley. I had one last card. The area's star signalman Mick York was on duty at Cononley. Mick was the youngest of our general purpose relief signalmen and officially knew every signal box on both sides of the area, about 20. In his spare time from working as many hours as he could on the railway he had been a finalist on the television programme 'Mastermind' and was always helpful. If I was responsible officer for single line working he was my first choice Pilotman. I suggested that if he passed the train to Kildwick and closed up would he drive to Steeton and reopen it to allow the train to proceed. No problem.

On a couple of occasions I used an obscure paragraph in the General Appendix (as opposed to the Sectional Appendix or

Rule Book) which stated that an area manager or his representative could travel in a loco cab in the performance of his duties. Having caught the 11.55 King's Cross train from Bradford Exchange to Leeds I would present myself to the driver of a Class 45 on the Thames Clyde Express. I was genuinely looking at the operation of signals on my patch from the driver's viewpoint. Sure enough on the first journey we were late in receiving a clear run at Kildwick owing to the late lowering of the level crossing barriers. On reaching Skipton I phoned the signalman who did not have to think twice before answering: "The moment I got up to pass your train I saw the flashing lights of an ambulance at the top of the road *(there was a long straight stretch to the crossing from the Skipton direction)* and I thought, 'Hmmm shall I delay the express for a few seconds or shall I make the poor chap with a heart attack wait a few minutes at the crossing'……" I thought for a split second about checking with Airedale Hospital ambulance control but I realised they probably had better things to do. In fact I realised that he knew that I knew that he knew what had actually happened!

4. FIRST DAYS

Many of my 'first days' seemed significant, including my early-1968 first interview for my Railway Studentship training scheme in Leeds Divisional Office in a 1930s-style office block next to the Queen's Hotel at the end of the Midland Concourse of the then Leeds City station. I fingered my blue card Edmondson ticket with Huddersfield to Leeds written on it in fountain pen ink and presented it to the ticket staff at the barrier on Platform 1 at Huddersfield, boarded the train and carefully read the letter stating where I was to report and at what time. I had an hour in hand but could restlessly squander only half of that time before finding my way to the 2nd floor office and knocking on the appropriate door, trying not to knock too loudly and then debating whether I should knock again when nothing happened. A clerk in his 50s eventually opened the door and looked at me curiously. I am not sure what I was wearing, it could even have been school uniform. I introduced myself and presented my letter. He looked at it and handed it me back "You are a week early," he announced, witheringly. It was one of those moments when you wish a chasm would open up and swallow you whole. I had decided I really fancied a job on the railway, operating trains and being paid for it and I had blown it. When I think about it now, the untimely death of my father less than a year beforehand had made me introspective and nervous. Some might even say surly. I never really lost any of these facets. I stammered an apology. I had blown it through carelessness, over-anxiety perhaps, but I now stood no chance. "Just a moment," said the clerk, "wait here a minute." He disappeared to the office next door and quickly returned. "It's alright, the divisional training officer will see you now." I was introduced to my interviewer Mr Trevorrow known by everyone, but not to his face, as 'Joe' – a man of huge stature, late 40s perhaps, avuncular ,quietly spoken, looked you in the eye. A couple of weeks later I received a letter of appointment saying I should start on Monday 16th September 1968 by reporting to the railway training college at Crewe. This was the former railway orphanage of 1911 endowed by chief mechanical engineer

43

Francis Webb with £54,000 (£6m at 2020 values) out of the half-million (£64min 2020!) he left in his will. There was my blue card return ticket ....and there was my salary. The application form had shown £525 a year. My spending money was 10/- a week (50p) which went a long way and, in my widowed mother's circumstances, was extremely generous. This letter said £680 a year, £13. 0s 9d a week (£10.4s 6d, it transpired, after deductions). I was rich beyond the wildest imagination, even after giving mum £5 a week, which she secretly saved and gave me back on my marriage. In that wonderful way that encompassed both the strengths and weaknesses of British Rail, if you wanted to know exactly how much per week your gross salary should be you were instructed to take your annual salary, calculate 6/313ths and there you had it.

Having started my career on the doorsteps of the railway orphanage that September, small suitcase in hand, wearing a somewhat plaintiff expression, the week started to improve, a bit like the 'Hello Mother, Hello Father' American summer camp song. A trip to a small panel signalbox at Stafford with another free train trip went down well and I went round Crewe diesel depot. Not sure if that was an official trip or an extra curricular excursion with my yellow jacket trying to look official. We had many classroom sessions which were just like an extension of school. I particularly remember the lecture on the new 1968 Transport Act. Barbara Castle's legislation transformed the future of local lines with the concept of grant aid and, more importantly, the creation of the passenger transport executives for the conurbations. I also learnt a lot about the transition of the railways from being common carriers, open to cherry picking of their traffic by road hauliers.

My first day at Tees Yard in early 1979 was an unmitigated disaster. I set off early by car. About 05.30 I think to be sure of being there by 9. Linda ran a mini to get her to school and our local garage had sold me a Hillman Imp ideal for getting me to my then job at Neville Hill. What a disastrous decision! It was more than cantankerous on a cold morning taking at least half the run from Roberttown near Mirfield to the other side of Leeds just to warm up and to prevent it from alternate stalling and engine flooding from too little or too much choke.

On my way to Middlesbrough the last problem on my mind was warming it up. Chugging down the A1 the temperature gauge shot up and steam emission took place from the bonnet. The cylinder head gasket had gone. Not that I had a clue what it was - I was told so later by George McVay, mentioned earlier in connection with guard Calman. My solution of finding a source of cold water and sizzling it into the engine would not have been deemed appropriate by anyone with the slightest mechanical inclination. Why did I not just find a phone and give in? I was in the RAC, or perhaps AA, at the time. I soldiered on stopping every couple of miles, whenever I found water, and arrived very late. 10.00 rings a bell. No phones readily available to inform my destination of the trouble of course. I parked up the Imp (by name, Devil by nature) on the dock by Middlesbrough signalbox and eventually had the car scrapped. In retrospect I am not sure it needed to be scrapped but at least I could savour a sense of retribution.

Such humdrum difficulties dim even further into insignificance compared to my first day at Bradford. This was my first day as a supervisor, one that I had been eagerly anticipating for such a long time. After finishing my management training I had a couple of months supernumerary at Healey Mills helping out with such impossible balancing acts as the daily return to match each guard with the type of work they had performed. It took a couple of hours every day for the 100 or so guards stationed there and I bet no one ever used the information. I was waiting for an opportunity to be placed in a suitable Grade C supervisory job. You can well understand staff in Grade B looking forward to a chance of promotion only to find one of these whippersnappers, all theory and no notion, parachuted in from the heavens. 'College kids' was the ultimate insult. Well, perhaps not the ultimate one. In fact the reception was probably better on the former North Eastern Region than elsewhere because the 'traffic apprenticeship' scheme had been in force since around 1909 and you can get used to anything in time.

When entrants turned up somewhere for training in some filthy office sited in the middle of a huge puddle in the cinders on a freezingly cold morning at say Hull they were never asked if they were on the Traffic Management Training Scheme. Just "You a traffic apprentice then?" Answer, an eager "Yes!" Reply, probably a shrug. By such brief exchanges the railwaymen knew all they needed to know and just what to do. To be fair that was usually to tell the youngster what to do, keep an eagle eye out, give the trainees enough responsibility to make them think they were learning something and bend their ear about two pet subjects. First: How busy this location used to be and how this was a quiet a day. Second: The improvements they needed in the hope it would reach the ears of management. Strangely, it all worked better than it had any right to do.

Anyway, while I was awaiting my opportunity, the 'Traffic Assistant, Bradford (Valley)' fell off a ladder painting the outside of his house. I knew the building concerned, a large terrace house with attics and bay windows by the traffic lights on the main Huddersfield to Bradford road on the steep hill out of Bailiff Bridge. It was a long way down and I do not think the poor man worked again. I met him only once, when he called in the Bradford Exchange area manager's office.

I had an interview with the area manager Alan Peak and Joe Trevorrow from Leeds. Alan Peak was not a warm man; self contained, an engineer not an operator. The drivers consulted and negotiated only with him, refusing to speak to the area operations manager Jeff Lawson because he was not a loco man and they resented transfer away from technical managers. Management let them get away with it. Mr Peak said I knew all the theory and was looking to put it into practice. I did think at the time that his statement was pretty obvious. Anyway I started the following Monday.

Believed to be the first visit of an HST to Bradford Exchange.

By 1976 the huge Victorian Bradford Exchange station had been closed and the land sold. The new station comprised only four platforms but the station was modern and integrated with the bus station which had been renamed 'Interchange'. I immediately suggested that the new Exchange railway station should be renamed Interchange but the idea was rejected on the grounds that the cost of re-signage outweighed any benefits. Clearly, management came from a different school from the legions now in charge whose mantra could be said to be "re-paint, re-sign and re-market" (re-gularly?). It did eventually happen some seven years later.

In the meantime I sat at my new desk in a modern office across from the 'Traffic Assistant Halifax', Geoff Armitage and 'Area Inspector' Horace Egginton. We had the usual British Rail tea ceremony to welcome newcomers which started with a debate about how many teabags should be used and whether to give the new member of staff a few days free tea club membership until 'subs' day, usually agreed but not without some reluctance, at least in the Yorkshire variation of the ritual.

Geoff Armitage was in his early 50s I guess, a product of the stationmaster era when they did everything, usually at remote locations. We used to pick each other up when we changed custody of the railway van for our alternate weeks on and off call. He seemed to think the fastest way from Dalton, Huddersfield to Bradford station entailed using the M62 from Cooper Bridge to some point where it tangentially skirted Bradford. This involved driving with the speedometer needle bouncing off the top of the scale with the steering wheel juddering ever more violently. This would continue until we met an inevitable traffic tailback where we would usually remain for a long time. When I picked him up we observed the 30/40mph limits via the A641 and reached the office earlier.

Geoff had a dry sense of humour. He had two favourite sayings. The first was to say whenever the word 'meeting' was mentioned, "A meeting a day keeps the traffic away." How wise he was. I kept this with me during subsequent jobs and was not averse to using it on frequent occasions. The second came every Thursday afternoon, after I had completed the pay run to nearly every staffed location north of Bradford (out to Cononley, across to Ilkley, back down the Wharfe Valley to Apperley Jct on the river Aire) before returning to the office with fish & chips for Horace and Geoff, who had been on a shorter circuit south of Bradford. Thursday lunchtime was when the weekly British Rail 'whole system' vacancy list was issued. Geoff used to pick it up and peruse it carefully. Every week he would hesitate and then stop with his finger on an entry. Looking increasingly excited he would scan the lines with his finger then say, "There's a good job here!" wait a few seconds and then deflatedly add, "Oh, it's mine!"

I have described Horace earlier in the book. He was a reliable source of advice and took a hard line with signalmen. If they were young then "They would soon learn", if they were old "They should know better." It was not that he was unkindly but he judged them by his own standard. He was always smart, in a sharp lounge suit, a full head of hair smartly cropped. He prided himself on always having £500 in notes in his wallet, I suppose the equivalent of £3,500 in 2020. I sensed he had come through the Depression when money was tight and he was simply relishing his success. Horace was a grade lower than me and might have had eyes on my job but he never betrayed it. The only time he used to fix me with a determined stare was if I did not want to work a Sunday turn and there was a danger of having to give it away to a divisional inspector. I did not like playing around with say a dozen ballast trains on the Ilkley line getting them on and off a possession in an orderly and timely fashion. On the other hand I would volunteer for single line working, especially overnight possessions for tamping midweek with some freight and the overnight pair of expresses about. If Horace or Geoff worked it they would go home about 16.00, turn out at 22.00, get to bed at say 04.00 and come back into the office for 12.00. This earned normal pay plus the overtime hours at night. I used to go home at 14.00, sleep, turn out at 22.00, get home at 04.00 and stay at home the following day for normal pay and no extra. When they were my age every penny mattered but, with my wife teaching and my earnings, time was more precious than cash. My policy was not popular.

Area operations manager Jeff Lawson used to be area manager at Huddersfield and I had worked for him on the studentship scheme when I was 18. He was a mild mannered man who clearly knew his operating but had trouble when required to be unnaturally forceful. We became friends after I had left Bradford and he visited me occasionally in Dawlish, after we had both retired, if he was on holiday in Torquay. On my first day at Bradford though he was on holiday, his job being covered by area relief manager Bill Lockley.

Bill was a real character and a bull of a man, forceful when it was not remotely necessary sometimes. He was stocky, medium height, heavily built, dark hair with a tendency to curl and a pipe that emitted foul black smoke. He would sit behind his desk and lean back in his chair, each puff from his pipe sending clouds of smoke up to blacken the patch on the ceiling above him. Drawing on his pipe indicated thought.

Exhaling was a smoke signal that a pronouncement was forthcoming. More often than not this would be his gruff Yorkshire catch phrase, "Leave it to me old boy," regardless of the age of the person he was addressing. Bill had been a relief station manager and, when I was on the studentship scheme, I associated him with South Elmsall and as a freight rolling stock inspector chasing errant collieries and coal merchants for standage, demurrage and damage. Beware if you misappropriated a wagon on his patch or if you were in Control and had not managed to pick up empties quickly enough after they had been declared available in those pre-TOPS days. He greeted me in a friendly manner but curiously, guardedly, in the way you might welcome an exotic pet into your household.

The phone rang. Bill extracted his pipe from between his lips, leaned forwards and picked up the receiver. "LOCKLEY", he announced in a way designed to throw the caller out of his stride, especially when he answered a phone they had expected to be answered by someone else. His ebullience subsided. "Yes…. Where?.....Yes…..Ok". He put the pipe to one side and announced generally, "The freight trip coming out of Valley has derailed and demolished Manningham Jct signal box." I looked at Horace, Horace looked at Geoff, Geoff looked at Bill, Bill looked at me, "Off you go then," he said and resumed his smoking. I grabbed my brief case and asked for the van keys. I left the office with a few directions of how to get there, it was only a mile from Forster Square, itself only ½mile across town.

My mind was divided by what I might have to do on arrival and how to negotiate the traffic. When I reached the box and parked the car I could see a scene of pandemonium. There were vans everywhere and perhaps twenty or so staff apparently from different departments. The box was situated at the neck of the yard complex which contained Valley goods yard and the marshalling sidings, both, even by then, sadly under-utilised As I opened the van door I was relieved to see the box had not been demolished but a Class 31 locomotive was sitting sadly on the ballast, leaning resignedly against the back wall of the signalbox for much needed support. As I approached, the signalman was peering out from the doorway with a box full of people chattering away competing with the incessant barking of the signalman's rather large dog. Others were poking the locomotive and another group was tending to the track. How was I going to impose on this lot that I was in charge and, if I managed that, what was I going to do next? Alternate words were drowned by the dog as I tried to introduce myself and check and sign the train register book. Traffic had been stopped in the down direction but I assessed the damage and decided it was clear to be passed at caution. The track circuits were occupied by the accident. At least I did not have to put in single line working. I checked the train had at least perfunctory protection, as it was difficult to do it as per text book, and started to establish the cause. Talking to the signalman in the box was impossible. I eventually plucked up courage to ask him to put the dog in his car and he surprisingly obliged. I think he had been wanting someone to give him leave to do it. At last it was possible to think clearly. The loco had clearly derailed owing to a relatively minor track defect which was at least readily agreed. The engineers were working on what was necessary to keep the box in one piece when the loco ceased to provide the support that was now a clearly mutual matter.

After an hour or two a van drew up. Bill Lockley got out and walked slowly over to the box, taking in the scene as he did so. As he reached the foot of the box steps I was standing in the doorway. "You alright then?" he asked. I said I was and I think he signed the train register. He took another look round and simply said, "Right then," and left. The Holbeck breakdown crane was now on its way. Attempting to rerail a locomotive without the breakdown foreman being present was vetoed in the appropriate mishap manual, a prohibition for which I was grateful. I had to work out where the crane was able to stand without fouling the main line by either its physical site or the swing of the jib. I guessed I was going to need to put in a 'between trains' T.2 possession when work was being done to prevent debris hitting passing trains in the event of a misjudgement. The breakdown foreman gave me short shrift and made a few alterations to the arrangements but this was apparently his normal treatment of the operations department. I had drawn back freight wagons into the yard for examination. I think there was only the loco, not more than one or two wagons perhaps, to rerail. It was done in what seemed like a few minutes when my back was turned but as I was to realise in future, it took longer to reassemble the toolvan train, have a fry up (usually on overtime of course) and set off back. There was nothing to say the rescue gang would not be called to an all night session and they needed refuelling just in case.

Suddenly everyone had disappeared and there was just the signalman, me and...oh, yes....the dog, now a well-behaved and docile animal who was happy to curl up near the stove, listen to the clear chimes of the block bells and have a snooze. I went back to the office. "All done?" I was asked. I nodded and looked for the teapot. Bill put his head round the door. "Don't forget to do the mishap form," he said before disappearing. No matter how I had done at least I felt I was now at long last working on the proper railway.

The questions of dogs in signal boxes was one that exercised my mind for a while. If I mentioned the Manningham Jct canine distraction to anyone there was a tendency for them to say I must not stand for it and it was not allowed. I was less certain. It was not really covered by the rules as far as I interpreted them. You could hardly say their presence was a breach of the instruction to keep the box private and a well behaved dog was not going to be a distraction, although I suppose barking at a second man signing the train register book in pursuance of Rule Book Section K (the old Rule 55 reminder to a signalman of a detained train) could be distractive. We were a long way away from the days when relieving colleagues were likely to complain of allergies. It seemed petty to enforce a ban and difficult to counter any refusal. What if I banned the dog and the signalman was subsequently attacked, perhaps on his way to his car at 22.00 one night?

Bowling Jct was a case in point. This was not on my north side patch but I went occasionally when Geoff was away and we were a visit short on the weekly tick sheet tally pinned on the notice board. Bowling Jct, like so many railway locations in those days had fallen on hard times. It was the point where direct Leeds to Liverpool via the Calder Valley expresses reached the Bradford-Manchester line via a chord from the Leeds-Bradford line at Laisterdyke. There was an intermediate box at Hall Lane level crossing which now saw one freight train a day and where it was rumoured the young signalman's idle time prompted mischief. Fortunately it was not my job to stop it.

Bowling Jct was only just over a mile from Exchange but it was nevertheless isolated, in a cutting and near an insalubrious part of town. The signalman there had a dog that seemed untroubled by the basic service of one train a way each hour. Only a little over a decade earlier the box had not only to deal with the expresses via Hall Lane but also a succession of light locomotives and empty stocks to and from Low Moor plus a local service. Only slightly earlier than that, it also had the South Yorkshireman to Marylebone via Penistone. In 2020 there are four trains an hour each way to Halifax and beyond plus the Grand Central King's Cross trains formed by modern streamlined multiple units. As one Grand Central driver once put it as I passed through Mirfield with him on a Class 180, "The passengers here look at us as if we were a spaceship." I left the Bowling Jct signalman to his solitude, memories and the company of his dog.

5. BRADFORD

The two other members of the Bradford management team were the terminals' manager Gordon Hull and the parcel manager George Carr. Gordon was perhaps mid-40s, an ex station master who lived in the station house at Guiseley. Gordon could not have been more helpful. He shared the south side on call with Geoff Armitage but he offered to turn out to my patch if I had any problems getting there or it was extremely urgent. Parcel manager Mr. Carr was a friendly individual with whom I had relatively few dealings. His duties were mainly to deal with the Grattan's mail order locations which, I seem to recall, were located in two converted redundant mills. I went there only a couple of times, once when covering Geoff's pay run. It was a bit like going back into the old mills of Huddersfield I knew as a child with windows open to the street on hot days allowing, the rhythmic racket of the power looms assailing the summer air and textile workers performing at a rate that seemed even to a five-year-old unreasonably fast. Back in Victorian times with long hours, children crawling under working looms, and pay that barely covered the essentials of existing in cholera-ridden tenements this work scarcely crossed the threshold out of slavery. Here in 1976 teams of mainly Asian-descent workers fought the conveyor belts firing parcels at them with greater rapidity than they could handle. Grabbing teapots for Teddington, dresses for Darlington, watering cans for Waterbeach, the 'porters' sorted them into their destinations, corresponding with the road van transfers to Forster Square and the allocated spaces on the trains of parcel vans that worked away from J.B. Priestley's Bruddersford, every evening to prevent the need for double handling at the trainside. I think there were only two other posts covered by Asian descent staff on the rest of the area. I felt that this was the effect of existing staff finding jobs for their friends and relatives and a lack of awareness, in this surprisingly insular city, compared with London at the opposite end of the spectrum.

I witnessed only three direct incidents of racial discrimination in my railway career, although I realise I must have failed to notice many more. I was aware that the situation in Bradford constituted a bias that would probably be termed institutionalised racism nowadays. It was probably a tacit, even subconscious decision not to encourage multiracial recruitment rather than downright malevolence but the resultant reduced opportunities could have been the nursery of the emerging problems two generations on. Trying to see the opposite side of the argument, many members of the Asian-descent potential workforce did not have the language skills to appreciate the finer points of the regulations but some did and many of the British-descent potential workforce also lacked those basic skills.

The only overt racism I saw which affected promotion was when I was a trainee at Doncaster and was invited to sit in with an operating manager at a suitability interview. The trade union agreement was that the senior suitable candidate should be appointed, not the most suitable senior candidate, even less the best prospect for the future of the railway. The suitability for promotion of signalman was handled by reviewing the senior applicant's disciplinary record. If it was satisfactory he or she would be interviewed. If rejected, the next senior suitable applicant would be interviewed until the vacancy could be filled.

On this particular occasion, one or two appointments had already been approved when the signalman from Bottesford West Jct on the Nottingham to Grantham line via Aslockton where it was joined by the freight line from Newark South Jct, was shown in with a view to taking the vacancy at Balderton level crossing which must have ranked as the smallest box on the east coast main line, located between Grantham and Newark, on the most minor of lanes, with a single stop signal each way. He was an early middle-aged man of West Indian descent. I think the questioning was much the same standard as the previous interviews but answers that were not fully correct were less tolerated. I did not think the signalman's answers were satisfactory but my expectations in that respect had yet to be compromised by experience. To be fair, I was not happy about the two previous appointments either. The manager concluded the interview by saying the signalman was not yet ready for promotion and to study his block regulations more thoroughly. As the applicant shut the door behind him the manager turned to me and uttered the words that have stuck with me for 45 years, "I'm not having darkies on the main line." My stomach turned over but I was powerless. Yes, I could have argued with him, I could have reported him but I did not have the courage to blight my personal interests.

The second incident was at Tees Yard when there had been a fractious exchange between the down yard shunters, of whom three were not particularly religious white Teessiders. The fourth was an immigrant from the middle-east, Egypt I think, who had been bullied by the others. The outside shift supervisor, known as the assistant yard master or AYM, had separated the staff involved in what might have turned to fisticuffs. I was the senior staff member around so I called the victim into the former yard master's office that had a panoramic view of the operation, as all the Eastern Region modern yards enjoyed. I asked what had happened but I admit to remembering his tears and his sniffling as much as the story he had to relate. There was no provision of tissues in a yard master's office and I distinctly recall the shunter removing his woolly hat and wiping his nose on it. He said the other shunters were asking him what it was like to have more than one wife and were making rude remarks. I tried to console him, saying their behaviour had to change and that I would speak to them. I then had the three individuals in. They genuinely regretted what had happened and said they would stop immediately. In fact I think they thought that, they might say, 'teasing' their colleague in such exchanges was really a way of including him in their informal team where it was normal to abuse someone on some pretext with the expectation of a robust response. If so, this was clearly the wrong subject. I heard no more complaints from this source but I came to realise that my action was probably ineffective and I should have followed up more than the once I asked the plaintiff if everything was alright when I encountered him outside the shunters' cabin.

The third example was encountered at Shipley passenger station. After the local trip engine had delivered what wagons it had in its possession to the wayside locations it served, such as Guiseley coal yard, Crossley's scrap siding at Shipley and Keighley yard, its next round of duties entailed the collection of water cans from Shipley station. The term 'cans' had survived the removal of metal containers and their replacement by large plastic carriers such as were used in the 1960s in caravans before they had been routinely connected to the mains. The working timetable retained the column note 'stops to set down water cans' which helped the term to persist.

Once the loco had half a dozen containers or so in the cab it would set off light loco to Esholt Jct on the Ilkley branch, down the other leg of the triangle to Apperley Jct then back on the third side of it to the Apperley Viaduct box with its pervasive odour from the nearby sewage works, not sure about Thackley Jct, and then back to Shipley station. Esholt Jct had a chemical toilet and the signalman had to bury the waste once a week in the undergrowth of the embankment.

A West Yorkshire PTE Metro Cammell dmu passes Esholt Jct with a publicity special.

The loco ran into the down platform at Shipley, the Sri Lankan leading railman appeared on the opposite platform to catch the empties being thrown across to him. The sport was to throw each one far enough away from the recipient for him to have to run as if he were in the outfield of a cricket match making a catch. I do not think they would have done this to a white leading railman and if they had done, a white leading railman would have had the confidence to either let the containers land on the platform, leave the train crews in no doubt what was thought of them or report it. Their sport was conducted in the full view of all the passengers, (all two or three of them mid-morning). I tried to put a stop to it but I am quite sure it continued and I did not enquire further. I told the regular, rather sour, senior railman he was in charge and he should not tolerate it but my actions, on reflection, were those of an inexperienced supervisor.

The freight trip working was handled by someone called George Lalley who sold whatever he could get his hands on to anyone who would buy it; eggs, firewood, probably nylons if we had been at war. He was an affable individual who took the view it was better to be a friend of the supervisor than an enemy. Nothing was too much trouble if you asked him to work extra hours or ensure a certain task was completed. One day, operations manager Jeff Lawson called me into his office. "Something's going on at Guiseley with the shunting and the trip engine," he confided. "I want you to find out what is going on. I suggest you stand on the bridge at the north end of the yard and watch. Make sure they do not see you." I did not have much experience but I did know that if I was spotted it would destroy any chance of cooperation ever again, and it would possibly even follow me to other jobs. I also realised that people like George Lalley knew exactly what was going on because he was probably the one who was doing whatever it was. Furthermore, his chain of information would pinpoint where my van was parked at the time any misdemeanours were discovered. I suspected something like fly shunting where the loco sent two or more wagons away to the sidings, the vehicles spacing themselves, to be berthed correctly by altering the hand points between them. Anyway, I told Jeff I would not be doing that but would put a stop to it. The following day I made my way to Guiseley for the arrival of the freight trip. Guiseley box opened on one shift to allow access to the yard so it was natural for me to be there at that time to complete a box visit. On such an occasion nothing wrong would be contemplated of course. I took George on one side and said that reports had been received about some shunting irregularities and I had been asked to find out what. "I do not want to spy so I thought I would just tell you so whatever it is would stop." George grinned and nodded. I think that probably worked.

The other problem I had with the signalboxes on the water delivery round was that there was no road access for coal deliveries. Every now and then the railway bought the contents of a 16 tonne mineral wagon. It was one of my jobs to book on an extra Saturday train crew and persuade a couple of the goods handling staff at Valley yard to work their rest days. Under my supervision the train of loco, brake van, mineral wagon and another brake van would draw up by the box concerned. The goods people would shovel the coal out onto the ballast and then into the signalbox bunker. I would have to pick suitable gaps in the train service and move them out of the way as necessary. This was not easy at Apperley Jct where the Ilkley branch left the Aire Valley main line. I worked alternate Saturdays and had alternate Mondays off so there was no benefit financially to me.

On the subject of coal wagons, my list of duties included visiting all the coal merchants on the area to inspect their books for evidence of extra charges being owed to the railway. I cannot remember the small print of the accountants' expectations but a typical example included delivery of roadborne coal. There was a premium to pay compared to it being delivered by rail and a surcharge if it came from a pit that was rail connected. I knew that the staff at most stations kept an eye on inbound coal lorries with strange ownership details on the doors and I was confident that my random visits did not spot similar events taking place. Nevertheless, I made an appointment with my first merchant who was located at Shipley and duly knocked on the door of his terraced house one winter's afternoon. I was ushered into the living room, seated under a dim standard lamp and offered tea and cake. I was then presented with a large tome opened at a page showing the current date with entries in copperplate fountain pen. No crossings out, no scribble. I duly went through about twelve pages and a couple of months of entries. I could not really understand what I was reading and I certainly had no intention of admitting I did not have a clue. I was sure of two points though. If there had been extra money due to the railway this book would not tell me. It could easily have been a duplicate and, where nothing showed a road delivery, the corresponding rail vehicle number could not be checked. I drank my tea, said thank you for my cake and left. Back in the office I told Jeff Lawson just how fruitless this had been, the best part of half an afternoon for nothing. It was my first and last merchant check.

I would sometimes engineer a visit to Halifax signal box on Saturday afternoons, if the visit list needed an extra tick, and return on a summer Saturday train headed by a Class 25 or Class 40 but we could easily become stretched if, for instance, we had a points failure at Mill Lane Jct where the Leeds and Halifax lines converged before Exchange. There was just Gordon Hull and me on duty so one had to be near a railway van all the time. Early on in my time at Bradford we had a telephoned bomb scare concerning the left luggage lockers causing the station, and I think the bus station, to be closed. Gordon thought it well worth the risk if we took the master keys and checked out every locker. Fortunately there was nothing untoward to be found and the train delay was limited to less than 15min.

Retuning to Shipley, the signalling there was one of the most complex installations that existed under absolute block regulations. At one time the three boxes at each corner of the triangle formed by the Leeds-Bradford Forster Square route, the Leeds-Skipton route and the Leeds-Bradford Forster Square route were: to the east Leeds Jct, to the west Bingley Jct and to the south Bradford Jct. By the time I arrived, Leeds Jct had been absorbed by the next box in the direction of Leeds, Guiseley Jct where the Bradford-Shipley-Ilkley line diverged via the newly re-opened station of Baildon. As mentioned previously, Guiseley Jct is now Dockfield Jct, Bingley Jct is Shipley West and Bradford Jct is Shipley South Jct. Simple. British Rail had no difficulty with locations such as Wath North (North) and Oakenshaw North (South Jct.) but the Shipley former situation did not suit Railtrack/Network Rail.

Double track existed on all three sides of the triangle with two platforms on each of the legs towards Bradford. There were no platforms at that time on the east to west leg from Leeds to Skipton. Trains from Skipton or Morecambe to Leeds had to call at the Skipton-Bradford line platform, reverse at Bradford

Jct and proceed via the Bradford-Leeds platforms. Loco-hauled trains could not cope with such a complication so skipped Shipley. Trains from Leeds towards Skipton that called at Shipley had to proceed past Bingley Jct and reverse into the down Bradford-Skipton line platform with the guard operating the buzzer to dmu drivers. Trains such as the Thames Clyde Express had no time to dawdle around performing this procedure and looked sniffily down on Shipley as they passed. There was an extra set of instructions when tail traffic (dmus hauling parcel vans) was involved.

This was complicated enough without two further problems. The Bradford-Skipton side of the triangle was on a sharp curve which I suspect could accommodate short Midland Railway passenger coaches but the throw of longer dmu vehicles fouled the opposite platform line making even a two-car dmu an out-of-gauge load. A Skipton-Leeds dmu therefore had to have the Leeds-Skipton line blocked with the 1-2-6 bell signal exchanged between Bingley Jct and Bradford Jct before the train was offered as a 2-6-3. The same applied to say a Leeds-Morecambe dmu needing to reverse at Bingley Jct into the Bradford-Skipton platform. The Bingley Jct signalman then had to send the blocking back outside home signal bell code to Bradford Jct (3-3). As per signalling regulation 7, the Bradford Jct signalman could not accept a potentially conflicting train until he had received the 3-3-4 bell signal telling him the reversing train was at a stand. I think I am right in saying that the Leeds-Morecambe train had to be signalled to Bingley box by the 3-3-2 'shunting into forward section' bell signal followed by 8 bells 'train withdrawn'. When station duties were complete it was signalled to Bingley as 4 bells, 'is line clear for express passenger train?'. 'Train out of section' from Bingley Jct to Bradford Jct and Bingley to Bingley Jct completed the procedure. Including calls for attention, the procedure for acceptance and 'train out of section' with Guiseley Jct and understanding by repetition I make this 134 beats on the Bingley Jct block instruments. I get a different number every time I check the figure!

I doubt whether it all happened by the book when I was not there. Every so often train register books had to be withdrawn for cross-checking. Horace Egginton was a wizard at this and I made myself his slow-witted apprentice but even I could see that the 1-2-6 was not being sent at all. When a train was offered and refused, one signalman might book the opposite line being blocked at that time but his mate often booked 1-2-6 when it was eventually accepted. They probably took the precaution of putting the block needle to 'train on line' though even if only to cater for the eventuality of a visit in the middle of the move. The occasional 'train out of section' entry was missing, especially the last entry when the page had been turned over for entries on the opposite line but standards were generally good. It was not unknown for a whole train to be missed though and some of the engineering possession entries did not comply with modern requirements under the 'new' rule book where wording requirements were specific.

There was only one signalman in the Shipley area with whom I could not get on, perhaps the only one in the whole of the Bradford area. This was one of the residents at Bingley Jct. He was a corpulent bear of a man who would sit in his braces on the raised Midland frame operating the block bells and instruments on the shelf behind and above him with his hand twisted back to the block bell over his shoulder. He could reach even the distant signal levers from this position and throw them around from his sitting position. Occasionally he had to rise to fill in the train register. It is hard to judge whether he hated me more than I despised him. I do not know his personal circumstances but perhaps he had good reason to do so, even if it was my basic earnings for what I did compared to his. When I visited he would operate the block bell tapper like a machine gun. Was that 3-3-4 he just sent or 10? Ten is not a signal but it might have been 9 or 11 to see if I could count. The block regulations specifically said bell signals must be made 'slowly and distinctly, the pauses between the sets of beats being clearly marked'. Good luck to anyone trying to enforce that one at Bingley Jct. By the time even the 100th of the theoretical 134 beats had been sent by very slow and very distinct beats with very clear pauses, the train concerned would be running late. Sometimes if two signalmen had a misunderstanding in ringing the bell codes, one would resort to 'slow and distinct', one signalman receiving such a signal code, when I was there, once saying, "That was just sarcastic."

The morning express to Nottingham passes Shipley Bingley Jct in the hands of a Class 40 before the provision of passenger platforms on this side of the Shipley triangle.

On one occasion I had not followed the order of bells being exchanged. Perhaps my concentration had lapsed or perhaps the large man sitting on the frame was having a joke at my expense. I made a feeble excuse that I had left something in the van and disappeared for ten minutes to check the green regulations book. As I thought, two of the signals had been rung in the wrong order. On my return I had the temerity to raise the issue with the signalman. He turned on me and snarled that he knew what I had been doing checking up on him in the rule books and that he could not look things up like that. I was well and truly caught. This was a classic example played so often by experienced railwaymen on the less wise of turning their wrong doing into yours but the sad part for me was that he was quite right. I should have known. I should have been confident enough to take him on toe to toe. Horace would have done. I was about to tell him to work straight up in future but the phone rang from Guiseley Jct. A voice said, "I've got a rubbish train here that I am going to send you to run round." The Bingley Jct signalman's lip curled before he retorted, "Run round your own expletive rubbish," and slammed the phone down. I took this opportunity to say I would go to Guiseley Jct to see what was going on. The day after, in a quiet moment in the office, I confided to Horace Egginton what had happened. He looked quite upset for me and said in a fatherly fashion, "Don't bother about him, he's like that with everyone." This may or may not have been true but I had heard some evidence of that with his remarks about the rubbish train. My lesson had been salutary and it was one I tried to remember: Keep one step ahead. Know your rules better than anyone else.

The method of working at Shipley was instrumental in pulling me out of a tricky situation at Exeter in the first couple of months I was there. A dispute with the NUR had resulted in a refusal to work overtime. The number of signalmen was being run down with a resultant high vacancy rate to ensure there was less of a problem absorbing displaced staff after the modern panel signal box replaced the manual boxes. I cannot remember now whether the dispute was national, divisional or local but the NUR was strong in Exeter, directed by the City Council leader Chester Long who chaired the staff side of the regional sectional council and had friends, sometimes appeasers, in high places.

Chester had tried to blacken my name in regional circles. Soon after my arrival the Bristol divisional manager passed on a letter from the regional personal manager's deputy wanting to know why proper consultation had not taken place over some emergency budget cuts. The letter to my boss Paul Witter had ended, "May I suggest you should teach your area manager the rules of consultation." I was seething as I drafted my reply. I had the minutes of a signed local departmental committee (LDC) consultation meeting I had chaired on the subjects. Few people were prepared to take Chester on though.

Whatever the origins of the dispute we were faced with being unable to cover Exeter Middle signal box. The West Box was legendary, being restored at Crewe Heritage Centre after resignalling. 'Middle' Box would have been called 'Exeter East' in any logical naming system and was similar in both size and importance to 'West'. The platforms of St. David's station were in the short block section between the two. My operations manager, Bernard Price, a former Shrewsbury area relief signalman, was away on holiday so the efforts to cover the afternoon turn fell to the signalling inspectors Derek Old and Bill Mardon, liaising with the roster clerks and conveying the worsening news in regular visits to my office. Compared to 1976/7 at Bradford it was now the summer of 1983 and I was in charge of the Exeter area with 965 staff of all operating and clerical grades. I had replaced a well-liked area manager in his 50s following his sudden death. My opening pep talk to the area team and clerical staff gathered in my office was that I was there to restore standards and improve safety and punctuality. I was subsequently reminded that I had ended my address with the words that, "The party's over," or something equally likely to endear me to my new staff. Delivered in a Yorkshire accent to gentle West Country folk it could possibly have sounded a shade harsher than I intended.

Class 50s Nos. 50050 'Fearless' and 50002 'Superb' enter Exeter St. David's with the 13.00 empty stock from Laira to form a Waterloo train on Sunday October 12, 1985.
Credit: P. Medley

Anyway, here we were working as a team unsuccessfully trying to keep the Western Region Main line to Plymouth open when we suddenly had a volunteer to work his rest day. Just as we all relaxed there was another message to say he could not make it because he felt unwell. I phoned him. He had obviously been persuaded to have second thoughts but was at least apologetic in his refusal. It was now approaching 14.00. The early turn man would be going home soon. Should I order a signalling supervisor to take over? If I did order them to man the box, would the signalmen at Exeter West, and Cowley Bridge refuse to work with him? More immediately, what were we going to do with the trains approaching from Newton Abbot? Time for some clear thought.

My mind went back to Shipley and I hurriedly drafted some new local instructions for Exeter West. Each box had a set of these on the back wall with exemptions from some rules, additional requirements and a few special bell signals and routing codes. My replacement ones for Exeter West gave special authority for signalmen to allow a train to shunt into forward section if the box in advance was closed. The block indicator would be normal, the bell signal should be booked in the train register as if sent and a reminder collar should be placed on the levers concerned.

While the instructions were being typed I followed up on the second string to the bow. I spoke to the signalman's union representative, starting by asking him what was going on. An innocent "Nothing" was the reply. We talked about how no one was available to cover Exeter Middle in a few minutes time. "We just seem to have run out of cover," I was told. I asked the key question. "We are not in dispute then, it is just that there is no one to take over?" The rep thought he had won. "Oh no Boss, there's no dispute," he said. I replied, "Oh, that's good, in that case I can ask a signalling inspector to work the box until we can find someone."

The next bit was the hardest, telling Bill Mardon to disregard a lifetime's union membership and his Labour councillor credentials to work the box until someone could be found. I think he contemplated a refusal, which would have resulted in my sending him home but he went with a heavy heart. I put my special instructions in a safe place for use the next time I was over a barrel. I believe the night man found himself available for 12hrs from 18.00 but, if I am mistaken, some similar cover did materialise.

My strategy had been learned when I was area operations manager at Middlesbrough. My area manager Arnold Wane was a Horwich trained loco engineer, a background that had forged the man he was. It also destroyed him when he later succumbed to asbestosis. But in his mid 50s he was on top of his game. I do not think it unfair to say he was not popular with his staff but that is not a criterion for judging effectiveness. The particular lesson we are studying came at Tees Yard when he wanted to discuss weekend staffing arrangements to move a backlog of traffic. Yes we still had those in the late 1970s. It was normal to have a Sunday shift rostered to move some trains to Tyne or York. The supervisors had decided they were no longer going to consult with Arnold as I suspect they thought he had taken them to the cleaners so many times. It was my job to go and talk them round to going upstairs to the office with the panoramic view to agree the weekend working. It took some doing but the yard planner, who was the supervisors' spokesman, eventually gave in, saying his members were not going to work this weekend whatever the Boss said. Arnold Wane went through every approach possible meeting with the same response. "Sorry, we have all been working so many hours no one wants to work on Sunday." When this was incontrovertibly established he played the card I had taken with me up my sleeve to Exeter. "We're not in dispute then?" "No we're not in dispute." "Then we will run the yard with management staff on Sunday." And he did.

I have always said that of all the people for whom I worked Arnold Wane had the clearest vision of what he wanted and how to get there. There was only one route; the most direct. He would achieve everything he wanted in a local meeting then take the staff side to the pub and take their money playing dominoes, at which he was an expert in the '3s & 5s' version. He owned a garage with the Leyland franchise at Hurworth-on-Tees.

Shortly after I moved to the area office from Tees he took me on one side to say that the family mini was not the sort of car he thought his deputy should be driving. If I went down to the garage one of his sons would sort me out with a really good deal. One son handled repairs and the other sales. I duly did as I was told but the really good deal amounted to little more than just a deal. We changed the car at Arnold's garage shortly before my next move to a Triumph Acclaim which served us well for another 16 years, well into my early retirement.

Arnold's wife Heather was a keen participant in Darlington amateur operatics, although Arnold regularly insisted she was shy. Together, they would lead a round of area dinner-dances at which attendance was semi-compulsory. Linda and I did not, would not, could not dance so they were a trial. It was at one of these that he first met Linda who was wearing a particularly stunning dress. He asked where I had been hiding this beauty for such a long time and repeatedly tried to make her dance. When we moved to Exeter the social scene had some similarities, with a few Western Region events also being held on the area. Linda and I thought we had better try to learn to dance and took some very private lessons. We tried out what we had learned at one event held at the Langstone Cliff Hotel at Dawlish which was a disaster as private lessons had not taught us how to avoid other couples. Nor had we learnt how to turn corners or even go back the way we had come. After one solitary and salutary attempt we gave up. I had a brain wave. "Hang on, it's the area manager who says what sort of social gathering we have so I do not need to have dances!" That just left the odd Regional jamboree for which excuses had to be found.

Arnold Wane taught me that every time I went to headquarters I had to make time to circulate round the various offices making face to face contact with people who might be of help in the future, also to ensure that any visiting superiors to my area had to sit on an uncomfortable chair while I sat at ease behind my desk in swivelling and preferably tilting chair, ideally with the light at my back to make my expression difficult to judge. He was disappointed when I chose to move to Newcastle Divisional Office after a regrading of my Middlesbrough job was agreed but I needed an extra job on my c.v. ready for my next potential promotion and I wanted to move house from Teesside. In fact I agreed the move to Newcastle only if I could move house, whereas most people tried to negotiate the opposite. The more I got to know Arnold the more I was aware of his otherwise invisible insecurities. I think his perception that the Middlesbrough area's shortcomings were treated more seriously than some other areas were justified and the opportunity his rules re-examination might give the divisional officers was a real worry to him. He actually asked me to tutor him for the test.

But we have strayed a long way from Shipley in search of these transferable lessons. I had learnt a couple more at first hand in my days on call. One late afternoon of leaden skies, dusk settled on the West Riding. The Guiseley Junction signalman sent a message that there had been a couple of point failures and needed help. The signalling & telecommunications staff were called, as well as the civil engineers. There was often a dispute into whose equipment was at fault. As signal engineers remarked their equipment was set to fine standards not the odd half inch or two. As the civils said, the signal engineers stuff failed if it had so much as a grain of dust inside it. In the meantime the operator in charge clipped and scotched the points and authorised trains to pass signals at danger. Obviously, the more complex the layout and busier the train service, the more the risk element rises and concentration becomes critical.

So with visibility hovering between needing a hand lamp and managing without, with staff of two departments wanting ownership of various bits of equipment, with their spirited exchanges about what needs doing and by whom, the ringing of the block bells, the horns of detained trains and the visits of traincrew to carry out Rule Book Section K, what are the chances of the operating supervisor and the signalman reaching a clear understanding? Virtually zero? Well that's my excuse and I am sticking to it. Normally you would politely request people to transfer their infernal racket outside the box but these were the ones upon who we were relying to salvage the problem. Between us we managed to release a couple of trains. On my reaching a recalcitrant pair of points with a heavy clip in one hand and a couple of chocks under the other arm the problem was where to put your handlamp to see what you were doing. Don't waste time seeking a solution – there isn't one. Point clips are beasts. They are one of the survivors from the Victorian Age of heavy engineering; one piece having a tendency to swivel away from the other. But, hope they do that or else you will not get it under the near rail and round to the far one. And greasy; thick black gunge that gets everywhere. Budget for a new shirt out of any overtime. Again, indeed hope there is a lot of oil on that clip because the last sort you need to pick from the motley selection on offer at most signalboxes is one without it and if you choose one showing the remotest sign of rust you are doomed to failure. Add a return to the box for a different one to your potential delay estimates.

Meanwhile an impatient dmu driver will probably be looking down his nose at you for taking so long. Here is the driver of the 17.12 Leeds-Morecambe, the prime Aire Valley commuter train of its day. Let's get that clip on. Test it, pull it, kick it. That looks good. Well, not good, it looks as if it will hold. Give a pre-arranged signal with the Bardic to the signalman or go on the phone. "Authorise the driver to pass the signal at danger and obey all other signals." I pass on the message and off goes the driver. The front coach has not completely passed me when the train stops abruptly. The driver drops his window and looks back at me and then down (in both senses). "Points not set." He says in a matter of fact tone. I was horrified to see that the trailing points from the Ilkley line into the down line had not been set normal for the train to pass. The signalman had not checked his route but I was in charge and I had not checked the safe position of all points on the route I had verbally authorised the driver to use.

I spoke to the signalman and I thanked the driver profusely. Heads were sticking out of the quarter lights of the dmu. As the train set off again I identified one of them as belonging to one of the signalling inspectors at Leeds. I waited a request for either an explanation of what had happened, if he had found out, or why there had been a second stop, if he had not, but none came. After a week or so I relaxed. Ten more yards and there would have been extensive damage, heavy delay and, quite possibly, a disciplinary charge for me. I reflected on what had happened and taught myself a few lessons in that intervening week, confiding in Gordon Hull. He was appalled, but not at my mistake, more that I had taken charge and therefore responsibility. His advice was to simply do the legwork on behalf of the signalman on the basis there was only one person in charge.

In fact I recalled having seen him in action doing this at Apperley Jct one evening. The layout had been relaid with modern clamp lock points and a single lead junction to the branch. These rapidly became unfashionable after a tendency to pass signals protecting the junction at danger had resulted in collisions. Newton (near Glasgow) was such an example. Thorne Jct on the Doncaster division was a 35mph single lead junction to Hull from the Doncaster-Cleethorpes line. But that was in the 1980s and this was still firmly in the middle of the 1970s. Gordon had honoured our arrangement about covering each other's on call when time was important and nipped down from his home in Guiseley to Apperley Jct, only three miles by rail but a good deal more by road, including a rough ride in the van down the track bed of the former fast lines which had been removed in a 1960s rationalisation scheme. When I arrived he was in the middle of a move checking everything with the signalman. I did not understand how he could justify not taking charge. I reverted to my normal methods.

The new Apperley Jct layout took a long time to settle in. The points were over-sensitive to movement and would not work if contaminated. The Rylstone limestone trains, loaded eastbound, often caused trouble from the cloud of dust that usually accompanied their progress. If good old fashioned points misbehaved it was not uncommon for the signalman to whack them with his coal hammer and resume normal working. These new fangled ones did not respond to such vulgarity. It was necessary to obtain a crank handle from a case in the box and sign for it in the train register book, then insert the handle and pump the points to the direction you wanted them. This action contained a dramatic moment when it became evident whether they had electric detection or whether they were still not fitting correctly. Sometimes they would jam half way and there was no option but to wait for technicians to free them. I think I am right in saying that there was no requirement to clip them if detection was restored but on one occasion, before the Guiseley Jct episode, a move I authorised from the down main line to the Ilkley branch passed over the single lead junction and took the up Ilkley Leeds line instead of the down Leeds Ilkley one. I could swear I had wound them 'normal' and the reliable signalman was sure they had been set properly. The driver set back and continued on his merry way without reporting the incident. I lost faith in clamp locks from thereon and always clipped them regardless.

When I went to the Western I was appalled that station staff were allowed to pump clamp lock points and that the handle was not subject to much in the way of security. I used one for the last time at Exeter Central when there was a point failure when I was doing a routine visit. It seemed to impress some staff and disappoint others that their area manager would stoop to such a menial task. At Bradford such failures had become part of the routine - I remember attending to clamp lock failures at Dryclough Junction, west of Halifax and Mill Lane, outside Exchange, on hot Saturday afternoons. Ah yes, clamp locks did not like excessive heat either.

I did have the occasional success when on call though and one of these also occurred at Apperley Junction one wild and stormy mid-evening. A parcel train from Forster Square towards Leeds was stopped at Apperley Junction's up home signal which was a long way from the box at the other side of the junction itself ... and then a substantial overlap besides. An Ilkley line passenger train was given preference but before the signal could be cleared for the parcel train it set off slowly towards the box. The conflicting moves were fortunately out of the way as the parcel driver presented himself at the box. The signalman correctly challenged the driver with passing his up home signal at danger only to be met with indignation. "You authorised me to come up to the box with a green light waved side to side," the driver claimed. No matter that this was not the correct way of going about such a move and there was no signal being displayed from the box window as the train reached it. Control became involved and the driver insisted he had received a green hand signal. The 'deputy' phoned me around 21.00 and I set off in my trusty yellow van, eventually bouncing along the empty track bed and walking out to the signal, my long, rubber lined, black mackintosh keeping everything except my head dry. When I looked back towards the box I tried to imagine myself at loco cab height. The trees were flailing fiercely in the gale. Sheets of rain were lashing my face and the light from the nearby chemical factory security lamps, when lined up with the signalbox roof from ballast height, was being windblown as if the fitting itself were moving. I noted it had a blue tinge but I was suddenly surprised to see that with certain combinations of wind and rain the blue looked more like green and the tempestuous conditions made it seem it was being blown from side to side, like a saunter's hand signal to a driver to proceed towards his lamp with caution. I explained to the signalman what I had seen, and then to control to tell the driver he was wrong, but not that wrong. I subsequently visited the factory and obtained agreement for the light to be redirected away from the railway. Many years later I was complimented by someone who was kind enough to say the Bradford drivers thought well of me and I can only think that, if it were indeed true, being thorough that night at Apperley Junction must have been the main reason. A lesson learnt though – treat what drivers tell you with respect and you will be right many more times than you are wrong. The other direct contact with Bradford drivers was instructing them on overhead line safety after east coast suburban electrification. All I did was to parrot the appropriate booklet and at this distance in time I am surprised I thought I knew enough about such a crucial safety subject.

The clamp lock point renewals at Apperley Jct and the consequential signal alterations of single-lead junctions, here and elsewhere, were shown to suffer more consequences if a signal was passed at danger. Hindsight might have prevented such problems but so would foresight. One of the management slogans of the time was 'Don't plan for failure' but hindsight suggested that, at least in signalling terms, this was the equivalent of "don't do a rigorous risk analysis." The term 'risk analysis' was still in its infancy, at least on the railway at that time where the reliance was on a disciplined application of copious rules; rule book, general appendix, sectional appendix, local instructions, weekly notices, emergency notice boards, signalling regulations, working manual (green, white, yellow and pink pages). Just looking at the nearest sectional appendix to hand the 1978 Southern Section of the Eastern Region alone ran to 471 A4 pages. The pink pages of the working manual covered only dangerous goods and ran to 115 or so A5 pages.

Even if criticism of the safety at single-lead junctions came after their installation, it was obvious at the time that it was impossible to plan parallel moves at them. This is the modern watchword for planning busy junctions to turn the otherwise requirement for two main line paths into one. As an aside, I believe that if having sufficient capacity depends on parallel moves taking place then you need more capacity. A classic example is at Manchester Piccadilly where the TransPennine trains to and from Liverpool were booked to cross simultaneously at the junction between Ardwick and Piccadilly. Given that the eastbound ones had just come through the congested Castlefield corridor and the westbound ones had come from, usually, Scarborough, the parallel meeting of the ways happened rarely and the late train had to be accommodated afterwards. My belief is that parallel moves should not be planned and if they do happen it will free a bonus path.

Turning back specifically to Apperley Junction in 1977 the worst aspect from my viewpoint was that the down main starter on the Shipley side of the junction was removed. Someone had doubtless had a look to see how often trains were stopped at it and found it was not very often. However, if there was an obstruction, say in Thackley tunnel which was in the block section, a train waiting for permission to proceed from Apperley Junction during the Apperley Viaduct unstaffed hours would be standing at Apperley Jct's home signal blocking access to the Ilkley branch. I had a couple of strategies in my mind if this happened. If it was a dmu and the driver had route knowledge I would run the Aire Valley train round the other two sides of the triangle to Shipley. If the train was loco-hauled or route knowledge for the dmu driver was absent I would have laid three detonators a train length clear of the junction track circuit and instructed the driver to proceed to the detonators and wait until personally instructed by me to proceed. The latter would probably have got me the sack I suppose. But the Ilkley trains would have run to time so the sacrifice would have been worthwhile! I could have kept shunting the train to the up line and back I suppose.

There were two other lessons that come to mind at this point, both occurring at Keighley. The first followed the derailment of a 'vanfit' (covered, brake fitted van) in the yard. The mishap book said that loaded vehicles should not be rerailed locally. The Holbeck breakdown crew should be called. I outlined the circumstances to Control, filled out a mishap form with the derailment cause left blank and went to the signal box for a cup of tea. I expected a road van to arrive with jacking equipment and a gnarled old foreman of at least 40 to effect rerailing by sleight of hand. The Holbeck shed boss at this time was the formidable figure of Ted Geeson, a legend at serious derailments where it was rumoured that by his simply glaring at a wagon it would jump back onto the tracks in fear of the consequences. My incident would be a good few layers beneath his contempt.

It was not that long before Bingley offered us a Class 1 train, 4 beats on the bell. There was no express due. Enquiries revealed it was the sub clause of the regulation that covered a 'breakdown train going to clear line'. A pedant, not me, might pause to consider whether if the derailment of one van in a quiet yard complied with that description and whether it should not have been a Class 2 covering 'a breakdown train NOT going to clear line'. The capitals are used in the signalling regulation. However, this was used only for toolvans going back to the depot. We cleared the points to get the rescue train into the yard. The foreman pointed to the van and asked if that was it. He snorted at my reply and rerailed it with jacks and packing in a few minutes. Time for a brew. Then there was the loco to run round its train, propel out onto the main line and set off back to Holbeck.

The Bradford trip engine crew had been watching the proceedings with an air of detachment but were now in a hurry to return to Valley Yard. They coupled up to the van and started to put it in the siding where it was needed. CLUNK. It was off the road again. I really do not know why I did not do my best to rerail it myself but there were so many eyes watching. Phone Control. The breakdown vans were stopped at Shipley, returned, did the same again and went home but not before the foreman had told me in no uncertain terms not to go near the van again. It would take at least a page to list the lessons learnt that day. It turned out that the van was unevenly loaded so the front axle was very light and the rear one very heavy so it was likely to be lifted off uneven track.

Another day at Keighley reminded me of a further lesson, one that I knew but had forgotten. On summer Saturdays each year the holiday extra trains from Leeds would start back at whichever town was having its factory holiday weeks. The holidays are sometimes known as Wakes' weeks, but I think that was more a Lancastrian term. The special traffic notice had the arrangements for empty stocks to run out to Keighley in this case and restart the train from the up platform. I guess there was a Scarborough, Yarmouth, Skegness, perhaps a Cleethorpes and even the Poole.

This was a part of railway work I liked best; getting passengers onto their train as quickly as possible, cutting station time, achieving punctual starts; the power of moving a huge train just by blowing a whistle and waving my hand. Bill Lockley was spare and had come out to direct operations. I well remember rushing to get rid of one train with a Class 40 on the front bang on time and turning to Bill at the other end of the platform.

"You did a good job there didn't you?" he asked.

I tried not to appear smug. "5 late in and on time out."

"And what do you say about breaking the rules?"

"How?"

"Were you authorised to start the train?"

"......Yes?"

"Who was in charge of the platform?"

"....you I suppose."

"No 'suppose' about it."

A simple lesson but one learnt. Only one person is in charge of train dispatch.

I had been at Bradford over a year when my rules exam came due. Jeff Lawson was going on holiday and Bill Lockley was going to cover him. Bill came in for a coffee and leant forward on the desk. "I'm going to take you on your rules next week," he growled with a dose of good-natured threat. I was not unduly perturbed, in fact I was confident that I probably knew more about the theory than Bill. He had probably not opened the signalling book for decades and would not be up to date with amendments. Or so youthful arrogance led me to imagine. On the other hand, I had learnt rules at evening classes, in signalboxes on the studentship scheme, on intensive courses as a management trainee and, most of all, I had received private lessons from Les Jardine, a softly spoken lowland Scotsman who was also a labour councillor. Les had been signalling inspector at Cudworth and moved to Huddersfield in about 1966. His son was a friend of mine in the sixth form and my best friend at school was more than smitten with Les's daughter.

He was now chief signalling inspector at Leeds and I used to travel with him quite regularly in my off-call van-less weeks. Lessons with Les were like having one's eyes opened to the world of railways, perhaps the difference between being read a story as an infant and being able to see the pictures as the pages were turned. The semi-legal phraseology of the signalling regulations came to life with sketches and anecdotes of how the rules were applied and what the dire consequences could be if they were not. Of course the supervisory rules exam covered more than the signalling book…a lot more. I was confident but not so much so that I did not spend a few evenings and a weekend re-reading bits I had difficulty retaining such as Single Line Working acceptances shown on the accompanying revision aid.

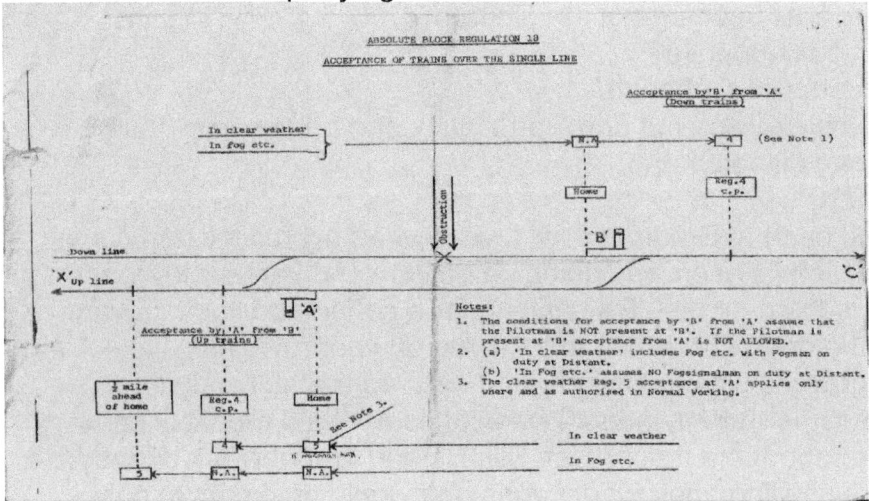

There was another one of these to remember for acceptance conditions approaching the single line.

Eventually Bill called me in.
"Right you bugger, I'm going to enjoy this." It was a joke….at least I thought so at the time, so I grinned. The advice to persons doing the examining, even then, was to put the person being examined at their ease. Ask some easy questions first. Be conscious of the image you are projecting and be careful not to intimidate. If Bill had read the guidance

he had either not taken it in or he was not going to have his fun ruined by it.

"First question," he said. I relaxed a little expecting an easy ball I could smite to the boundary.

"When does the pilotman wear a blue armband?"

"Blue?"

"Did I say blue?"

"Yes"

"Then I meant blue."

I thought hard. He was referring to single line working over double track (or more) lines. There was the red pilotman's armband and provision for what could be tied on to the upper arm if one was not immediately available. Then there were route conductors, for drivers who did not know the route they were booked to cover, called pilotmen in the railway vernacular. They did not have armbands. Or did they? I hesitated and answered that it could only be during single line working when the proper armband was not available and only a blue piece of material was able to be tied on instead.

"Wrong." The one word response was an invitation to guess again but I was not going there. I had fired my only shot.

"In that case I don't know." Not a good answer to the first question. I felt a little crestfallen, even punctured.

"On the Humber Ferry. Next question....."

At that time the shipping operation was still under the British Rail umbrella. It probably did require a pilotman in certain tidal conditions I supposed but we were not issued with a navigational manual. Bill had enjoyed my moment of discomfort, then proceeded normally and I passed, with what amounted to a resounding Yorkshire compliment ending the session.

"Not bad," he said as I left the room.

I have related this story many times at many rules exams I have conducted as examiner, usually as an anecdote to indicate just how fair a person I was being not to do that, without much success in that respect probably. Only if I knew the person I was examining very well would I actually ask it as a first question and only if I was confident they were going to pass regardless of the Humber Ferry. After the early privatisation of the British Rail shipping division its relevance was reduced of course.

The greatest challenge of being on call was the suicide problem. I do not intend to dwell unduly on the subject, just to indicate what was involved. We were not allowed to call someone being killed by a train a suicide as this could be done only after a coroner's verdict. This instruction was reinforced and applied more rigorously as the years passed but back in the 1970s it was still called a suicide in railway conversations. A point of contention with us, and particularly the unlucky drivers involved, was that the verdict would be misadventure or whatever, instead of suicide, if there was the slightest excuse not to bring in an alternative verdict. I think that was in deference to the sensibilities of the family and possibly even for insurance policy safeguarding but it did not do much to reassure the drivers or the person involved with clearing up the mess. Many of the issues involved surfaced during the Area Manager's Diaries I wrote so I will not repeat them. The worst location on the Bradford area was Menston on the Ilkley line which was near a traditional mental home, or 'institute' perhaps. There were approaching double figures in my eighteen months and they all occurred on Horace Egginton's on call week opposite to me. I thought at the time that I had a guardian angel but in later years I wondered if Horace and Gordon Hull had shielded me from them. I would have found out afterwards from signalmen and control logs though. I had a near miss one bank holiday Monday when there were no trains on the Ilkley branch until lunchtime. One unfortunate individual waited on the footbridge with a rope attached to his neck ready to jump in front of the first train. When it eventually arrived the rope snapped and the train stopped. The action would have injured and even killed the train driver. It was rumoured that the escapee was run over by a train a few months later though.

I was at Bingley Jct one sunny afternoon completing a box visit. Bingley had offered a Class 6 Rylstone stone train, probably 1200 tonnes plus two locomotives. After a while we received the dreaded 'six consecutive beats', legally and logically without 'call attention' and described in the signalling regulations as quite simply: Obstruction Danger. It is worth pausing to mention that the bell signal for removing an obstruction was just call attention and send the 2-1, the same as train out of section. Basically, drama over let's get on with the job. After rapping out the acknowledgement 6 bells the Bingley Jct signalman answered the phone. The Rylstone freight had hit someone who had jumped in front of it at Bingley station, the damage a mass approaching 1,500 tonnes hitting someone at 60mph being scarcely able to be contemplated. The Bingley Jct signalman had to send Obstruction Danger back to Bingley to block the up line and place lever collars on the appropriate signal. I did not have my van with me, as I tried to do visits by train where possible.

The Morecambe dmu was in the platform at Shipley, its crew looking impatient at the delay. I crossed the line to speak to the driver and guard, who had come to the front of the train when he had seen me. I explained what had happened and how a substantial delay was likely, while I tried to work out what to do in the other half of my brain. Obviously I could not sit here. I could get a taxi but then I would lose touch with what was happening for 20min or so perhaps. I went back to the box. Was the line clear to Bingley's home signal? It was, so the Obstruction removed signal was sent and replaced with Blocking Back inside home signal. The Morecambe could then be accepted to Bingley under the Regulation 5 arrangement where the line was clear only to the home signal with no clear overlap available. Normally this acceptance was available only where specially authorised but there was provision in accordance with five more signalling regulations. Regulation 14 (b) allowed the acceptance to be used "when the line is clear to the outermost home signal but is occupied by a train or otherwise obstructed ahead of that signal and it is necessary to work a train forward to a point in rear of the obstruction." I was covered for this move although I would not have remembered it was clause (b).

I discussed what was planned with the dmu's train crew. There were two dangers. We had lost the ability to detrain passengers to road transport in the event of a heavy delay, but we tended not to do that in those days except for limited distances when another train was ready to be turned round at the opposite end of the obstruction section. We could always bring the dmu back to Shipley under the provisions of the situations in which a wrong direction move could be authorised. A bigger danger was that passengers might be subject to distressing scenes but we had no need to go as far as the home signal if this seemed inadvisable. Off we went. Despite my previous good fortune this one was to be mine. We stopped at the home signal and I went forward on foot. I could see the train not far away and there seemed little fuss. I had probably beaten the police and the ambulance but, no, there they were on the platform all the clearing up done, no mess on the locos, a last bit of tidying up to do with remains on the platform. There was no one around who had seen it other than the loco driver and he was happy to go forward. I do not think I have entirely got over even the limited sight I had, if I have to chop up raw meat for instance, but I could not believe how lucky I had been. I waited until the scene was fit for passengers to see, saw the stone away and returned to reassure the dmu driver he could safely proceed when his signal was cleared.

On the subject of quoting regulation clauses and sub clauses there were certain ones which were used as shorthand. If for instance there was a failure of signalling equipment and telephones we worked to the time interval arrangements described in signalling regulation 25 (a) (iv) and this mouthful was a shorthand regularly used to describe the situation being handled. Another Regulation needing a good memory was No. 15 Examination Of Line. This listed what types of train could conduct the examination in what circumstances; if there was a tunnel in the section, if it was dark or in fog and falling snow, which conditions had to have another person competent in rules in the cab with the driver etc. I learnt all this with the efficiency of one of the prize parrots my uncle in Fleetwood owned. I was ready to apply the regulation when the time came. Shortly after I had arrived at Bradford the supervisors were in the office around 16.45 when the call was received that youths had been reported putting stones on the line at Crossflatts (where a new station was to be opened in 1982). I took out my timetable to see what trains were around to examine the line and what to tell the signalmen. Geoff Armitage, my south side counterpart, asked what I was doing. I curbed myself from asking if it was not obvious but I managed to ask why. "Get yourself out there and examine it on foot," he said with uncharacteristic impatience. I duly did so and pronounced the line clear without having put a train in harm's way. The majority of line examinations are in fact done on foot but the regulation is about trains and does not mention it. Another obvious but important lesson quickly learnt.

A feature of signalbox visits was the need to examine detonators. These were round metal casings with flexible lead clips which could be manipulated into position to secure the detonators to the rail head in order to alert the driver of an oncoming train of an obstruction. They were chiefly used to protect engineering possessions and failed trains but they were also to warn an oncoming train of an emergency such as a landslide or road vehicle on the track. Their theft was a cause for concern in the days of an active Irish Republican Army threat but I never knew of any thefts other than from robberies when locations were unstaffed. Spare ones were kept in innocuous grey boxes on the signalbox shelves. Most boxes had levers painted with white with black chevrons that operated detonator places. These put two adjacent detonators on top of the rail if the lever was pulled after a train had passed a signal at danger. In some locations they operated automatically in conjunction with their adjacent signal – in place on the rail when the signal was at danger and clear when the signal showed proceed. The general appendix had a set of instructions about when these detonators fell out of date, at which time the supervisor had to take them away for safe disposal in large locked containers that could not be carried off under someone's arm.

The funny thing about detonators (the only one perhaps) was that, no matter how often you visited a signal box, when you decided to check them – ones in the placers, ones on the shelf, ones in a storage box, ones on hooks by the door ready for the signalman to grab on his way out to stop or protect a train or developing dangerous situation, it was commonplace to find ones that were out of date. No matter how often you checked, old ones would materialise. I used to put this down to the civil engineering staff at times of a possession palming their old ones off on the operating department and taking our new ones. There were a few occasions when I found some with 1940s dates stencilled on them. Another signature feature of my signal box visits was to check the bardic handlamp usually sitting on the block shelf next to the instruments. When I had visited boxes in the Huddersfield area on my studentship scheme with Les Jardine he had always inspected the handlamp and ensured it did not have its green lens showing. The theory was that if a signalman picked it up and turned it on train crew would see a green light. I preferred the red lens to be the default position but perhaps white would have been more sensible. You could hear the signalmen grind their teeth when I insisted on this but they could not summon a counter-argument.

Finally in this chapter it is worth admitting to failing to get on top of the issues at Bradford Valley Goods. This was a location where arriving material such as steel or newsprint would be taken by lorry to the consignee. There was precious little traffic left and even less outward business offered. There was a Grade B supervisor who knew the business inside out and who was hostile. There was no job for me to do other than endorse an order for extra transport from National Carriers if the normal requirement could not cover it. My absence prompted a claim for regrading from the 'B' grade supervisor, unsuccessfully, but I realised the railway had a way of catching up with such situations. I also failed to get to grips with the shunting roster there which seemed to have lots of overtime to cover three posts on each shift. Perhaps not nights. The ring leader was known for being militant and I did not take him on. I might excuse myself by saying I had all on to keep up with my round of box visits which were classed as safety of the line issues but, if I had been area manager, I would have directed my traffic manager to get himself out in the yard to define the work needing to be done and how many people were needed to do it, probably doing the equivalent of a work study survey. When I reached Teesside I think I had learnt that approach. Then when I wanted to take out the night turn supervisor at Newton Abbot between 22.00 and 04.00 I personally sat there noting everything that was done until the supervisor said he had nothing else to do until 04.00. This was not how the Western did such things but I knew exactly what needed doing when I chaired the consultation meeting. Bradford Valley taught me a number of lessons which were eventually reflected in my own budgets but it did not help my boss at Bradford. On reflection of course Jeff Lawson should have given the task to me as a specific objective. In the meantime I chose to write a report concerning the Aire Valley service to Scotland and how it could be improved, based on a project completed as a management trainee at Doncaster seeking to justify extra stops in the proposed Anglo-Scottish High Speed Train timetable. By moving the two daytime leisure trains further apart they could cover business requirements and save a set of coaches, or so I suggested.

I was followed into my Bradford job by Chris Dickinson, another young trainee with a bright future ahead of him arguably blocking the job for the local junior supervisors or senior signalmen for instance. I am not sure what Chris did about Valley. I also acted as host for the management trainees allocated to the Leeds area for them to receive their practical signal box training, one of whom was Stuart Baker who rose to the upper echelons of the Department for Transport and who former Chiltern chief Adrian Shooter holds responsible for the bi-mode elements of the Inter City Express programme of the '20-teen' years. Stuart was researching his famous railway atlases at the time and in later years used to rightly boast that he had been an objector to the Ilkley line closure proposals of the mid-60s when he was at Bradford Grammar School.

Looking at my excuse for not tackling the profligacy of shunting provision at Bradford Valley, one of my main problems was most of Thursday being absorbed by the pay run. This was governed by instructions in the cash regulations, another tome of instructions to absorb. Pay distribution was to take a variety of routes at different times. The motor vehicle used should be changed regularly and there must be two people involved. I am not sure what this last requirement was meant to achieve. Two serious injuries instead of one in the event of an attack? My normal escort was a young clerk from the office. We picked up a large box of cellophane pay-packets from the Bradford cash office then some more at Keighley, around 100 in total I think, and distributed them around the Dales. It was hard to find different routes, especially to signal boxes down country lanes, and different routes extended the time involved. You had to finish before the morning shift went home. We always used a yellow van with a red B.R. arrow signal and we always finished the run at Apperley Jct as the fish & chip shop was on the way back to the office from there. Guiseley box was, I think, the repository for the permanent way gang's wage packets. I thought I would innovate and in discreet words asked the local taxi firm we used for call-outs and emergencies what their price would be for a taxi for three hours on a Thursday morning running however many miles I had calculated were involved. The taxi dispatcher, someone who dressed like Danny deVito in 'Taxi' and had the same winning means of expression, looked me in the eye and said, "Pay run is it?" So much for security. I made my excuses and left.

Fortunately developments in banking meant that weekly pay packets delivered to outlying locations eventually became a feature of the past but I realise we were lucky to get away with this week in and week out. I knew early in my Studentship days that the cash regulations often amounted to simply a safeguard for management to hide behind. When I was at Brighouse for a brief time (the station closed for 30 years or so from 1970 before reopening as an unstaffed location and I must be the only person still alive to have issued a ticket at the booking office there) I had to escort the clerk to the bank on foot to collect the cash. There was only one feasible route, across the huge River Calder bridge. So much for varying the route. The pay packets had then to be made up before the early turn staff went off duty - relief signalmen at outstations, track gangs etc. The notes had to be clearly visible through the packet and arranged so that they could be counted accurately because shortages were not made up if the packet had been opened. It took me a long time to get my first one right. At Healey Mills a few months later the Thursday morning cash delivery came by armoured car and half the office was involved in the compilation. The end of the process was a tense affair. Would the last note be there to enable closure of the last pay packet? Would there be a fiver left on the desk? The last eventuality was easy. It was put on one side to await someone reporting their packet was short but the former relied on both honesty and observation coinciding.

Mention of National Carriers at Bradford Valley brings up the only real weakness in the 1968 Transport Act. British Rail's 'Sundries' division was hived off to a new concern called National Carriers. 'Sundries' made a hefty loss on carrying small consignments (bigger than a parcel, smaller than a wagonload) in a system of through vans that were supposed to make guaranteed connections in marshalling yards in the middle of the night all around the country. Before TOPS was introduced there was a sort of 'TOPS lite', to use modern terminology. It was called Advance Traffic Information, a system based on Telex that notified yards of priority connections requiring to be made so that hump shunting priorities could be established. If you opened the doors of twenty vans you might find forty consignments weighing 30 tons. And that might be on a busy day. Staff had to choose whether to stay with Sundries in the form of National Carriers or return to British Rail. I think there were a few incentives promised in the form of shares but many chose to return to the sanctuary of the parent company. British Rail, perhaps with the exception of Freightliner, was tied to hiring all its road vehicles from National Carriers, the only exemption being in case the new firm could not supply the order in which case private operators could be used.

You can tell how far the collection and delivery service lagged behind the times just by the name we used: 'Cartage'. The newly transferred drivers had lost any incentive to safeguard the goods traffic they were handling. Supervisors seemed to take the view that the British Rail order would be there regardless of what they supplied. In fact if the traffic was lost to rail there was a good chance they would benefit from a trunk haul too.

We had to take the area vans to the National Carriers workshop and the mechanics' attitude was clear to me the day I complained that the relatively modern Escort was leaking water onto the driver's seat every time it rained hard. The foreman said, "Yeah, common fault with these vans," and that passed for the pinnacle of their customer service. When it came to parcel deliveries it was just the same. In the 'autumn peak' season approaching Christmas it was normal for National Carriers not to be able to cover British Rail demands. I was on the management training scheme at Hull in 1975 when private operators were brought in to cover the shortfall. The parcel supervisor grinned when National Carrier said they could not cover because he knew the privateer would achieve 50% more 'drops' than normal even on a NCL regular round.

Once I had seen the year round in any job I became restless, looking for the next challenge. If you had done the Easter box openings one year the old adage of 'not two years' experience, one year's experience twice' kicked in. I was enjoying my job at Bradford. Linda and I had moved to a new detached former show house at Roberttown on the Bradford side of Mirfield and Linda was teaching at Dewsbury. In retrospect it might have been economically, and certainly socially, sensible simply to have stuck there for as long as railway reorganisations permitted. But for the time being ambition was thwarted as negotiations took place to make more headroom within the supervisory grades by creating a new Grade 'E' off the top of the existing scale which ended at 'D'. The need had arisen because of grade inflation (or 'creep') resulting in jobs of widely differing responsibilities being squeezed together in the existing structure. As a result there was a long-standing freeze on advertising Grade 'D' jobs. Eventually the dam burst and there must have been about twenty or more jobs advertised on one vacancy list. To mimic Geoff Armitage I saw at least half a dozen that I could claim at least 'should be' mine.

There was station manager Harrogate which I did not want as the operating content was low and secondary to the booking office supervision. Assistant Yard Master, Tyne was on shifts but also had some on call responsibilities. I would not be comfortable with both. Most of the others required a house move but still I applied for a large selection. This was a naïve error. I should have applied only for those I really liked because a carve up would result in those who had applied for virtually everything being given the one for which there were fewest applicants. In my case this was rest day relief senior operating supervisor Neville Hill. To accept it was a big mistake.

≢ British Rail Eastern

LEEDS (NEVILLE HILL)
COMBINED DIESEL MULTIPLE UNIT
AND COACHING STOCK DEPOT

Booklet issued on opening of the diesel depot before the addition of HSTs.

On paper the job looked as if it would be easily encompassed. The rest day relief supervisor covered late turn on Monday and Tuesday. Wednesday and Thursday were spare and Friday and Saturday were early turn. No nights, which in terms of experience was not good news because this is where the hard work was done and the difficult problems without back-up were to be encountered. I looked forward to perhaps having some interesting tasks pushed my way on my spare days. How wrong I was. First, I had not discovered that there was no general purpose relief supervisor so the three people in the shift jobs, and me, had to cover our own sickness and holidays. One of the shift supervisors, Ray Rix, was permanently detached from his roster to undertake special duties on anything to do with cleanliness, especially external cleaning standards. 'Rixie', to friends and foes alike, was a legend in his own imagination, a larger than life character who acted as if he had been placed in charge of the others. Second, the rest day relief was shared so the shift supervisors worked a rest day cover week after their night week. Third, when anyone was off all rest days had to be worked. Fourth, if two were off then it meant 12hr shifts and all rest days worked. So the roster was often 7x9hrs nights finishing 06.00 Monday. Return 8hrs later at 14.00 and work 6x7hr late turns finishing at 21.00 Saturday. Then back at 06.00 Sunday for 7x8hr turns finishing at 14.00 on Saturday and then, at last, what was seriously termed by my colleagues (laughingly by me) as our 'long weekend' until 22.00 Sunday; 32hrs without seeing Neville Hill. There was no late turn requirement on Sundays. Even then I usually gave my Sunday morning turns away to my colleague Clarrie Fletcher who would fit it in to his 'long weekend' for an extra 14hrs pay. He would finish at 21.00 on Saturday, come back on Sunday 06.00-14.00, back home and then onto seven nights at 22.00 (21.00 Mon-Sat). Only a dilettante like me would give up his Sunday turn. On a week with two of us away, heads down for an 80hr week. If someone, me for instance, refused a rest day 'Rixie' would reluctantly give up his special duties for a day but he made it obvious he was not happy. On the other hand, I suppose I made it obvious I was not happy most of the time.

My colleagues were all time-served shunters and guards who had reached this senior supervisor position on a newly refurbished depot after decades in the morass of marshalling yards and chaos of carriage sidings around West Yorkshire. They were all about 60 so most had worked in the 1930s, through the war and weathered the closures of the 1960s. I was aware that most had probably suffered deprivation, were facing retirement without their full complement of years in the salaried superannuation fund and that this was their time to make real money. For me, it was the previous generation or two of my family who could identify directly with how they must have felt.

The most affable was Cyril Hackney who took on my training. He was helpful and tried to explain how we could not allow the job to be uncovered or allow one of the 'B' grade supervisors to cover on higher grade duty. After all, one had been passed over to let me have the job. What Cyril did not do though was leave me at the 'west end' to run the job on the mini panel and by hand signals so I was always afraid of having to cover the duties, not for myself but because mistakes could kill people. Clarrie Fletcher was a huge man, a gentle giant he did not say much and the less he said you knew the more he disapproved. I used to follow Ben Curry round the roster and therefore I used to take over from him. He was also a man of few spoken words and virtually no written ones. We could park our cars between the sets of tracks in the middle of the yard so I would see him, as I shut the car door, standing in the office doorway that opened onto cinders covered in spent tea bags, smoking his pipe with his black mackintosh buttoned up to the neck over his serge uniform. As I approached him, about 10 or 15 minutes early on the appointed time depending on the traffic I met crossing Leeds, he would take an extra puff before breaking the rhythm of inhaling and exhaling simply to say, "It's all in t'book." And off he would go. I would go to the log book and review the entry. Supervisor B. Curry on duty, a few perfunctory lines if something dramatic had happened, then the 'off duty' time. At the other end of the spectrum I recorded a lot, probably far too much, and Cyril, who followed me, probably did not bother to read any of it. Of course I resorted to my supervisory uniform in this job after I had rediscovered it hanging in the wardrobe brand new for a couple of years while I had worn a lounge suit.

I must say, there was very little in the way of sickness from these veterans. There were a couple of occasions when Cyril did not arrive for the early turn and I had to work until 10.00, calling out Clarrie for an eleven hour 10.00-21.00 turn, trying to balance not waking him up against giving him sufficient notice. Ben, and I think Clarrie, said the railway did not pay for their telephones so it was not available for calling them at home. Again, telephones were still an expensive luxury to some in the 1970s and acquiring one was an important step towards demonstrating prosperity. I had no such reservations but if Ben wanted me he still sent a taxi with a 'take duty' request. It was easier to say 'not available' than on the telephone. I do not think I resorted to not answering the door and hiding behind the net curtains but it happened no more than two or three times. Linda and I were once on our way out to Linda's mum & dad's for Boxing Day lunch and tea when the taxi rolled up as we were backing down the drive. Take Duty 13.00 Staff Shortage. I heard Cyril's words ringing in my ears about not letting down the side but I nonetheless refused. Ben and Cyril would probably be glad to work 12hrs each and Ben had probably asked me only out of courtesy!

Neville Hill was opened as a steam locomotive shed mainly serving the North Eastern Railway's workload around Leeds following the expansion of services that had caused overcrowding at the Midland depot of Holbeck. As such, it was allocated to the York (50A) motive power district whereas other Leeds area sheds such as Stourton and Farnley Jct were grouped with Holbeck and ones such as Copley Hill and Stourton were in Wakefield's fiefdom. Following rationalisations and boundary moves Neville Hill went from being 50B to 55H, the alphabetic demotion being necessary to accommodate it at the end of 55A Holbeck's ownership group after 55G Huddersfield (Hillhouse) rather than shuffle smokebox door allocation plates around the whole of the West Riding fleet. By the mid 1960s Neville Hill was the prime home of the Leeds Division's diesel multiple unit fleet. There was also still a depot at Bradford Hammerton Street which was the original base of West Riding dmus. There was a considerable amount of loco-hauled work to be handled because all the London and cross country trains were still loco and coaches, plus a midland main line set that started work from Neville Hill every morning.

Trains approached Neville Hill from Leeds via Marsh Lane Cutting (see figure) and were allowed to enter the depot by the west end supervisor. This normally meant access to the examination point, a small shed where arrivals were booked for repairs and fuelled. Another supervisor would attend with clip board in hand, but the data he needed stored in his brain which operated as a dmu and working timetable database. He would liaise with the mechanical foreman in the five-road red brick former steam repair shed. I was always fascinated to know the background to some graffiti on the side of this shed which read 'VE Day 8th May 1945'. To a 28yr old in early 1979 35 years sounded like pre-history but of course it is now 41 years since I noted it. Many of the people with whom I was working would have been my age when the paint was applied to that wall.

The good dmus were then sent through the washing machine which was controlled by a wash plant operator from a small cabin. Every time I hear Gerry Rafferty singing 'Baker Street' it reminds me of that cabin at 02.00 in the morning when I was doing my rounds with it on the operator's radio. It caught the mood of nights at Neville Hill perfectly. Once washed, the dmus would bypass the carriage cleaning and repair shed and enter the departure sidings, marshalling as instructed ready for departure. The timetable of those days still had morning and evening peaks; more trains and longer ones. There were many departures up until 08.00 and by 09.15 others would be coming out of service. There was a similar rush of departures around 15.00-16.30 and arrivals after 19.00.

A typical array of Neville Hill dmus outside the repair shed. Note the white livery one is, as usual at that time, clean.

Loco-hauled trains would be routed to the reception sidings. The loco would be released to go to Holbeck or its next working and the stock would be watered. A pilot would propel the coaches through the washer and haul them back into the cleaning and repair shed before going to another job. When the maintenance staff had finished, the west end supervisor would send one of his two pilot locos to haul them out onto one of the twelve departure sidings. A team of cleaners, the word 'gang' might be more accurate, operated in the cleaning shed under the eye of a Grade 'A' supervisor.

There was a strict clockwise operating discipline. If the depot manager saw a set, for instance, being put into the repair shed directly from the west end to save time then senior operating supervisor beware. The same went for getting too near his precious, and expensive, doors of the dmu shed. The old steam roundhouse and loco servicing shed shown on the diagram had just been converted to a high speed train repair shed initially for training on the new sets and then for initiation into service. Over on the up side of the line were rakes of Mark 1 stock used for summer Saturday extras, football specials, Working Men's Clubs or Women's Institute specials and the like. These usually needed remarshalling to the requirements of the party size and then being brought across for cleaning and a once-over from the technicians, usually on the lighter-workload day shifts.

Diagram of the Neville Hill layout (prior to the construction of the HST sheds on the site shown as 'steam shed' on this plan).

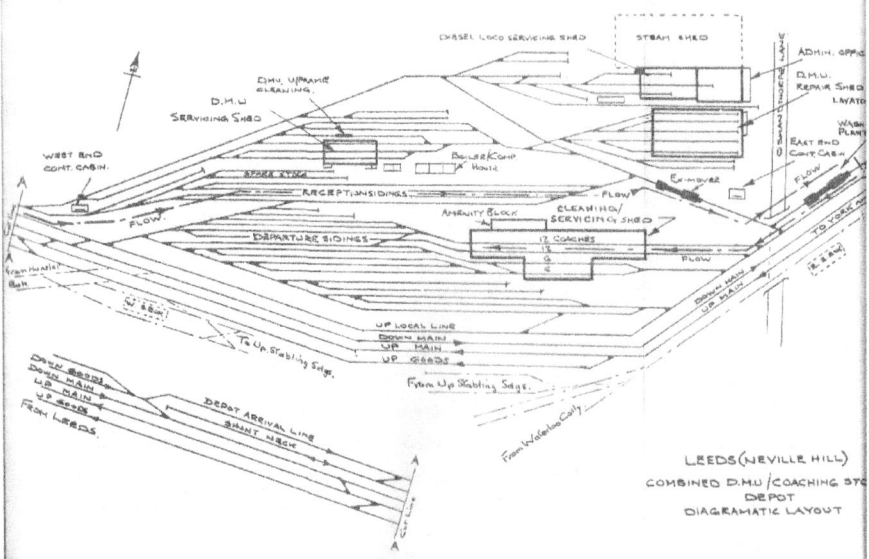

The Devonian cross country set was a case in point. It was usually on the depot around 18.00, a twelve car formation of Mark 2 coaches with two brake second open (BSO) vehicles at the northern end. It was the aim to keep these marshalled brake to brake to assist the guard and station time keeping but if a replacement was required for one of them we had to be enjoying a very quiet shift if we were to send a pilot through Leeds station with it and round the triangle to turn it. I used the Devonian quite a lot for holidays and courses at Derby. Even if the train was busy, which it often was, the rear BSO was usually almost empty because people did not wait at the end of the platform to join it and those walking through gave up after reaching, if not the first guard's brake, then definitely the second. The set was put on one side until morning to receive the attentions of the day shift as it did not leave the depot for Paignton until about 10.15. If there were problems, a late start could be at risk. It looked pretty silly to have a late departure after it had been in the depot's possession for 16hrs. I remember being near the departure sidings one morning when I heard it start towards the outlet signal with a loud thumping noise from a flat on the rear vehicle. I radioed my usual west end shift supervisor John Smith (not an alias!) to put the outlet signal back on the driver, then the carriage expert from the shed. He made an examination and pronounced it was just scale from being moved with the hand brake having been left on. I would have just detached it and run one short but at least I had not let it go unseen.

The Devonian had two sets working just one direction each day, although the Western used the 12-coach formation to form a local from Paignton to Exeter and back to Newton Abbot in the early evening. The standard of cleaning and maintenance at Newton Abbot was exemplary and sometimes we were put to shame by the attention given to what in their eyes was a 'foreign' set. Many years later I mentioned this to a former colleague Reg Renshaw, who had worked in the depot at Newton Abbot, and who was kind enough to return the compliment. I believe this is the one and only time in fifty years that I have heard depots indulge in reciprocal accolades.

The depot used to operate with only one fixed signal for the whole layout; the depot exit ground position light. The rest was done by hand signals but I never worked a shift where there was either a derailment or a collision and I cannot recall one on other turns either. This was remarkable. For instance the departure sidings were split into two groups named, for want of greater originality, 1 and 2. The sidings in each group were named with even less creativity 1, 2, 3 etc. In many older yards they would have had names the history of which would had been lost in time, such as Klondyke or Factory etc. So a supervisor would tell a shunter to call forward the train in '1 in

3' or '2 in 1' to draw forward to the shed outlet. This was done with a hand wave, preferably with a copy of a white publication in hand, and in darkness with a Bardic. Still no collisions from misunderstood instructions or misread signals.

Neville Hill from the washplant.

Perhaps the nearest I came to a derailment was one evening when I arrived at 20.45 for nights to find Ben Curry standing in the doorway as usual. Instead of his usual reference to non-existent log book entries, this particular evening he had a new one for me. "Devonian's off t'road in t'washer." And away he went home. That was one advantage of a shift job. No matter how bad the situation when your relief came on duty that was you gone.

I donned my big black mackintosh and went to the washing machine control room. The operator could not help much. Everything had been normal until the train had stopped. The driver thought he was off the road by the jerk he felt. Not sure there was a shunter with it but, if so, he was no more help. There was only one thing for it. Having come to a clear understanding with the driver about just how intrepid I was going to be, I set about examining the train.

The washing procedure started not with the opening saxophone solo of 'Baker Street', playing again in the back of my mind at the very mention of the Neville Hill washer, but with a spray of clean water from a double-arched spray 140ft before the next installation. Next was the dreaded Exmover plant, negotiated at 3mph, which applied an acidic solution, capable of removing metal brake dust from the coaches, and 220yards further on the washing plant attacked the side of the coaches with water and rotating leather flails. A final rinse at 220 gallons per minute was supposed to wash it all off and dispose of it safely via an effluent treatment plant to local authority discharge standards. The specification for Exmover was 82% oxalic acid, 16% synthetic detergent and 2% capryl alcohol mixed with water to a 5% solution. Trains coming out of service at Leeds were supposed to have their windows closed by the guard before arriving at the depot. I would often ride on a set through the washer on its way to the cleaning shed looking for anything needing special attention and I was doused by the pre-wetting spray more than once with a drop light wide open.

The part of the operation furthest from humanity was the toilet flushing apron. Again, 'senior operating supervisor beware' if the depot manager saw evidence of toilet flushing anywhere else on the premises. It is probably also worth mentioning that train tanking required two sets of hoses, one of non-drinking water for toilets and the other for catering cars. These hoses were a different colour and had to be stowed with their nozzle in a bath of antiseptic solution. If you saw one of these on the ground, that meant trouble for whoever was involved.

Anyway, back to my incident. If there was a derailment it was in the Exmover plant and there was only one way of finding out, to crawl in on hands and knees. The plant was switched off but the liquid was dripping from all the fittings. I thought it would be likely to blister my head or remove my hair but I soldiered on. There was no derailment but a wheel chock (a block of wood with a wheel profile curve in one side of what would otherwise be a triangle, designed to stop unbraked, brake isolated, or brake exhausted vehicles moving. Somehow this had been dragged off the reception lines, past the wash plant operator who was probably too busy illegally listening to Gerry Rafferty to hear the noise it created and into the washer where it had stuck. Much manoeuvring back and forth eventually released it and normal working could resume.

The only time I remember Ben making idle chit-chat concerned the day in January 1977, he recalled, when the northbound Cardiff had arrived with a Class 52 D1013 'Western Ranger' loco to be sent back on the early afternoon Plymouth. This loco had appeared at Leeds because there was no replacement to take over so a Gloucester traction conductor had agreed to work through on the proviso the loco would come straight back. Do I believe this was not deliberately engineered? Probably, if only just. After all Western steam 4-6-0 loco No.6858 Woolston Grange steam locomotive reached Huddersfield on the 08.55 summer Saturday train from Bournemouth West on August 15, 1964 in similar circumstances except that it was Nottingham and Sheffield that could not provide a replacement. It is said the Low Moor crew was reluctant to take it from Sheffield Victoria but did so with the presence of a loco inspector. Unfortunately it was out of gauge on the Penistone line and its cylinders made contact with Denby Dale platform, and probably some unreported others. However, in that endearingly unpredictable way you so often meet when managing enginemen, by the time they reached Huddersfield the Bradford crew was so attached to the Grange they insisted on keeping it and had to have it prised out of their possession.

If the 'Grange' reaching Huddersfield was the most unusual working of the 1960s, and the Class 52 making it through to Leeds was the rarest of the 1970s, then photographer Peter Medley suggests his photo of No. 58002 on the 12.10 from Liverpool Lime Street on September 1, 1984 was the most remarkable of the 1980s.
Credit P. Medley

Eastern High Speed Train depots operated on the basis of integrated management. Operating and technical staff were under the technically qualified depot manager and procedures allowed for maintenance and cleaning to be done simultaneously, usually reducing the servicing time by half. Precautions had to be taken against water meeting electricity but otherwise it worked well. When both cleaners and technicians were clear one pilot moved the set and the other brought in the next one from the shunt neck. It should also be mentioned that there was also a ground frame at the east end in case the west end single outlet point was unavailable. On early turn it was the senior operating supervisor's job to let out an HST, I think the prototype when I started there, by obtaining the signalmen's permission and setting the points.

My first meeting with depot manager Jim Walkden took place in his office the morning I started there. He was a chunky individual, overweight, a no- nonsense pipe-smoking Lancastrian. When I say 'no-nonsense' I also mean to include an unwillingness to accept what was 'common sense' if it was contrary to his entrenched opinion. Despite that, we did not get on too badly. He might not say the same. The problem of integrated depot management was that operators were held in less regard than technical staff. They were there to provide a service for the engineers and do the dirty jobs whereas I saw both sets of staff as being there to provide a service for the wider railway and its travelling public. Integrated depots on the other hand tended to be introspective but they were still much better than those that retained separate management. When I went to Exeter, and when I left, Plymouth Laira was not integrated. The shunters and cleaners worked for the area manager and the technical staff for the depot chief. As a result, if a train was detained during maintenance the cleaners had less time before it was due into service. In an integrated depot the cleaners actually had more time cleaning if this happened and less time drinking tea waiting work. At Exeter I saw this to my daily cost waiting for Class 50s on 9 Mark 2s to appear over the horizon at Ivybridge every morning.

There were two distinct groups of shunters at Neville Hill, I was told by the boss. The east end shunters worked for the dmu supervisor and were not involved in main line stock. The west end shunters were the opposite. "Shouldn't they work flexibly as one dual-trained group?", I naively asked that first morning. It must save time and would save money if one less post were to be required at slack times of day. No reply, although I suppose a sour look amounted to the expression of a contrary opinion. "We haven't had an ex- management trainee on the operating side before," he said, "so I want you to go in and sort out the west end shunters." This sounded like trouble. I wanted to know more but I was not told what I

104

needed to know. Off I went to learn the job in two weeks working on three shifts before 'taking on' and then I set about sorting out the west end shunters. I should have taken at least three weeks.

When I moved on to my next job and reflected on my time at Neville Hill I came to realise that when I was told to 'Sort them out' Jim Walkden really meant 'Keep them quiet' because he and his admin assistant were relatively obstructive to processing disciplinary cases quickly enough to stop them building up into a backlog. The east end shunters were exemplary. They did not cause trouble and they expedited their work. It is significant that I can remember none of their names whereas most of the west end names are etched in my memory. There was a group of, I think, three brothers and their father who was away long term sick and then one or two cousins. In my training period I was told that there was no point booking any of the family group off on their rest day because their sibling would just go sick to allow his brother to work his rest day at enhanced pay. Tolerance of this was endemic to the operation of the depot. I was told that there was a history of prison but I never tested this out. I did not think we employed people with that background but, if we had done so, who had gone along with it? The implication was that nothing should be done to upset them.

My three shift colleagues and Ray Rix were all better shunters than the actual west end staff. When an impasse was reached they would just do the job themselves and the shunters knew it. 'Job and finish' was the west end's motto, meaning you did the basic work and went home. 05.00 for an 06.00 signing off time would be considered late. If you wanted some extra refinement after the main work had been completed then prepare for a battle. In the middle of the night it was down to you. In fact in the middle of the day too. I was determined not to fall into the trap of doing their job for them, partly because, unlike my experienced colleagues I was worse at it than the shunters but mainly because if I started I would end up doing as much shunting as they did. There were one or two occasions when I gave in, when the shunters were genuinely busy with other work and an urgent job needed doing. I vividly, too vividly and too often, recall standing in the cleaning shed pit road uncoupling an HST power car with its pipework coated in excrement from the flush-to-air toilets. To uncouple the jumper cables it was necessary to hold a flap up and pull on the stiff (and at that time new) cable at the same time, which took two hands. There was a flimsy chain, provided to hold up the orange flap but it had broken off - a regular occurrence I discovered on examining more power cars. This was clearly a basic design fault by someone who had never done this job. The solution was not difficult. A bolt was necessary. I pursued the matter with the boss and eventually an answer came back that a bolt would cause an increase in weight and so the suggestion was declined.

Forty years on and the new Spanish-built Mark 5 sleepers have had similar design difficulties identified. The failure of the brake system at Edinburgh Waverley one morning has been ascribed to the brake cock handle having been inadvertently knocked shut by one of two highly experienced staff members who were underneath the train trying for ten minutes to release a jumper cable out of its socket. I wonder just how many hours of shunting the designers of couplings have to undertake before working on their technical drawings?

When it came to design faults there was none greater in any aspect of railway activity that I discovered than the HST power car emergency drawbar coupling. This was a huge lump of metal in the brake van which had to be manhandled out onto the ballast. The nose flap on the power car had to be raised and the bar affixed to the equipment inside. There were two drawbars, one for fixing to a locomotive and the other for coupling two HSTs together. The loco had then to be positioned to allow a large metal bolt to be inserted through the other end of the drawbar and the draw hook of the loco. This required moving the loco backwards and forwards until it was in the right position to about a centimetre accuracy. On all but two occasions I saw this happen, out of probably at least scores of them, the shunter had to duck between the HST and the loco to secure the bolt. It was known as a pin. Some pin. In every occasion I saw it done I was the person in charge who condoned the irregular method but it was the only way of ever getting on the move again. The nose end flap itself was the first problem. It should open by unlocking two fixtures with a carriage key but this never happened smoothly owing to under-maintenance. I remember a power car and barrier vehicle, heading back from tyre-turning at Thornaby, failing at Eaglescliffe one day when I was at Middlesbrough, visiting Tees Yard. A Class 25 was sent to assist it but the crew could not get the flap open and had to await a fitter with a large screwdriver to remove it entirely. Fortunately it had come to a stand on the platform avoiding loop line so delay did not ensue.

East Coast main line diversions via Eaglescliffe were frequent events. A Class 47 calls with a Newcastle to Liverpool train to pick up and set down Darlington passengers.

When the production HSTs arrived on the depot it was still the intention to maintain full set working with the same power cars. I don't think that lasted more than a week when it was found we were two sets down with a power car failure on each one. Mix, match, one set down. It was also decreed that the coaches would always be marshalled in numerical order, including identical 'second open' coaches. The shunters, even in recalcitrant mood, knew the formations should be right but shunting a power car and four coaches out of the shed, detaching one in a dead end siding, putting the power car and three back in the shed and detaching one, going and picking up the first detached one from the dead end with the remaining power car and two coaches then going back to the HST shed and coupling them all up and performing continuity and 'pull' tests to ensure the buckeye couplings had engaged? At 04.00 in the morning? Insist on it and you would find there was time for nothing else before the day shift came on. And for what?

Whenever the west end shunters felt aggrieved by anything at all they would decree that they were 'working normal' This phrase was an insult to the use of English because it meant exactly the opposite. Normal was racing around the yard with the pilot doing jobs in a hurry for more time playing cards between tasks. Their 'working normal' was imposing a 3mph speed limit and double checking everything they did, finding fault wherever and whenever possible. It was a 'work to rule' or, again more accurately, a work to rules they had made up. I cannot remember what had annoyed them one night when I took duty with the rain lashing down and clouds scudding across a watery moon but I was informed they would be working normally. One of the 'brothers' climbed onto the pilot Class 08 loco and duly informed his driver what was going on. The driver was an old hand who had stepped down from main line work owing to ill health. "Normal then is it?" he asked the shunter. "Yes", it was affirmed. "Then your position isn't in the cab with me it is out there," he said pointing to the fitted stepladder by the loco front buffers. It took one shunt before a reversion to management's version of normal.

Another cause for grumbling came if the carriage maintenance supervisor said one of the loco-hauled sets required to be 'buckeyed'. This meant the train had to be separated between each carriage by about 10ft and the buckeye coupling secured in the raised position. In winter it was a cold, dirty and heavy job. In summer it was a hot, dirty and heavy job. There were no volunteers to be had to do it so plenty of time had to be created so you could insist. I suspected my colleagues did it for the shunters sometimes. If the separation job did not get done there would be a (justifiable) hue and cry from the maintenance shed and then the boss.

One strange relic of pre-integration was that the drivers and guards remained under the control of a separate train crew supervisor. I rarely visited their lair, mainly because there was no need to do so but I think my colleagues spent a lot of time there with people they had worked alongside in the past. There was rarely a problem. Occasionally a pilot driver might be uncovered for an hour but there was always the means of covering the work, even if it meant cashing in a favour a driver owed the train crew supervisor. The conclusion might be that number of 'shed and ferry' drivers was too high and that the depot was too far from scrutiny by the area office.

The automatic carriage washer was vulnerable to cold weather and if there was anything worse than a mild frost for a couple of pre-dawn hours it would be shut down immediately. Perhaps two or three sets might be squeezed through before a close was drawn but the external condition of the loco hauled sets went down hill quickly. The dmus did not suffer too badly because most of them came on depot two or three times every two days, and more, so they stood a good chance of a daytime wash three or four times a week. We had some Passenger Transport Executive liveried dmus in white livery with painted coloured bands which were affectionately known as the 'white ladies' which only rarely declined to the status of 'grubby old girls'. After a week of cold weather, 'Rixie' would appear with a special pilot turn driver and a shunter. That was 42hrs pay against the budget before we started. The dirty coaching stock would be held in the Exmover plant going backwards and forwards repetitively either as a set or individual vehicle. It would be left for the acid to penetrate the grime and then eventually washed off. Eight hours on a Sunday was the regular shift, even in relatively good weather, to keep on top of external cleanliness. The modern railway does not seem to have any 'Rixies' but I suspect that neither does it have much in the way of Exmover either. I think the acidic concentration might have found itself occasionally stronger than 5% too.

A Neville Hill 'White Lady' on a publicity special at Burley-in-Wharfedale photographed as the author pretends to join as a typical passenger.

I was convinced the other supervisors used to turn off the wash plant far earlier than necessary, working to the forecast temperatures and not waiting to react when the frost actually set in. My mind was fixed on the reason I had been told for the shut downs taking place. True, severe frost could burst underground pipes which would disable the plant for perhaps weeks, but the main reason was the freezing of the leather flails that could then damage the coaches or break a window. I was having a cup of tea in my office about 03.00 one morning, reading one of the many newspapers that constituted one of the few perquisites of this job and congratulating myself on how long I had delayed the wash plant shut down when a driver stumbled through the doorway with blood gushing from his leg. He had been climbing into the cab of a dmu via the wooden steps when his foot had slipped on the ice, gashing his shin. That was another lesson learned, but at his expense. Take into account likely icing of surfaces.

In terms of pre-heating and items such as dmu door locks there was never much problem because it was normal to keep all engines running all the time on the basis that if you stopped one it might never start and delay other trains marshalled behind it on the departure siding concerned. The coach interiors were often choked with fumes from the notorious dmu heaters by the time trains entered service. They were warm though.

Fumes were the most noticeable in the dmu repair shed. Should you venture in there on a cold night with the doors closed it was impossible to see more than 10 or so yards owing to the blue fog swirling around the vehicles. I saw a complaint from fitters' staff representatives claiming the fumes were dangerous and a reply that said there was 'no evidence that diesel fumes were carcinogenic.' That's one letter I would not have signed and sent.

The dmu supervisors were masters of ensuring the right power/weight ratio was supplied to meet each diagram's working timetable. It was also relatively rare to short-form a 3-car diagram with a 2-car 300 h.p. set. If a unit had a bad history of an engine dropping out, or even being temporarily irreparable, they would try to match it with a good unit on diagrams requiring two sets. Hence, if I was taking a log of a run with a double set I automatically suspected one of the sets would be defective. There was a slipstream effect of the second set which also gave some assistance in the case of a defect. Some of the sets had 180h.p. engines compared to the normal 150h.p. It was well known that the Class 110 Calder

Valley sets were 720hp 3-car sets with two power cars and four engines, but some of the ones that otherwise looked like Class 101 Metro Cammell 600h.p.3-cars were actually 720h.p. Class 111s. The number series were 50134-7, 50270-89 and 51541-51560. The '50xxx' cars were renumbered 53xxx.

Another complication concerned the longer trains of dmus we sent up to Leeds station, often with units for three trains. If this required more than eight engines (say 2x3cars with four engines in each of their two power cars, plus a 300hp twin with 2 engines), then the front set had to be fitted with 'twelve car panel lights' so the driver could see which engines were working …or not. Many had just 8-car light fittings so a swap of front to middle might have to take place. Until I worked at Neville Hill I had considered dmu work boring but I realised this was short sighted. On the subject of long trains into Leeds one summer Saturday found two trains coupled departing from the upside which stopped the station for a while detaching the rear set of coaches to wait for its loco there instead.

The number of carriage cleaners available for work varied widely. Saturday nights were less well attended than say Tuesday nights even though the workload was the same. I have seen as few as five on duty which amounted to one person cleaning something like 18 coaches each plus a few dmus. Once work was completed there was often an excursion train to be cleaned. These were often not in too good a condition to start with - clean enough superficially, but do not look too closely, and in many ways shabby. I would try to walk through these as well as the other stock. They were never good but sometimes they were bad and I would instruct the carriage cleaning supervisor to bring the cleaners back to it. This was unpopular for a number of obvious reasons but one more obscure one was that it was an insult to their work. The vast majority of the cleaners were women, most of them in what I would then have called middle age, perhaps 40 to 50. Any older and the combination of nights two weeks in 3, or 14 on the trot if you turned up for them all, plus the agility needed getting in and out of trains, added to the weight of carrying water, vacuum cleaners and stretching to the far corners of seating bays, windows and racks (not to mention the condition of some toilets) meant it was not work for anyone older. Younger women had not yet settled for this being the best paid job they could find – poor basic but shift enhancements, unlimited night turn overtime and weekend pay. This was a way to pay the bills and the kids' treats on a poor Leeds housing estate. They gave me very little trouble bar a bit of teasing. I was a shade too old to be the son but the right age to be their little brother perhaps. Their supervisor on my shift was a kindly individual who reminds me perhaps of the benevolent prison officer in 'Porridge' who was so nice the inmates found no fun in taking too much advantage. To put the gang back on a set to do a better job at 04.30 on a Sunday morning was pushing it though.

The other cleaning operation performed at Neville Hill was an early foray into the world of privatisation with a contract held by a firm called Holdsworth to do heavy cleaning of dmus, initially the Swindon TransPennine sets. It was a long way from the privatisation of the whole railway, back in 1978, but I really could not make the figures for heavy cleaning contract stack up. British Rail paid low basic wages for work like Holdsworth's. How could a firm do it cheaper than we could? If they produced higher standard work then surely that was simply a function of better supervision. All became clear to me in due course. It was said they would tour Leeds city centre late at night for rough sleepers and promise board and lodge in return for cleaning work. It might not have been entirely and completely true but one or two incidents I observed on the depot involving alcohol led me to believe it might be the case. Incidentally, I did not have a single alcohol/drugs related case on any shift involving operating staff including the west end shunters and the cleaners.

Our prime train was the Leeds Executive breakfast car train that left Leeds at 07.30 and ran nonstop to King's Cross in 2hr 32min for the 186 miles, hauled by a Deltic with eight coaches. The front two were 42 seater 1st class (FO) open coaches

113

which had an at-seat meal cooked freshly in the kitchen car. When I travelled on it during my time at headquarters for a meeting in London with management staff I could have breakfast on the train or, I think 3/6d (18p) breakfast expenses. I always chose the latter.

One of the FO vehicles had been under repair for a few days. A replacement had not arrived and a first class compartment (FK) coach had to be used instead. When I came on duty the FO had been released from repairs but Ben had not replaced the FK with it when it had arrived from the station just before 19.00. I told the west end that they would need to do it during the night so it was ready for the empty stock departure in the morning. They objected. The gist of their argument was that jobs like this were down to the day shift, and the late turn they had relieved should have done it, or it could wait until Sunday when they had more time. I knew they would be looking to get off home around 04.30, leaving just one of their number to mind the shop so I insisted it must be done. When the evening's work was squared up with the last two trains in the cleaning and maintenance shed I made sure I was in the west end cabin to intercept an early finish. As expected, the shunters refused so I said they would be booked off at the time they refused work without pay for the rest of their shift and formal disciplinary proceedings would ensue. After the shunters' had vented their feelings, the Leeds Executive got its FO.

The following week I was working 14.00 to 21.00 on the Saturday and some of the shunters involved were working 12hr days 06.00-18.00. As I made my way from the car to the office I saw the three shunters walking down the yard. When I asked where they were going they said 'home' they did not want the overtime. As they passed I said that they had accepted the roster with overtime so going home would be a disciplinary offence. They did not trouble to respond. An offence it was, but that did not get the yard shunted.

Fortunately the first few hours on a Saturday afternoon were not busy and, as usual, the east end shunters did not want to be involved in any display of solidarity with their west end comrades so worked normally- the management's definition of 'normal'. I did a couple of moves as they became necessary, pulled a few point levers, but not much until a Class 45 arrived from Holbeck with a single-manned driver to work the empty Mark 1 stock from the departure sidings to the station for a Leeds-Carlisle fixture's return football excursion. Perhaps my memory deceives me as it would be a strange choice of loco to send to Carlisle without a balanced working. A London Midland Class 40 would appear to have been the natural choice. Furthermore, a trawl of the internet reveals no such football match.

After the loco had backed down to the train I walked across from the cabin to the train side. The driver was looking out of his cab window when I said I was going underneath to tie him on. I was 6ft tall and slim, not particularly strong. The grease of the screw coupling smeared itself on my shirt, I banged my head twice and then did battle with the brand new vacuum hose on the coaches. I fought with it as if it were an anaconda, in size and hostility but far less flexible. No matter how much I twisted and strained I could not get the lugs of the two hoses to engage. By now the driver had wondered what was happening and was looking over my shoulder. I tried again and eventually he tapped me on the shoulder. I looked to see what he wanted. "Come out of there, he said. "Our lass could do better 'n that." The ultimate put down. I believe that the word 'lass' in that Yorkshire context and location meant his wife not his daughter so perhaps it could have been worse! His wife was probably an able bodied woman used to getting jobs done. Shamefacedly I let him swap places. The coupling was completed in no time, the driver was back on his loco with a shake of his head and perhaps a 'tut' or two. After the event I should have felt humiliation I think but I suspect the driver was saying 'At least you tried." At least I would like to kid myself into thinking so. I was sure of one thing though and this (rather than my need to get some vacuum brake shunting practice) was the lesson I took from the incident: if I had not offered to do it he would have stood on ceremony and waited until an 18.00 shunter had come on duty. I had feared they too might have decided they were not going to work overtime and not show up until 22.00 but they duly arrived at 18.00 and worked as if nothing had happened.

To complete a trilogy of awkward brushes with west end shunters another difficulty occurred in early May. I had been there about 6 months when it was time to sort out the rakes of coaches in the up sidings. To do this a special shunting turn, driver and pilot were booked to spend the morning over there. The various rakes of excursion stock had to be converted to the booked formations of the summer Saturday extras. I had the existing plan of what vehicles were in each siding in the right order and how we wanted it to finish up. The youngest of the brothers, Stephen, my age or a little younger swaggered into the office for his orders and I explained what was needed. He pushed the papers around the desk for a moment before saying, "It's up to you to tell me my moves." It really wasn't and most shunters would have taken exception to the supervisor having the presumption to tell them. That included 'young Steven' standing in front of me. It was not worth a fight. "Go into number 2 pick up five, put them in 4. Go to 3 pick up one put it in 2....."I jotted the instructions down as I devised them. When I had finished I passed the paper to Stephen who looked them up and down and after about a minute replied, "I can do that in three moves less." I think he meant 'fewer' but I let it pass. Off he went with a smile on his face, his objective completed to plan.

Although I felt my life was being dominated by getting the west end shunters to do their job properly, and although the routine of the depot was usually conducted quickly and safely, there was an anarchic sub-culture at play even then. It was hard to define. We would speak with civility to each other nearly all the time. Instructions issued in their messroom were greeted without hostility but by no means devoid of a challenging atmosphere. Most of the time everything was done without an argument. An example of the mixed values of the shunters came around midnight on one night shift. There had been a series of incidents involving the theft of axes and ladders etc. from the emergency equipment stored in guard's vans across the main line in the up sidings. It was likely that this would be discovered by a guard who had come to take a train out so delay could ensue, especially if a few vehicles had been robbed. It beats me how this annoyed the down side west end shunters who were not involved in finding or financing replacements or minimising the delays but it aggravated them nonetheless. I concluded it was something about having one's patch invaded.

On this particular night one of the shunters burst into the west end cabin exclaiming, "There's torches on the up side." His colleagues were with him in an instant. "They're pinching from the vans again." As one body they rose and set off across the sidings. I shouted after them, "Where are you going?" One of them looked over his shoulder with disdain, "We're off to sort 'em out." Before I could assimilate the implications, they were crossing the main lines, illegally, and heading for the rakes of coaches. I was not entirely clear where the Health & Safety legislation stood on such an eventuality although I was aware it would no doubt say I had to forbid what they were doing. Some chance! And call the B.T. Police? Wrong timescales. I was aware that dangerous weapons were involved and imagined myself explaining why I had stayed in the cabin talking to my supervisor friend while a pitched battle was being waged in Neville Hill up sidings. Of course this was pre mobile phones but at least I had a radio to the yard to call help.

Off I set behind them, catching up despite the tripping hazards. When I reached the last in the column he turned to me to offer a piece of kindly advice. "Got your carriage key with you?" I never went anywhere without it. I took it out of my pocket. "Hold it like this," he showed me, "handle across your palm and the key through your knuckles. If they come for you hit them downwards with it in the face, like this," he demonstrated with a sharp movement of his forearm. The tutorial did little to pacify my doubts about the expedition but by now we were by our first van. I was relieved to find no sign of present or past nefarious activity and we moved on. We fancied we saw someone sliding down the embankment as we reached the far end of the sidings but there was no one else around. The disappointment of my group was palpable as we trudged back to the cabin for a cup of tea. The verdict was that the trip had been fruitless but they'd get them next time. On someone else's night shift I hoped. It was a strange situation sitting there in those circumstances for once feeling and being accepted as one of the team.

Some of the problems to be overcome were not the product of either laziness or misbehaviour, they were structural problems within the depot and time pressures. One of the last trains to come out of the carriage shed each early morning was the nine-coach set that formed the 09.30 Leeds-King's Cross. This was a two-portion train, the front three going empty to Halifax to form a portion that ran via Huddersfield to be attached to the remaining six coaches of the Leeds portion at Wakefield Westgate. It is worth considering the journey of the Halifax portion. It ran via the Greetland and Bradley Wood curves which were mothballed for decades before the current local service was introduced between Huddersfield and Halifax/Bradford via Brighouse. The loco ran round its train at Huddersfield and then did the same at Wakefield Kirkgate. When it reached Westgate it stood in the middle road and then backed onto the rear of the Leeds portion. The return portion was detached at Doncaster and ran via Hare Park and Calder Bridge Jcts to Kirkgate, not needing to run round until it reached Huddersfield. I think the Class 31 used at this time (having replaced a Class 25 that had in turn taken over from a Fairburn 2-6-4 steam tank engine) worked a Doncaster-Hull and back portion of a King's Cross Leeds train around lunchtime. The train had replaced the old 'South Yorkshireman' from Bradford Exchange to Marylebone via Penistone and the Great Central main line.

Back at Neville Hill, it was obviously necessary to have a brake van in each portion. If a vehicle had to be knocked out of the set for a defect or examination we usually had a replacement available but it was difficult to attach it at the east end so time usually dictated it was added to the Halifax portion at the west end. This made the Halifax portion four coaches and the Leeds one 5. Next time it happened it became five and four but when one day the Halifax ran with six and the Leeds portion with three I decided we had to spend time putting it right. I think even the shunters had realised the process had to end sometime.

There was never any instruction from the depot manager on operational issues like this and there was very little contact with the outside world at all. Perhaps no man is an island but the same cannot be said for some railway depots. They become an end in themselves separate from the living organism that is a railway system. Jim Walkden's deputy was Chris Kinchin-Smith who had good family connections with senior Eastern region management. Chris was nearer my age and understood both what I was doing and what needed to be done. I guess he had suffered problems with the west end shunters at disciplinary hearings and the like. Our paths were to cross many times in our careers and I always thought we had a tacit understanding about the difficulties we had experienced at Neville Hill. It was, as the modern idiom might have it, a journey. It was certainly a learning curve.

The blinkered view was never clearer to me than the day I prevented major delays on the Leeds to York and Hull main line outside the depot. It was late morning when I was down at the west end cabin. A train was at the outlet signal but it did not clear as expected. There was a dmu in Marsh Lane Cutting that was also stationary. I asked Leeds Panel box and they said there was a point failure at Neville Hill West Jct so I offered to sort it out. There was some surprise that a depot operator might feel comfortable on the main line and knew how to use the clamp lock points crank handle. There were some clips in the cabin. What was the problem? After clearing it with Control I got the trains on the move again until the signal technicians arrived. It was child's play and offered me a bit of variety. At the following morning's 'prayers' Jim Walkden instructed me that under no circumstances had I ever to leave the depot in future. "Your job is here," he said firmly, inserting his pipe to enforce the last syllable. To say I was demotivated would be an understatement. It was not even as if the depot had not benefited – it had got the empty stock into traffic.

I did go off the depot shortly afterwards when children were placing stones on the main line one lunchtime. I chased them off and followed them back to a nearby school, whence they had originally absconded. I told the headmaster what I had seen and he promised to deal with it. I had to notify the B.T. Police when I returned to the depot though. It was not really my job to pursue vandals off the premises and in retrospect I think it was a symptom of feeling increasingly caged and not learning much that was new. 'Lesson 1, How to deal with stroppy Shunters (or not)' had been learnt and revised (in both senses of the word) many times over.

I sought advice from my training officer Joe Trevorrow who was still at Leeds eleven years on from my first interview but he was of little help. Jim Walkden was angry that I had asked someone at divisional office and not him. Would he understand that anticipation of his anger was the reason I had gone to another source in the first place? Better not say that. I was told that a move would be considered after I had been there a year which does not seem unreasonable in retrospect but seemed arbitrary at the time. Arbitrary, because it was!

"Another year and you'd be happy
Just one more year and you'd be happy
But you're crying
You're crying now."

The promise was kept though and 13 months or so after my arrival I was in my troublesome Hillman Imp with the blown cylinder head gasket on my way, albeit very slowly, to Tees

Yard. The grade was MS1 and I had free first class tickets for myself and Linda but a good deal less income, a bigger mortgage, Linda had given up her teaching job and we were away from friends and family. Such was the stuff of railway promotions.

7. STUDENTSHIP

The length of the Neville Hill chapter, especially in relation to the time spent there, shows that I probably learnt more than I thought. Certainly no other group of staff held any terrors for me in the future but perhaps I never quite learnt that there were other ways to win a battle than slugging it out toe to toe. As indicated in the preface I am now going to go back in time ten years to my earliest formative railway experiences.

When I was released from the Francis Webb Orphanage at the end of my induction course I received my orders where to report the following Monday. I do not think I am being unfair to suggest that most people might guess it would be a passenger station, perhaps Leeds even, or a signal box, or a marshalling yard, obviously Healey Mills. It was none of these. My first week on the proper railway was to be spent at a modern Freightliner Terminal. I had just spent a week being told how 'liner' trains, 'merry-go-round' coal trains and trainloads of raw materials such as oil and steel were the future of freight by rail. Although massive investment in marshalling yards had been undertaken in the early 1960s and had come to fruition in the mid 1960s the tide had already turned against them. The Eastern had pulled the plug on another huge investment, by coincidence also at Stourton. A strategic change had already decreed that marshalling yards that were to have a future were to be in the centre of industrial areas, not greenfield sites. The future of Whitemoor, Carlisle and Perth was already threatened by the time I entered my second week on British Rail, on September 23, 1968.

I reached Stourton from my Huddersfield home via a stopping train to Leeds. There was no express until 09.30 anyway. Then it was a Leeds City double-decker out through the Victorian district of Hunslet until I alighted for a walk down a long metalled drive to the brand new Freightliner terminal with its giant yellow gantry cranes spanning two rail lines and a roadway. Rows of neatly stacked silver containers with red stripes inscribed with the Freightliner brand name were the only 'boxes' that could be seen because 1968 pre-dated the use of gaudy maritime containers moved to the centres of consumption from deep sea ports. Most of the traffic was domestic, some poached from road but much of it transferred from other less efficient rail transport.

There had been a dispute the previous year concerning the access of privately owned lorries to these British Rail owned terminals. I think the short sighted NUR policy had won out. They might have saved a few jobs immediately but lost ten times as many in the long term. These were the days of the growth of 'own account' freight operators (i.e manufacturers using their own lorries) and private hauliers. For Freightliner to win the traffic, firms had to be convinced to containerise their business in the first place and then rely on Freightliner to collect their traffic at the right time, trunk haul it usually overnight and deliver it on time the following day. The operation was beyond the firms' direct control. If British Rail had industrial relation problems allowing private lorries into its terminal then the customers could experience their own trade union difficulties in transferring business away to British Rail.

The dispute had been exacerbated by a further objection from the National Union of Railwaymen to the removal of brake vans from the rear of some trains. The ride quality of a brake van wagging along at the back of a 75mph Freightliner was apparently not obvious. Freightliner countered by using the North American term for a brake van and calling their new invention a caboose. It was a small 10ft container with windows and the guard's accommodation located inside. According to legend the occupants suffered from a general shaking about and susceptibility to travel sickness. I am not sure how this was worse than a ride in an ordinary brake van, with the snatching experienced on partially fitted freight trains, and have no desire to find out, but it was experienced at much higher speeds. The apparent solution was soon abandoned but the cabooses made snug cabins compared to waiting out in the open at the exposed extremities of the terminals.

I was met by the terminal overseer. These modern terminals had returned to Victorian titles apparently. I met the operations manager and technical chief then the shift managers and clerks. When a lorry arrived with a container its paperwork was checked and the consignment allocated to a space on the next suitable service, unless it was part of a block booking by contract. The priorities were notified to the crane driver perched high above the tracks and the container was duly picked up. The lorry might then retrieve a container that had been stacked or receive one directly off an arriving train.

Most departures were in the evening and most arrivals in the morning. It was disappointing to hear that pessimism had already set in. The staff felt they had already been let down not only by the disputes but also from a failure of management to expand the range of destinations quickly enough. If they did not have a suitable service then traffic had to be refused. Firms offering all their long-haul goods were reticent about transferring only a part of it leaving them with a split operation. The alternative was an extended road delivery from the nearest terminal available which undermined the economics of rail before the container had even left Leeds.

Despite the obvious problems, I set about learning what went on with enthusiasm. I was invited to civilised 3-course lunchtimes at a small café up on the main road and made to feel part of the team. The paperwork and updating of display boards with mini magnetic containers was interesting but not a patch on driving the crane.

I had four weeks there and a full week was to be spent with the crane drivers who were not slow to suggest that I should have a go. Working to the instructions of a team-mate on the ground we sat in our glass cabin and ran up, down and across the terminal with containers from road to rail and back. The crane had top lifting apparatus that fitted over the corners of the container, depending on its length. Twist locks and spigots ensured a safe lift but it was nevertheless prohibited from standing underneath an airborne container. One of the key factors was to ensure the right length of containers were put on each wagon to maximise capacity. 10ft containers were rarely used even by then, the most common being 20ft ones, so three on a 60ft capacity wagon. Imperial measurements were as a result of the American domination of the market.

Two photographs taken from the control cabin of the Stourton Freightliner gantry crane in September 1968.

The terminal operations manager questioned me on what I had learnt and I took him through all the handsignals and consequential crane actions. He seemed surprised that I had actually been driving the crane. In the background of the spanking new terminal was the old Stourton steam shed, an abandoned hulk of a red brick building now devoid of rails. It had closed less than two years earlier but it seemed an irrelevance to this modern railway I had joined with its diesel services far below me, even if an unfashionable Co-Bo went past occasionally as a reminder of the folly that marked early diesel purchases.

My next destination was small station work with an allocation of three months at Woodlesford. This was not the most convenient place for daily travel from Huddersfield, especially early starts and late finishes so I negotiated a change to Mirfield on the four track section of line shared between Lancashire & Yorkshire and London & North Western Companies prior to their 1st January 1922 amalgamation and

1923 Grouping. It was also the location of the experimental L.M.S speed signalling system that was aimed at provision of a fourth aspect (the modern version being double yellow) and coping with the dense advection fog associated with the confluence of the Colne and Calder rivers, the canals that mixed with air pollution from the mills. There was still a station master in residence, also in charge of Brighouse on the Calder Valley. He was responsible for the three Mirfield signal boxes. Heaton Lodge Jct where four lines split into two further four-track routes, Bradley Wood Jct, where the curve from Huddersfield joined the Calder Valley and Brighouse. His two stations retained a booking office and a parcel office.

The station master was a Mr Horsfall who had a part time clerk. He sorted me out with a training programme covering the booking & parcel office. Better to come early morning because ticket sales for the sparse off-peak train service were few. The Normanton to Sowerby Bridge service of three-car Calder Valley 720h.p. sets was still running but even that succumbed to closure in 1970, taking Brighouse station with it. I made friends with the booking clerk and his regular relief who was a genial man, seemingly amused to have an apprentice he could teach the many wrinkles of the relief system. I think his name was Charlie Mayes and I now wonder if he was a brother of tricky signalman Ernie whom I was to encounter later in my career. They had similarities. We had parcels for the House of the Resurrection monastery at Heaton Lodge (I think it was a training seminary actually) and a few puppies that had to be fed watered and kept muzzled before the local kennels picked them up. We were not really aware of the term at the time but I guess they were from puppy farms.

I spent as much time as I could in signal boxes. Coming west from Leeds the first signal box was Mirfield No. 3 which was a large box that converted track circuit block from its boundary with the new Healey Mills panel box into absolute block to Mirfield No. 2. Mirfield Nos. 4 and 5 had been abolished when the Bradford via Spen Valley line was closed, following the Beeching Plan, in 1965. No. 3 would have been the box where

I needed to train ten years beforehand but the routine of absolute block bell signals and block indicator working was not available and there was a booking boy looking after the train register so I felt to be muscling in if I sat and watched and if I tried to take part it felt to be doing the booking boy out of some variety. Did I sense some resentment too, as we were about the same age? Probably. Mirfield No. 1 was closed, redundant after the closure of the steam depot, Heaton Lodge fitted all requirements except it was probably too complex for a learner to tangle with the levers and, as a result, setting up routes too slowly, there was a booking boy, it was remote from public transport and I could not just drop in for an hour now and then. Not really suitable at all then. The Calder Valley boxes had only half the traffic, or less, than the middle section so Mirfield No. 2 it was. Even this was not really satisfactory. 100 trains on the early turn, I think, the majority freight, meant there was enough traffic but the west end bay platforms with the exchange of parcel vans had been removed. The marshalling yard entrance was on the track diagram but it was mainly used for storing excess westbound coal traffic to free capacity at Healey Mills (yes, it was so busy then). Locos would then arrive to work a westbound freight special starting out of the yard.

Because of the short distances between boxes, when we accepted a train from Mirfield No. 1 we had to offer it straight on to Heaton Lodge Jct but we often had to wait for train out of section and immediately offer the next train, usually a freight.

The three regular signalmen became my friends and there was no problem in being allowed to work the simple box for long periods. Occasionally I might turn round quickly and find a pair of eyes keeping a watch on me from over the top of the then non-tabloid sheets of the Daily Express. Closure was not far away and by the end of my time there the fate of my three friends had been decided. One lived in the Aire Valley so he was moving to a vacancy at Cononley. When I was appointed to my Bradford job I looked forward to re-acquainting myself with him but he had moved on, and no one even seemed to remember his being there, so I wonder if he took redundancy. Another friendly old man (of perhaps 50) was accommodated as railman (porter in effect) at Ravensthorpe & Thornhill, perhaps the luckiest station to escape closure in the 1960s' West Riding. When I used to wave to him on my stopping train to Leeds and, later, York I used to ache for the indignity I felt he must be suffering. He retained his signalling rate of pay of course and he did not look unhappy. The third signalman was single. He had seen the writing on the wall, applied for another signalling job and was on his way before I left. Destination? Holloway South Down on the main line just outside the tunnels at King's Cross.

I always thought that the diverse fate of these three friends encapsulated the problems of reducing staff on the railway. I was to reduce numbers wherever I went, even if traffic was stable or rising. Modernisation of the Exeter area signalling was a case in point but the watchword of Arnold Wane at Middlesbrough rang in my ears. For all his single-minded pursuit of his objectives one sentence stuck in my mind. "Cut out as many jobs as you need to but make sure you do not cut out the people." In the Area Manager's Diaries I said that as far as I knew no one left the railway against their wishes in the Exeter scheme. Those who chose to go had a redundancy pay cheque and those who did not want to go were fitted into jobs. A few of these were on passenger stations but all were in more responsible positions than Ravensthorpe & Thornhill and there was a path back to the power boxes for those who wanted it. Some others went to remaining manual boxes in Cornwall or Wales. I think I have discovered one who went with an ill will but there were complications over his choices, timing and last minute changes of mind. The repercussions of modernisation at Mirfield stayed with me but imagine my surprise when a visit to a recycling emporium (aka junk yard) in the old Exminster station building near Starcross in 2018 revealed the signal box diagram of Mirfield No. 2 hanging on the wall. It was the layout just before I went there. It had a cracked frame and water damage. It needed the former tender care it used to have from my friends. Despite the price tag I just had to have it. The dealer came down from about £200 to £160. I came up from £100 to £120. There we stuck. I didn't have to have it that much! Last time I called in it was still there. Time to go back and renegotiate perhaps, starting at £100.

As I looked at the diagram my eye was drawn to the facing points from the down slow to the down loop that had earned my first ticking off from the station master. He had seen me replace the home signal before the train had cleared the points. I tried to defend myself by saying it was electronically interlocked by the track circuit but he just looked sourly at me and said, "Not what t'book says." Conversation over. The brief episode helped formulate my view that the observation of the rules was not divisible or, for that matter, negotiable.

The signal posts in the Mirfield area were the same ones installed for the 1930s' speed signalling, a fact that probably provoked the modernisation scheme. The modern meaning of 'double yellow' was conveyed by a 'yellow over green' aspect. In terms of identification during fog each signal had a red searchlight half way up the post so it was, in its original conception, I believe, the only place on the network (ever?) where a green, yellow and red aspect could be applicable to a driver at the same time.

The afternoon Red Bank newspaper empties hauled by a Class 45 overtakes a Class 47 alongside the remnants of the old Mirfield steam shed. Mirfield No. 1 signal box was sited on the photographer's side of the line opposite the Class 47. Mirfield No. 2 was located on the former loco shed side of the line between the two large buildings near the rear of the freight train.

Incidents were mercifully few but one sticks in my mind. I was on duty with Norman Whitworth, the signalman who went to the Ravensthorpe job, in a typical thick fog. The large mill across the line was invisible and you had to peer into the gloom to spot tail lamps on the furthest line (then the up fast – now the up slow!). We had a train in section to Heaton Lodge Jct on the then up slow line and a Class 8 partially fitted freight train standing at our home signal at the west end of Mirfield platform waiting acceptance. It was not too long before Heaton Lodge Jct cleared the block and accepted the Class 8 (3-2 on the bells). The train started away and I sent 2 beats 'train entering section' which was duly acknowledged with the block indicator needle placed to 'train on line'. As I watched the train pull away I was alarmed to see it had only around eight wagons and no brake van. Short trains of fully fitted vehicles were not that uncommon, but not that short, it would have been a Class 6 anyway and these were in fact mineral wagons not the more likely vanfits.

I turned to Norman for inspiration. He was already on his feet. I knew that the bell signal for 'train passed without tail lamp' was 9 beats but this was train more accurately 'half a train passed without the other half'. Still, 9 beats it was and, as the regulation prescribes, 4-5 to the box in rear instead of train out of section of course. Norman was clearly not happy with this and picked up his block signalling regulations from under the lid of the desk where the train register book was kept. Regulation 19(d) obviously applied, "during fog and falling snow no train except an engine in accordance with Regulation 15 (examination of the line) must enter the section until it has been ascertained that the line on which it is about to run is not obstructed." Yes, yes, but that was not what Norman wanted. Here it was: Regulation 14(e). "should a train pass without tail lamp and also without side lamps, the signalman must assume the train has become divided. He must send the 'Train Divided' signal (5-5) to the box in advance…." Oh, not '9', '5-5'! Wait a second, "unless he has reason to believe that the second portion will not enter the section in which case the 'stop and examine signal (7 beats) must be sent." Well, if the second portion was to follow it would have done so by now and in any case the gradient is slightly rising. Norman picked up the box-to-box phone to Heaton Lodge Jct. "That '9' signal I sent you was a '7'. That disposed of the inaccuracy nicely. How to shift the back portion? By now the guard was back at Mirfield No. 3 to say the line was clear so it was just a matter of propelling the second portion through to Heaton Lodge to recouple to the first portion. What is the next train? What luck, a light Class 47, an unusual enough occurrence at any time. Couple up. Speak to Heaton Lodge and send the train entering section again, authorise the class 47 driver to pass the signal at danger. Text book stuff was recorded in the train register.

Not quite though. There was a shallow gradient of 1-in-573 back to Mirfield No. 1 so Norman and I should strictly speaking have employed the last sentence of 14(e). "If, however, there is a rising gradient in the section from the box in rear, the signalman must carry out the provisions of Regulation 22, in which case it will not be necessary for the 4-5 bell signal." True, it would indeed not be necessary but only because Regulation 22 required the 2-5-5 bell signal to have been sent 'train or vehicles running away in wrong direction' As if there was a 'right' direction, one might say, but there was and that had a 4-5-5 bell signal!

Note how the regulation states if 'there is a rising gradient in the section from the box in rear'. It does not say 'if the gradient from the box in rear is a rising one'. There might be a substantial drop in height from the rear box to yours but if the downhill gradients are interrupted by an uphill one that might be where the train had become divided and it might be running away back to the box in rear. Clearly the regulations were designed for long sections. If it came down to minutiae some might say Norman and I should not have been reading Regulation 19 at all as 'Train Divided' Regulation 20(f) says much the same about sending 7 bells not 9 or, for that matter, 5-5, but specifically says, "Should a train become divided in starting and the first portion proceed, leaving the rear portion stationary....." you should send 7 to the box in advance and not send 4-5 to the box in rear. Because it was foggy we did not know whether the rear portion was stationary or for that matter, that it had divided on starting and not before.

I have run through this incident in exhaustive, probably exhausting, detail with a few aims in mind. Even a relatively straightforward incident without much danger is not so simple; what signalmen have to know; even if they don't know it they usually know how to square it up; how you can think you know what to do but fog, falling snow, darkness etc. can change what is needed and, finally, that studying the regulations in response to having experienced an incident is productive. I never needed to revise Regulations 19 and 20 much after that.

It was exactly how my signalling coach Inspector Jardine would have taught it to me.

In subsequent jobs I was sometimes involved with trains passing without tail lamps and had to employ the lessons of that foggy day in Mirfield. As Exeter area manager I was visiting Exminster box, by coincidence right opposite the emporium where Mirfield's track plan was to be found for sale. The up Cornish Riviera express was signalled and passed normally. It was a bright summer's day with the sun in the south directly behind the HST. It was obvious the train was complete with a power car on each end but the sun had drained all colour from the red tail lamp/s. I asked the signalman if he thought the tail lamps were lit. He said he could not tell so I shrugged and said, "It's 9 bells then isn't it?" He looked as if to say it definitely wasn't and made a counter suggestion. "Shall we let it run to Exeter and check?" My actions would have brought the train to a stand at City Basin only 1¼ miles short of Exeter St. David's and incurred delay. The signalman's proposition was sensible and I knew it but that was not the indivisible discipline expected of the rules. Yes, City Basin stopped the train. Yes, the light was showing red. No, it did not matter how important a train it was. No I don't suppose it did me too much good to insist on applying the letter of the law even if that was my expectation of others when box visiting. And no the signalman was not right when he then suggested it was necessary to send 4-5 to Dawlish Warren (the box in rear). We were in regulation 19 territory not 'Train Divided' Regulation 20. Clause 19(f), right at the end of the regulation says, "should a train pass with a tail lamp out when it should be burning, and the signalman can plainly see the lamp and is satisfied that the train is complete, the signalman must send the 'train out of section' signal to the box in rear and the train passed without tail lamp (9 consecutive beats) to the box in advance." So, no 4-5 signal was necessary in this case. Note, nowhere does the regulation say 'or give the next station a ring to have it checked.'

Back in Mirfield there was no tolerance shown to dmus with tail lamps out or missing in similar situations to Exminster. Over a cup of tea with nothing 'on the block' one chilly evening, with the Romesse stove roasting us as if we were sunbathing in Lanzarote, I was told an anecdote that probably subconsciously resulted in my arguably over-zealous treatment of the Cornish Riviera. Norman told me of a Normanton-Sowerby Bridge dmu that had run without a tail lamp for the whole journey. But the signalman at the penultimate box, Milner Royd Jct, sent '9 bells' to Sowerby Bridge. Every signalman from Normanton to Sowerby Bridge was disciplined with a 'Form 1' for failing to apply regulation 19. I reckon at the time of the incident that was about 25 signalmen, although my memory suggests the signalman said it was 16, possibly at a later date than I have calculated. Apparently the Milner Royd signalman was not spoken to by his colleagues for quite a while afterwards.

When my late younger brother Allan was working as a signalman at Marsden, after having abandoned university a couple of times, he rang me at Exeter to tell me how worried he was concerning an incident in the middle of a night shift. He had noticed a red tail lamp between the locomotive of a Manchester eastbound newspaper train and its first van. He rightly sent 7 bells 'stop and examine'. The driver was apparently somewhat annoyed and had said there was no such red light, thereby exonerating every signalman on the south side of the train all the way from Manchester, preventing Allan from the approbation of his colleagues but leaving him open to criticism for delay, to an important train as well if you like. I laughed it off, saying, "You know it was lit and so does everyone else. If anyone tries to tell you the driver said it wasn't just say 'Well he would say that wouldn't he' and that will put an end to it."

From Mirfield I was posted to cover the Leeds 'Full Loads" department. This prosaic name was chosen to differentiate the activities from the, by then, hived-off sundries division. It covered everything from the old-fashioned wooden containers, steel requiring cartage, vans needing old-fashioned porterage, to trainloads of oil and cement. Jeff Lawson was in charge, whom I was going to meet again at Bradford a few years later. He set me a programme of visiting all his terminals and writing a report on what I had discovered.

I started off at Hunslet Lane, a freight terminal located at the side of the Midland Main Line not far from Stourton Freightliner terminal. This was old fashioned goods yard working. A trip delivered the traffic in the morning and took it away in the evening. National Carriers provided the road transport for onwards delivery to the end user. The staff received a bonus for the tonnage they moved with their low capacity gantry crane. Much of the steel was short haul from Teesside or Scunthorpe where production was geared to rail so it was easier to send the lot by rail rather than segregate short haul from long haul. The road networks were of course undeveloped compared to now and there was no M62. If the gang put the steel from a bogie bolster rail wagon to a lorry they entered the tonnage on their bonus sheet. If they took it off bogie bolster and put it on the ground, subsequently putting it on a road wagon they could put it on their sheet twice. Very little was therefore placed directly from vehicle to vehicle. Sometimes this was for a good reason. Perhaps the consignee could not accept it and we needed to release the bogie bolster. Perhaps National Carriers could not supply the road transport required or the lorry had been delayed at the last delivery point or in traffic. All these were valid reasons but some others were not. I was not entirely convinced that all the direct transfers were booked as just one lift either so suggested that some bonus payments were being over-claimed. I was not there as a management spy or an auditor and as an 18 year old I had not learnt the meaning of discretion. I even thought I would be better regarded for my powers of observation. I think it might have simply embarrassed everyone. On reflection I even wonder if everyone already knew and it was a sort of 'staff retention' premium.

135

Moving on I had a shift at Hunslet East, watching how dangerous goods were treated and how the oil tankers from Immingham were discharged, before moving on to Wellington Street Goods. This was even more old fashioned than Hunslet Lane. It comprised just two sidings in what was known as Caley Yard. The origin of the name interests me now but I could not have cared less back them. Most railway sidings had strange names and I did not want to set people off on a trip down Memory Lane by asking about it. Rail vehicles arrived after reversal at Gelderd Road signal box to be greeted by four goods porters, two tractor drivers and a supervisor. The office staff for all the terminals was located here and I listed their duties in my report, strangely using the old gradings rather than their recent replacement Clerical Officer 1 to 4 (later 5) scale. There were six people (plus one relief clerk) engaged in the staff work of payment, consignment notes, charging, hiring and retirements and checking bonus sheets. The latter not very well I suspect. The Victorian office had high desks and commensurately tall stools. A rotund coke stove in the middle of the office baked those close to it but those on the margins needed gloves – the sort with no fingers so a pen could be wielded effectively. I think the quills had recently been replaced. A tall, spidery man, who must have been well past retirement age I thought, commanded his territory in the way Scrooge must have observed Bob Cratchit, on one occasion looking over his pince-nez to remark that I was a worrier. I did not consider this true but on reflection he was spot on whether it had been the pressure-cooker atmosphere at school or coping with bereavement. I also now realise it was not to change.

My feel for the clerical workload now, and indeed then, was that there might have been work for three of them. I suspect the establishment had been set for higher traffic volumes and not been reduced proportionately. Perhaps I learnt a lesson subconsciously here that, in any large body of clerical staff, there was usually scope for doing it without at least one of them. Harsh but true I'm afraid. The truism comes from clerical staff not working flat out for long periods of time and the perpetuation of procedures within the agreed workload that are no longer necessary.

I moved on to Marsh Lane for a day where cement traffic and coal were handled. My report noted there was a working foreman and a clerk whose duties (and I list them all to make the above point) were to compile the daily and weekly freight rolling stock return, keep delivery records for coal, cement and Hunslet East's oil, mark invoices and compile an opening and closing of work position. I took a passing look at the Cardigan Road coal terminal in the meantime but was unimpressed.

Then off I went to Whitehall Road, located on the inside of the Engine Shed Jct (Holbeck) to Whitehall Jct Midland Railway chord that skirts Leeds City station. Rail access was difficult through the passenger service, even the relatively sparse one of those days. There was an ungainly and old-fashioned overhead crane a good few generations older than the Stourton Freightliner one, but it worked. We still had traffic in the old containers and I remember securing a house removal from a telephone enquiry after consulting a tome entitled the 'book of rates'. It was a different world back then! I wonder if I won the contract by quoting too low? Moving on from that thought.... The clerk in charge was a dapper middle-aged man called Joe Moynihan. He was a union officer and a city councillor who had some sway, which annoyed me, with the new Passenger Transport Executive. His view of the railway and its future was worse than negative - even jaundiced - and he had no hesitation in transmitting his trenchant views to me. I remember he once finished a diatribe with, "What's a bright lad like you doing working for this lot?" I was young and keen but another month in the Leeds Full Loads Department and the propaganda would have changed my outlook..

Joe spent a lot of time out of the office, leaving me in charge. I suspect he did that even when no one else was available to mind the shop but I enjoyed it. I answered the phone, took decisions on a few aspects of loading and unloading priorities and watched the trains go by.

Two private sidings at Farnley were served by a trip that delivered traffic to Whitehall Road. One was Dunlop & Ranken's steel siding SP on a branch to the north and west of the former steam loco shed and the other was across the main Huddersfield line serving Cadbury's, mainly with traffic from their Keynsham factory. Both of course are now gone.

A couple of pages of my report have survived the ravages of house moving and I think it is worth repeating the conclusion in full, written by an 18 year old with no more than five months' railway experience. It shows what should have been more than obvious to senior management but perhaps they were too close to the problem to see it with fresh eyes. The style of the conclusion is too flowery for modern tastes of course but I had not learnt the style of business reports and even those were more fulsome than nowadays. It was written more in the style of a school A-level history essay and of course pre-dated the TOPS freight control computer system by 5 or 6 years.

"The lack of centralisation, to some extent an heirloom of the pre-grouping era, precludes any gains from economies of scale. However, had there not been a series of unfortunate occurrences – if the Whitehall Road crane had been at Hunslet Lane, if the entrance to Whitehall Road had been simpler, centralisation could have been done much earlier and much more easily. There is talk of a new Full Loads Depot at Stourton Up Sidings, but any such development would be extremely costly. To some extent a pre-advice system on a nationwide basis could solve many of the cartage problems so long as reliable transits could be guaranteed. Until such improvements occur there will be many anomalies, inefficiencies and wasted resources in what is still a very necessary service to the community. The sheer volume of goods in rail in the Leeds district each day could not be accommodated on the roads of the West Riding. However, to retain the railways' share and expand, modernisation must come to the Full Loads Department; a department which is, unfortunately, saddled with equipment which served the

Victorians well, but is inefficient and cumbersome to modern operating techniques."

Perhaps Joe Moynihan had got his point across. I moved on to a 'medium-sized passenger station' - Huddersfield.

Getting to work on a ten minute trolley bus ride was a pleasant change and my day release course was being done at Huddersfield Polytechnic, although I think it was still a technical college in 1969. Now it is a university specialising in rail transport studies, only 50 years too late for me. It's a bit like the hourly through trains from Huddersfield to Middlesbrough now, whereas I had to wait around on Darlington station (surely amongst the top ten draughtiest stations in Britain) for connections.

There was nothing much new at Huddersfield that I had not learnt at Mirfield other than how to do more of the same and faster. I was attached to the booking office and encouraged to perform as one of the roster. I found myself opening up at 06.20 because the other staff had taken all the overtime they wanted and left the most unpopular shifts for me. I did not mind as I relished the responsibility. It irked me a bit when I had a face at the window that I recognised from school and I could see them smirking about their university life, or teachers thinking I had fallen short of their expectations. The low point came when I was given a cloth bag and told to empty the toilet cubicles of the (old) pennies that were charged for their use. I was quite close to resigning at that moment. I don't think it was snobbery on my part unless thinking that I had been educated to be capable of doing a lot better counts as such. It probably does. In fact I felt like that for possibly the next decade, except for the time I was on my full management training programme and probably while I was at Bradford.

No. 45061 on the Red Bank newspaper empties on October 30, 1978 passing through Huddersfield with a Calder Valley Class 110 dmu standing in Platform 4. On the right hand side of the photo Platform 1 has now been widened and the through line used by the 'Peak' is now the platform road.

The most useful talent I developed in the booking office was learning to add up £.s.d. across the columns of the large account book. We were still issuing Edmondson tickets from large tubes, containing many different destinations, mainly in alphabetical order except for the most popular stations that were within arm's reach. Some had child and adult variations, others had to be cut diagonally a third of the way along to become a child ticket. Some had the price printed on them, others had to have it scribbled on. Some had the route specified, others had to have it endorsed. I was impressed to find that the route to be written was always the shortest station name en route so a ticket to the west country via Crewe, Shrewsbury and the Severn Tunnel (the standard route from Huddersfield until about 1970) had to be endorsed 'via Wem' a small station just before Shrewsbury. I presume it was thought that inscribing 'Via Shrewsbury' might have caused a queue. I learnt that I had not to be distracted by people asking questions when I was processing payment as it was a ploy to be wrong-changed to their benefit and that almost any enquiry, even if you knew the answer, had to be directed to the Enquiry Office a hundred yards or so along the station front. Huddersfield station was joint Lancashire & Yorkshire/ London & North Western and each had their own booking office on the wings of the station frontage. The LNWR one was the enquiry office in 1969. The functions are integrated now, although at the expense of having destroyed the art-deco frontage of the booking office windows in the former concourse. I also found out that if you told passengers, in effect, how likely they were to be killed or maimed on their journey you could get them to buy an insurance ticket and make yourself a few pence commission that added up over the week. It was practical to describe such dangers only off peak of course.

The starting numbers on each of the Edmondson tubes had been recorded so about ten minutes before the end of the shift the finishing numbers were recorded. The difference was multiplied by the price (without a calculator or adding machine) and entered in a column. Half fares and other bits and pieces were added on the destination's line and entered in the far right hand column. The vertical columns were than added up and cross-totalled. If the figures balanced in the bottom right hand corner you could go home. If they did not, you had to stay until you discovered your error. It would have been difficult enough even in decimal currency of course. All tickets were paid for by either cash or business/forces' warrants and there was one bus ticket style machine for adults and children to Leeds that represented the full extent of automation.

During my time there a new system of weekly balances replaced the daily shift calculations and as a result the deficit between the value of tickets sold and the cash collected grew. I could not really see the gain for the few minutes saved per shift and it struck me that some of the deficit could have resulted from clerks pocketing the odd fiver. I also realised that if the losses stopped when I moved to another posting it would look as if I had been doing it. I heard stories of auditors doing spot checks to trace the losses and resolved that I would go to work with my bus fare home and my sandwiches. And money for the tea club at the end of the week of course.

I took this lesson through to Exeter. Sometimes the sectors would look at the figures and demand shift balances should be reintroduced. I never opposed this. Then someone would propose abolishing them. Perhaps I exaggerate when I suggest the provincial sector would go for one way when InterCity was pursuing the other option but, if I am, it is not by much. I had to sign the monthly accounts at Exeter, a huge pile of returns from every booking office. I used to feel I was potentially signing my career away and it depended heavily on trusting the clerk who compiled them but here were a number of questions I had stored up my sleeve from my time at Huddersfield and accounts' correspondence courses to try to make it seem I knew more than I did. One was the 'outstandings' where tickets had been issued prior to accounts being settled and the other was the losses which were also a focus for travel centre managers' appraisal objectives that I set.

I also spent some miserable shifts in the parcel office. There was an open door to the road and another to the platform so it was always freezingly cold even on a summer's day. The volume of parcels can scarcely be imagined now. There were barrow loads out on the platform and a fleet of vans to perform collection & delivery. Every parcel had to be entered on a delivery sheet - consignee and address. The poor delivery driver was then supposed to identify the parcel and obtain a signature. The sheets came back at the end of the day with all the signature boxes filled in about as legibly as the parcel identity. It was a farce. Despite the shortcomings, how did British Rail manage to lose all its business to road hauliers? The Red Star service between any two staffed stations served by a through train with customers doing their own collection and delivery, was a strong product but it was watered down with a system of supposedly reliable transfers to and from a trunk train that did not serve the parcel's origin and destination stations. The whole parcel business had been costed as a marginal activity on existing passenger services with only a few dedicated trains of its own but sectorisation resulted in a rapidly growing beanstalk of overheads especially when passenger trains gradually lost their van accommodation. The beanstalk did not have a pot of gold at the top. Parcel consignments have constituted the biggest single freight growth business of the 21st Century and railways do not even have a foothold. Had I known what was in store I might have done even less time in that draughty old office.

My favourite work was in the enquiry office. It was warm and a kettle was always on the boil. In hot weather the chief clerk Norma would make iced tea. It was all very civilised. Work was shared between the counter and the telephones. I can still remember the phone number. If there were two or three of you on the phones the 'concentrator' lights would flash as a call came in and somehow I always managed to beat my colleagues to the button and they had to take another sip of tea to console themselves.

Passengers had to pay for seat reservations. Each station had its own allocation so if someone wanted to book a seat on the 08.30 Leeds-King's Cross we took out a chart and crossed off the seat the passenger chose. If none was left we had to ring another station for one of their allocation and they would cross it off their chart. A counterfoil was then made out in duplicate and the top copy was sent to the starting point of the train, often Neville Hill yard, by internal post for the counterfoil to be affixed to the seat. Duplicate reservations occurred if someone forgot to cross off a seat that had been allocated. The modern computer scheme does not permit this to happen. But it does, even allowing for the stupidities such as seats being shown as 'airline' a word that is perpetuated even though does not really fit the situation. This results in a ticket showing seat say 24A that passengers regularly interpret as Seat 24 Coach A. If it is actually seat 24A Coach M it can be a long walk.

The chief difficulty in the enquiry office was the lack of trains to Leeds as some genius had decided to withdraw the stops at Huddersfield in two pairs of the four Liverpool-Newcastle trains that ran each way. On top of off-peak local train withdrawals that meant there was just one train to Leeds between the 09.30 and the 13.30. The first train to Manchester on a Saturday was 08.15 and even during the week the two earlier ones were the 07.13 and 07.53 all stations ordinary dmus. The Newcastle express schedules somehow managed to lose the odd two or three minutes gained from passing Huddersfield at 20mph instead of stopping. They were rerouted from the closed Ripon line to the York main line but did not deign to stop there because, one senior manager opined, there was no demand.

I had one more location to sample before I was due to do an extended tour of all the divisional office. This was Healey Mills. The year was 1969 and traffic was still, to my mind buoyant. In fact I was mistaken because the base load Lower Aire Valley power stations had begun the process of depredation they were to exert on the TransPennine traffic upon which the construction of Healey Mills had been predicated. Gas consumption was switching from coal to natural sources as quickly as possible and 200,000 tonnes of coal a week was now being sent to the Ferrybridge 'C' and Eggborough plants by merry-go-round trainload services.

I spent time with the assistant yard masters on all the shifts; kindly and experienced men who took a lot of trouble to show me what was going on. A lot of time was also spent in the hump top cabin. This was the key location in the yard. If I had been the right age and had summoned up enough courage to be a bomber pilot there were two locations where a modern marshalling was vulnerable, the hump top and the outlet, probably the latter first. Photos I have seen seem to show indeterminate damage to the primary sidings which yard staff can easily circumvent.

The next chapter will cover marshalling yard detail at Tees but it is worth running through what happened at Healey Mills in 1969. There were 12 reception sidings reached directly by east bound trains and via a flyover for trains from the east. No reversal was necessary even for these loads as the loco was simply detached and sent for a return load or to the depot which was within the yard complex. A shunter uncoupled the wagons by destination or, in the case of empties not required at a specific location, by type. There were specific maxima concerning the number and weight of wagons to be included in one 'cut' so if there were say ten loaded wagons for one destination in the middle of a train followed by two for another destination there might be three cuts of three, one of the tenth and then the cut of two.

A pilot loco went to the west end of the siding and propelled the wagons up a short steep slope over a summit before a sharp falling gradient served to separate the cuts from each other. The machinery and the operator decided the weight, 'rollability', wind direction/strength, destination of the cuts and how full the destination siding was. The left or right side of the yard was decided at the King points. Gravity sent the wagons towards the appropriate 'queen' and then 'jack' points etc until the wagons entered the allocated primary sorting siding of which Healey Mills had fifty. Each one would be dedicated to a specific requirement such as Tyne Fitted, Tyne Unfitted, Whitemoor, or empty hoppers. If the staff and equipment had performed properly, not least the wagons themselves, they would gently roll up to the rear wagon in that particular siding and nestle cosily against it. Get it wrong and there would be a loud clang of buffers. Get it really wrong and the wagon might have to be taken to the trans-shipment siding along with a similar empty wagon, or a shifted load would be rectified using the mini crane. This took place far less than one might have thought it would but there were usually one or two casualties detained overnight. One of the worst events was if one cut caught up another and perhaps side swiped it. The result was often a derailment and sometimes a big pile of coal on the slope of the hump. But again this did not happen often. Hump shunting in fog was dangerous but so were the primary sidings as wagons could approach with the stealth of a deadly assassin.

When the yard shunters wanted to make up a train, either because a booked departure was imminent or a primary siding was getting full, they would arrange for the hump top cabin staff to close off the siding. They should also have pinned down wagon brakes on the rear three wagons as a fail safe precaution against errors but I cannot remember seeing this too often at either Healey Mills or Tees, although the yard shunters were so adept at working quickly perhaps I missed it. Hump shunting would continue and if there were wagons for the primary sidings being cleared a spare siding would be allocated or doubling up of a suitable one would be undertaken. A hump yard in full flow was a true thing of beauty; a fully functional industrial design.

Occasionally a wagon would get away from the system and run into an empty primary siding at too high a speed, running straight through to the marshalling area putting staff in great danger. There was a tannoy loudspeaker available to sound the alarm with a warning. I recall a lady from a nearby house once ringing to complain about the foul language that had been emitted which she had clearly heard when pegging out her washing. There was no excuse of course but there was some amusement around the yard about her comment during the phone call that she "could not believe railwaymen would address each other in those terms."

Part of the problem that I learned at Healey Mills and tried to address at Tees concerned the mix of fitted and unfitted wagons. Most of our trunk wagonload trains were partially fitted so perhaps ten out of say 40 vehicles might have been (usually) vacuum-brake fitted. Because you would need a fitted head for the next train, the tendency was to take the minimum number of fitted vehicles you could get away with having and make up the full load with unfitted vehicles which often carried lower priority traffic. The fate of important fitted vehicle traffic could be even more adversely affected if the traffic on offer exceeded the capacity of the scheduled trains. Spare loads would be made up and drawn out to the departure sidings waiting arrangement of a special train and perhaps be by-passed by traffic that had been shunted later. Brake vans were cleared from a primary siding onto the 'brake van kip' which was a steeply inclined siding at the rear of the departure roads. The guard of a departing train would climb into his van, release the hand brake and gravitate it to the rear of his train trying not to hit it too hard but definitely avoiding the ignominy of stopping short and requiring the pilot to give him an extra shove.

At Tees I will mention that our spare loads were made up for a Class 31 being found instead of the Class 37s of booked trains so that there was no need to reduce loads if a Class 31 turned up. The corollary was that if a Class 37 was indeed found it went without a maximum load, hauling the spare train. There were decisions to be made at almost every turn. It could not be taken for granted that a loaded wagon was more important than an empty because a steel works might be crying out, not just for more obvious bogie bolster wagons, but, for instance, empty light weight 'runner' vehicles to accommodate the overhang of a long length order being prepared. The system was biased in favour of quantity rather than quality.

The hump operators had a bonus system which, I had learnt, was not always conducive to safety. There was pressure to hump shunt everything that moved. If a 65 vehicle empty mineral was approaching from Lancashire with wagons to fulfil orders being made from local coal mines there was a temptation to run it onto the receptions, make 15 cuts of five wagons to the empty mineral primary siding and count the figures as genuinely humped. Of course this meant that the marshalling shunters had to draw it out and put it somewhere. Their opinion, expressed in terms that would justifiably shock the lady with her washing line, usually resulted in this practice being avoided. The assistant yard masters kept a watchful eye out as well.

Most of the eastbound destinations had primary siding allocations on the north side of the yard and westbound destinations on the south side. The trains made up for the utilities of Lancashire were drawn into the up departure sidings where two parallel departures could be made to the up slow and up fast lines respectively. Such were the expectations of the designers in the early 1960s. If you remember, there was still an overflow to be accommodated at Mirfield Up Sidings. There was also the former Midland Line from Royston Jct to (appropriately) Midland Jct, just west of Healey Mills, via Middlestown and a large viaduct. This was kept open for a while for four return coal trains each day from Woolley Colliery Sidings to I.C. I.'s Oakleigh Sidings at Northwich to avoid Healey Mills because of congestion.

Some sidings were allocated to a pick-up goods train such as the one that served Barnbow tank factory at Cross Gates and Garforth coal depot, both on the Leeds-York main line. The traffic from this siding was drawn into secondary sorting sidings prior to departure and re-sorted to the best order for the trip to deal with them. Through trains requiring traincrew relief were held in the up or down staging sidings, in later years used for merry-go-round trains that needed no shunting.

Modern marshalling yards were efficient in the use of staff with a complement of perhaps fifteen or so yard staff each shift. I spent some time on nights. The atmosphere was electric, the huge floodlight pylons beaming a white light into every nook and cranny and the yard living its own life like some nocturnal animal plodding through the bush. The difference in atmosphere was akin to that between a floodlit football match and one played at 15.00 on a damp and dismal afternoon. Nights were spent mainly at the hump top and included going through the routine of hump shunting consecutive trains riding with the driver on the Class 08 locomotive. On nights, two locos worked continuously except for a 20minute meal break. As one pushed its last wagon over the hump top the next prepared to push the next one and the first ran down an empty road behind another train. About 50 trains a night were shunted and even so it was not unusual for two or three arrivals to be standing on the flyover awaiting a spare reception.

While I was there, a large scale training programme was being undertaken into the assessment of train loads. I studied it hard, having the advantage of being a blank sheet of paper unfettered by allegiance to the old system, and did some instruction. Every wagon was to have a yellow panel fitted showing a matrix of figures. The left hand column had lines for weight, brake force, route availability and maximum speed. Across the top were columns for its loading condition; heavy, medium, light and empty. The guard or, in a large yard, train preparer would walk along the train with a pro-forma on a large clip board, probably in the pouring rain with water dripping from the neb of his grease-top cap onto the plastic bag being used to stop the form going soggy. He would look at the wagon label and see if it was shown as H, M, L, or E and note the appropriate weight. He would add the appropriate brake force to his total, check the route availability was within that of the train's expected journey and mark the speed if it was the lowest he had met so far on this train. He also had a column for 'excess length units'. A standard length unit was 21ft and excess length units shown on the yellow panel had to be added up and added to the basic total. If a wagon had no panel for some reason the working manual had to be consulted for the detail needed. Section 6, the 'white pages' entitled 'Preparation and Working of Freight Trains' ran to 65 pages in the copy with which I retired. A vacuum bogie bolster 'D' (BDV) weighed 65/49/33/23 tonnes in the H/M/L/E categories and had a brake force of 12, route availability of 4/4/1/1, a maximum speed of 55mph and was shown as having 7 extra length units. An airbraked BBA steel carrier was 102/69/47/28 tonnes, 50/40/25/14 brake force 10/6/3/1 route availability with a speed of 60/75/75/75. A BAA was the same except for the speed being 60mph under all load categories and when empty. Of course, if a BDV wagon was loaded with steel girders weighing 27 tonnes it would gross at 50tonnes when the tare weight of the vehicle was added. Because this is one tonne over the medium category limit it would be classed as heavy and assessed as weighing 65 tonnes. Despite an apparent search for accuracy, the goal was never reached. Nevertheless, compiling a train list pre-TOPS was a complicated task.

There were very few routes that were classified as RA 10 so vehicles requiring to go on lower classified routes could not travel on them unless the driver was in possession of a form of authority specifying any special speed restrictions to be observed such as over a weak bridge. 8ft 6in maritime containers (and, later, even higher ones) were similarly treated with the driver given the bridge number or mileage of structures where he had to squeeze the containers through the gap available.

Another white pages' table showed how the basic load for a route could be converted into a maximum load depending on brake force available and concentrating the tonnage into a shorter length with consequentially reduced resistances. So a basic load of 850tonnes could become 1350tonnes, as applied for Class 37s from Tees to York. Across the Pennines a Class 40 was quoted a lower load than a Class 37 despite its higher horsepower.

My best days at Healey Mills were spent riding with guards. I have vivid memories of visiting Ackton Hall colliery with Class 40 No. D349 on a 'control orders' trip that also served Glasshoughton colliery and the nearby Yorkshire Coking Company. If someone in that great marshalling yard in the sky had intended Class 40s to be used in tight Victorian colliery sidings he would not have given them big noses. As for adhesion, the only way of getting out of the colliery was by spreading sand liberally all over the track to the main line. Even then the loco made some agonising noises that would have alarmed a Class 40 Anti-Cruelty Society.

This spell at Healey Mills pre-dated the closure of Horbury & Ossett station which was located at Horbury Bridge at the east end of the yard neck. I travelled via a local train to Mirfield and a convenient connection into the threatened Sowerby Bridge-Normanton train to Horbury. Here I would alight with a posse of bleary-eyed Healey Mills trainmen from unbalanced westbound overnight workings and follow them across the tracks, through the Chas. Roberts 100 tonne tank repair yard and up to the modern yard admin block. In early March 1969 it was suggested that I might go on a longer brake-van trip so I elected to use 8M59 07.40 Healey Mills-Oakleigh (Northwich). Getting from my home on the Bradford Road out of Huddersfield for that time of the morning without a car was a problem but the first Bradford-bound bus to Brighouse and then the 04.25 Manchester Victoria-York parcel train would get me to Horbury & Ossett on time. I awoke to find at least 2ft of snow. Making my way down to the main road it seemed unlikely that any buses would be running. My Brighouse rail/road connection was too tight for comfort anyway. Eventually a bus turned up and took me slithering down the steep hill into Brighouse. I was relieved to find the loco-hauled train was also running late and when I reached the yard around 08.00 I found the Northwich train's guard drinking tea in the up departure sidings awaiting the provision of a loco.

Eventually D6865 appeared and attached to its train of 24-tonne mineral wagons, with double doors, that were used on this important traffic flow. I did not log my journey but I enjoyed my trip past my childhood haunts and up the Colne Valley to Standedge Tunnel. I thought it would be interesting to lean out over the veranda at the back of the van watching the rails pass below my wheels, practising the insouciant expression I had seem so many times from guards in my youth. Those ideas were soon dispelled as regular violent snatches from the partially fitted train meant that the best that could be done was to wedge myself on one of the two seats and look out along the side of the train from the small forward facing spy window. There was no warning of the snatches and I remember having nightmares about it the following night. Welcome to the world of the goods guard.

We came out of Standedge Tunnel into bright sunlight and not a flake of snow. We negotiated Stalybridge and then Stockport station where our 30 or so wagons apparently loaded with snow caused London-bound passengers some amusement. We took the Northwich line from Edgeley No. 2 signal box and deposited the vehicles in the I.C.I. sidings. The earlier Northwich train was ready to go back with its empties so I hitched a lift with D6950 and made my way back towards Healey Mills with just as many snatches. I had asked the driver to drop me off in Huddersfield if he could. We were routed through Platform 8 so I hopped off while it was on the move as Huddersfield schoolchildren were taught to do from infancy jumping off the back platform of trolleybuses before they stopped. What a missed chance this decision represented. The convenience of an early finish compared to waiting for a train from Horbury to Mirfield and then home had taken priority over such the rare opportunity of a brake van trip on a revenue-earning freight.

My next transfer was to the Divisional Office in Leeds adjacent to the Queen's Hotel but around that time I was given some time to visit the Leeds Division's control offices. In 1969 these were housed in three 'district' offices. No one had really tackled combination, and claimed the likely economies of scale, partly perhaps as there were no suitable premises. The Leeds Control took a full floor of the Aire Street office block. Compared to the pen pushing on the other floors, the atmosphere in the control office was one of earnest endeavour. There was the hum of conversation over telephones but it was generally quiet. Someone in the corner might be consuming fish & chips before getting back to work and the junior would be performing continual rounds with a large metal teapot containing dark brown pudgy tea made with a greater concentration of tea bags than was medically advisable, justified by the fact there was no greater insult than to be accused of making weak tea. A tray full of chipped and tannin-stained mugs, many with the fresh tea having been poured onto the dregs of the last brew, would be distributed to their owners. The first task to be learnt when entering the control grades was to be able to unfailingly identify everyone's beaker.

Leeds Control had recently converted from graphing the trains on each section to recording the details on cards. Late running would be scrupulously entered at each timing point with a large letter 'T' of almost any semi-recognisable shape scrawled on the card in the eventuality of any of these long distance trains every reaching such an elevated status. I had seen the punctuality clerks scrutinising the old style graphs on the following day and sending out 'please explain' chitties to the station master concerned, in the event of perceived signalling delays, and the depot concerned for train crew or loco problems. The length of time taken to complete the procedure of dispatch, receipt, investigation and reply was staggeringly inefficient. The instances of identifying lost time and preventing a recurrence were relatively rare. A cynic might say it would be likely to happen only if the member of staff identified was a novice in knowing how to reply. Many requests to drivers would come back with a corner of the letter folded back with the classic response 'No knowledge' inscribed on the back. If nothing had been received after perhaps a week or ten days a 'repeat' would be sent out to little effect. Even by that stage of my career I had seen what happened when the mail was opened and a flurry of these billets-doux fell from the correspondence wallets onto the desk along with many other 'multiple address' envelopes. These thick brown paper foolscap envelopes would have perhaps twelve address boxes to be used for many journeys back and forth.

A station master at a small station might mutter something to himself usually about clerks in headquarters having nothing else better to do. If it was a serious delay he would have heard of it already. Delays of two or three minutes were often just untraceable inaccuracies. Minor mishaps were treated in a similar fashion although the request for reports was given a higher priority at both ends. A typical request for a report about a door open on a passenger train leaving a station would yield the person in charge of the platform saying all doors were secured when the 'right-away' was given and a passenger had either tried to jump on or, if some variety was being sought, jump off. The guard was not likely to say he waved his green flag or light with a door open either. The purpose of all the exchanges was probably no more than letting staff know that someone was watching and it was probably a good idea to do the job right than have the annoyance of having to frame a reply.

I was not too impressed by my time in the Leeds control office as I felt they had been reduced from the status of controllers to recorders. On my L&Y/LNWR patch the signalmen regulated their own trains through junctions and over long block sections. If they had any doubt they might ring control to ask how a certain train was running. At Heaton Lodge Jct there were a couple of freights to the Liverpool area each day via Diggle and a couple via Hebden Bridge but they did not need telling by control which was which or, for that matter, the Western's complicated and impenetrable routing bell codes. The standard method of margining was to give a train a run on the Monday and see how it went. If it ran badly it would be held back the rest of the week. Other turns were well known as good runners. My friend Noel Proudlock in his time at Wortley Jct, as recounted in The Railway Magazine (Oct.2019)' always let Lancaster men on the evening boat train have a run in front of anything and learnt to give the Saltley express freight lodge turns the road unless you wanted your ear bending by a Brummie. In these circumstances, control was an irrelevance.

To be fair, this was not the case in the event of a serious incident where the coordination of emergency responses and reorganisation of train services was the top priority. I took this opinion with me through my career. Control also had responsibilities for loco and unit provision which in later years I found to be so restrictive, particularly after sectorisation, that it became an obstacle to actually managing to run trains.

York District control was located in a Dickensian office block in Tanner Row the opposite side of the North Eastern Belle Epoque headquarters' building that is now the top price Grand Hotel. I remember very little about my time there and, fortunately, there were no major incidents. Across the road in the original station building known as West Offices sat the regional controllers who oversaw the work of the divisional and district controllers. Some might suggest there was a certain amount of duplication and that one or the other could be slimmed down. Goodness knows what goes on now in the palace that Network Rail has built at the York Yards side of the station.

Wakefield District control was a different matter. It was again to be found in derelict Victorian offices that should have been bull dozed no later than the then recent Wilsonian white heat of technology iconoclastic period. It was here though that I saw one of the finest bits of control work that I have ever experienced. Arguably it was no big deal. It did not involve coordinating response to a major collision or bomb incident, it was a simple train failure and rescue.

The 13.10 King's Cross-Leeds had failed at Hampole, approaching South Elmsall from Doncaster. Adjacent to South Elmsall station was Frickley Colliery, served not only from both the Great Northern main line but also the Swinton & Knottingley cross country line that crossed the Doncaster-Leeds main line on an overbridge between South Elmsall and South Kirkby Jct where the main line was joined by the curve from Moorthorpe currently used by Cross Country Voyagers. When the word went up that the Class 47 needed assistance, the deputy chief controller (shift manager) stood up and, in a commanding voice, asked a simple question, "Who's got an engine?" The S&K line controller shot his hand up. "Light Class 47 York to Tinsley passing Pontefract". It went into the S&K colliery entrance, through the colliery yard, out of the other exit and onto the front of the train. It was only after the event that I wondered which depot's crew was on the rescue loco and how their task squared with their route knowledge. Presumably Wakefield Control had landed upon a crew conscientious enough to respond, but not too much so that they would say they did not know how to observe a signal out of a colliery yard; or they had found the crew wanted overtime.

The local coal workings were organised from this office on a huge blackboard with a large scale version of the train graph fixed to it for each section of line. The process of planning local services from there was called 'pin & string'. After seeing what coal traffic was standing at which collieries, the demand for empty wagons (by type) and the forecast of production for the rest of the day the controller would approach the train graph. Starting at Healey Mills he would pin his string there and apply standard running times to the destination of his choice. He would roll out his ball of string until he encountered a clash with a higher priority train either at a junction, or one which needed to overtake his path of string, in which case he would wind back to the previous recessing point for the clash to be avoided. At this point the diagonal line of the string path on the time/distance graph would obviously become horizontal until a suitable departure path was identified. Off the string would then go to its destination, sometimes needing to stop and watch the world go by a few times.

Having reached what was usually a colliery (but could be a coking plant, power station, yard or run-round point) the string would then be pinned for the standard allowance applicable for the planned operation. 'Detach 30 empties, pick up 20 loaded HTOs' would have a longer allowance than 'detach 30 empties, light diesel to ....' Similarly 'Detach 30 empties, attach 30 loaded HTOs" would have the longest of the three times to allow for the guard inspecting the bigger train and walking back from talking to the driver. The next move might be to take the wagons back to Healey Mills so the process of pathing the move would start again. The controllers knew what they were doing of course so they might know that there was for instance no point in trying to get from Healey Mills to Goldthorpe on the S&K at a certain time of the morning because too much time would be lost in loops waiting for expresses to pass.

The strength of the system was that optimistic programmes of work were less likely to be issued to the crews which would leave a shortfall of traffic moved by the end of the day. The weakness was that the paths actually taken by the trip freights often bore no resemblance to the plan. A signalman would take a chance and give a train a run, possibly because the driver had come to the box and diplomatically suggested the signalman was being a tad over cautious or because a passenger train it was being held for was running late. Equally, the path could be destroyed by events. In either case, the controller could intervene, unpin his string, and transfer it to a different destination or time. Overall the system worked well but I was never quite sure if it was necessary. The same controllers who were so skilled at designing the programmes could probably have guessed it sitting at a desk doodling on scrap paper. Computers would render both pins and string redundant, not to mention doodling, as would the reduction in traffic or its transfer to merry-go-round operation.

One of the snags I found in these control order turns was that they did not appear in the timetable so were not really in anyone's consciousness or calculations. I once met the divisional operations manager at Norwich when I was about 21 trying to introduce a trip book system at Cambridge. "How can the signalman at Ely North Jct plan his margining if he has no access to planned times of the trip working?" he demanded. I did not convince him, partly because I saw his point and partly in deference to his substantial seniority. I remember suppressing an urge to say that if Wakefield Kirkgate could manage to regulate its trip book trains then I was sure Ely North Jct could cope. When I went back to Healey Mills for a couple of months in 1976 the task was being done in the TOPS office, without pin or string I think. I remember one of the controllers gently suggesting to a guard

157

that the next task he might consider should be, "27 o' coyal to Wath next, lad". I had lived in Yorkshire all my life and I knew his Wath with a hard 'A' was the 'Woth' we used in my part of Yorkshire but I had the temerity to check with him that 'coyal' was coal and not steel coil. I received a withering confirmation that it was indeed the case.

I did not resent my subsequent incarceration for nearly a year in the Divisional Office. There was a lot to learn. I spent time in the passenger commercial office where public complaints were handled. I had a shot at sharing the workload with the helpful person whose job it was. I did not understand that 'without prejudice' was a widely understood legal phrase and told him I thought it might cause offence to some people. That did not get me very far.

One of my favourite trips was to bank holiday relief train planning meetings. Two people went from Leeds, neither being management grade. One was armed with the timetable and another with 'passenger count' information. We used to sit round a big table at York. The Cross Country one was, in those days, known as 'North East/South West'. North West/South West, North East/South East and North West/South East had yet to be invented and Scotland, as it was served by only one daytime cross country train via the east coast, was excluded from the title altogether.

The representatives of Eastern and London Midland Regions and their Divisions would go through the timetable. I was fascinated by the lack of bureaucracy involved in putting together a bank holiday programme. One person would say. "Full and standing from us last year." Another would say, Same here" and the chairman would probably bring such a full discussion to a close by saying, "York–Birmingham relief then. If Newcastle had information about heavy loading from their stations they might ask for it to start back there. If the LM said the parent train was under pressure from New Street they might say, "Extended to Bristol" and that would be it. A few weeks before the holiday a special traffic notice would appear with times of the train, diagrams for the loco and crews would accompany it. It really was just like that! East Coast, TransPennine the lot. Sometimes the process would be cut short by the suggestion, "Good Friday, same as last time?" Then another person might say we don't need the 18.35 from Manchester Vic to Leeds it was empty last year and the next agenda item would be opened, perhaps for Easter Monday. I was impressed and I think I took the lessons with me. I hated meetings that dragged on and I detested chairmen and, later, chairwomen who reopened a closed argument. Asking the question, "Anyone got anything to add," once was enough. A second invitation would invariably provoke someone to start the discussion all over again.

While on the passenger commercial side I spent some time out on the road with passenger sales representatives. I think there were three or four for the division. Their task was to meet representatives of the organisations in their patch. This included pubs and clubs, schools and women's groups. The aim was to fill a special train. Thirty here, a hundred there, negotiate free places for the organisers. Regular events such as the Rugby League Cup Final were targeted. No one cared who was likely to get to the Final, the ritual was what mattered. Destinations such as say Chelsea Flower Show or the Edinburgh Tattoo were other possibilities or girls' schools and a hockey international at Wembley. On one trip I visited my old primary school and sat with the sales rep in the headmaster's office. It drew on a poor area and expensive excursions to exotic locations were not how it did its business. I thought people would be glad to see me back. It was, after all, only eight years or so after I had left. Instead I left with a sense that I had let them down and, I thought some years later, even undermined their pleasure in what they thought they might have achieved for me. I was not asked about what I was doing and they would not have comprehended the training process I was in. 'What was wrong with being a passenger sales rep anyway?' I would have thought at the time and more so now. It was linked to the working class industrial ethos of educating yourself out of poverty and achieving what sociologists termed 'social mobility'. I enjoyed my days riding around in the cars with the reps. What did I care?

The majority of my time was spent in the operating offices. These worked with little management contact at all. I would not have recognised the Divisional Manager if I had met him in the lift, or his deputy George Potter the divisional operating manager either. Surely they should have made an appearance on their divisional 'shop floor' now and again. I moved around the punctuality, accident and coaching stock sections, usually each a bank for four desks or so in a huge office.

I particularly enjoyed the time on coaching stock, ensuring formations were right, or able to be put right. My favourite part of the day was when York Carriage works rang in the mid-afternoon with a list of vehicles being released into traffic. We had no prior knowledge so jotted them down then assessed what would be best sent where. If there was a post office sorting vehicle it might be put on a parcel train to Edinburgh, a brake gangway vehicle might be needed at Newcastle. Catering vehicles were especially important. One might be in need of repair at King's Cross so a similar specialist vehicle was sent there overnight.

One Friday, York was short of vehicles for its summer Saturday trains. It seemed that the Llandudno might have to run up to three vehicles short, even after we had sent them all the Mark I vehicles we could. By coincidence three of the coaches released from York were Metro-Camm Pullman cars. No one had need of them so I sent it to Clifton carriage sidings for use on the Llandudno. When this was discovered someone in authority said the Pullman name must not be besmirched by using the vehicle on such a service. It ran anyway. I went to York the following morning for a trip with them. The Class 40 No. 345 backed the Llandudno train into the bay platform opposite what was then 8 South, (probably 7). It kept coming and coming. I don't know whether someone had told the driver the wrong number of coaches or the shunter was not relaying

160

his signals properly, or even if the addition of my Pullman had not been noted but back it came until…CRUNCH the stock hit the buffers with a noise that could be heard across the station. Everyone froze, then various inspectors and carriage examiners came running across. They prodded the coaches and looked underneath, pulled them up the platform to the starting signal then pushed them gently back. The danger was that the bogie pins had snapped and it seemed my Pullman trip would not happen. I even wondered whether my initiative was going to have been the cause of a cancellation but after a while every one seemed satisfied and the train departed. My notes reveal the run to Huddersfield was unexciting except for watching the reactions of my fellow travellers.

My chief guide at this time was David Laycock, a CO 4 in charge of the passenger traffic section. He gave me a lot of work on engineering possession planning, compiling the weekly engineering notice and checking it. He planned what possessions could be granted to the engineer by keeping a board for each weekend with a map of the Division on it with possessions already granted marked with a huge cross. That way he made sure that a suitable diversionary route was always available. My lesson was that you did not need a complex system to keep control of what was happening.

David was the operating presence at the relief train meetings and kept an eye on loadings. My train home at night was the 15.42 Newcastle-Liverpool loco-hauled train booked for a Gateshead Class 46 with 8-11 coaches depending on the season and day of the week. On a Friday in the summer timetable it was the full eleven which was within the D385-tonne timings that were used. The Class 46s did not always turn up though. If a Class 47 was the substitute the train would be nearer to time than if it was a Class 40, for obvious reasons of design horsepower. The general public was not aware of such niceties and I remember waiting on a bitterly cold night on Leeds station for the train to appear past the signal at Leeds East. Our blood was close to freezing in our veins when the nose of a Class 40 dared to edge into sight and as it spluttered further into view a young lady standing nearby uttered the immortal words to her friend, "Oh good, its one of those big engines tonight."

The train was often 'full and standing' from Leeds, especially on Fridays despite the full eleven coaches being provided. The previous Manchester train was an hour in front and the next one an hour behind, both 6-car TransPennines (soon to be reduced to 5 with the withdrawal of their 'griddle' cars). On Fridays the 15.46 Hull-Liverpool, which left Leeds at 16.50, used to have a twin 300hp dmu attached to reduce overcrowding, returning on Sunday evenings. A reference to the griddle cars I have seen says that Aberdeen Angus in a bread roll with butter was 1/9d or around £2 at current prices. I never tried one but it is hardly surprising the venture made a loss.

Swindon-built Class 124 Trans Pennine sets were booked to serve York only once a day in the early 1970s with a westbound scheduled 15.15 departure.

Younger readers might be bemused by this concern over passengers not having a seat but it was unusual around any of the Leeds network for this to happen on other than the shortest journeys to or from the nearest station. In 2020 most trains leave Leeds with scores of standing passengers for the Huddersfield direction, even in the shoulder peak and often in the so-called off peak. No one worries or cares much although efforts are made within the franchising system to double up three coach trains to six if possible and the standard formation of the new bi-modes and loco-hauled trains will be 5 coaches. Providing five coaches instead of 11 does not seem much of an improvement but their capacity is only 20 seats short of the winter weekdays 'load 8' which had one full brake and a buffet car. True, it is only 62% of an eleven coach formation but there are around five trains an hour instead of one on the central Leeds-Manchester section.

The British Rail of the 1960s responded in the time-honoured way and a relief train was ordered to run at 17.04 from York to Manchester Victoria every Friday until further notice with eight coaches I think – sometimes it mustered only 7 and, I believe, a York Class 40 although you could not really guess the locomotive diagram from what was provided. The combined attention of Control and the York depot foreman seemed to plump first for an unbalanced London Midland engine to get it home and in times when Type 4 power was scarce, then occasionally an English Electric Type 3 or even a Type 2. Looking at my notes for a ten week period in 1971 when I used it every Friday from York to Huddersfield we were given a Class 45 (D35), 46 (D186), 2x47s (D1566/1914) and 6 class 40s including D225 Lusitania and Haymarket's D261. In order to justify the extra expense a special count of the passenger numbers between Leeds and Huddersfield was required so David asked me to ensure I caught the train home to provide the figures. I would willingly have done this of course but the office staff insisted I should book overtime for it. I reluctantly agreed to sign myself off at 18.10 but they said I had to claim the time back to my 'home' station which was down as Leeds. I explained I was not going to go back but they said it was immaterial, that was the agreement. In the end I tried to get out of the job as it was embarrassing to do that. The guard should have been prevailed upon to do it but I am not sure of the agreements in those pre-train manager days and it was likely that he (always a he) would have said he could not get through to do a count. This would have been evidence in itself though that the train was justified, if it were true.

One of the offices looked after the merry-go-round trains. The C.O.3 Don Thompson was a keen fellow cricketer whose assistant had moved on so I covered the job for a few months at the end of my training. A new cycle of work started each Thursday afternoon, sometimes around 15.00 but often later. Don and I would sit there twiddling our thumbs waiting for the crucial phone call and wondering how much overtime we would end up working. This was a strange concept because I was doing day release for my business course on Thursday mornings and would not get to work until 13.00. Incidentally my train from Huddersfield was a Newcastle express with a buffet car. I would go to the counter for a cheese and tomato sandwich and a can of cider. The steward would make the sandwiches freshly in front of me, probably using his own raw materials. I would take it back to the buffet car table with its free-standing dining chairs, consume my meal in a leisurely fashion while timing the train and still have time before reaching Leeds because the schedule for the 17 miles was 29min net and gross caused by a 60mph line limit with many very low intermediate restrictions including 25mph via Dewsbury platform at the foot of the climb through Batley to Morley tunnel. Modern trains pass Dewsbury at 75mph on a through line.

Class 40 No. 40004 enters Huddersfield with the 17.04 York to Manchester Victoria on June 25, 1982 after conversion to Mark 2 stock on a Pennine evening close to the summer solstice.

Eventually the Central Electricity Generating Board would ring with the allocations of coal to Ferrybridge 'C' and Eggborough power stations. As I have said before, this was usually at least 200,000 tonnes from a wide variety of Yorkshire pits. The nearest to Eggborough was Kellingley which was more or less underneath the power station. Nowadays it is considered greener to send Biomass from the Mississippi via New Orleans and Newcastle than to use this local fuel source. One of the more difficult mines was Peckfield, adjacent to Micklefield station at the junction of the Leeds to York and Hull lines. We had a matrix of standard running and terminal times and applied that to the loco programmes. I think it was 45min to discharge the load in the power station. The programmes we devised had to space power station arrivals so there was no wasted time waiting discharge. Some of the collieries such as Frickley had rapid loading bunkers to turn round trains on the move as per the merry-go-round name. The power stations actually had a loop so the trains did not need to stop, although most of the collieries did involve stopping and reversing on what were often industrial revolution-age sites. The wagons were loaded on the move. Some pits would do four or five trains a day, 900tons of coal in each 30 wagon 1,350 trailing-tonnes train, headed by a Knottingley Class 47.

Other pits had to use traditional loading messages and an empty train would be left with a loaded one being picked up. Most programmes started light loco Knottingley to Gascoigne Wood to pick up empties. We did not pin & string the moves but instead used standard running and terminal times as if no delay would be encountered. If two trains did clash at the power station then extra time would be added though. We inserted crew relief at appropriate locations no more than eight hours apart. I think the agreement with the Knottingley drivers was that they would accommodate the excess over 8hrs on overtime. I suspect that the actual running and the plan bore little resemblance but, if so, it would not be the only piece of railway timetabling where that happened. In the meantime two clerks were working on the computerisation of the process but I never saw any real feedback from them although our paths crossed every day.

It was the normal arrangement for the following week's drivers' rosters to be posted on the notice board no later than the Thursday but, again, the Knottingley crews were, I think, happy to compromise in view of their major customer being unable to comply with the constraints of doing that. Don and I would beaver away as quickly as we could with the aim of urgently getting the information to Knottingley in the guard's van of a local dmu. The last train was about 20.10 which I do not think we ever missed and we usually made the one before that. I had an enjoyable day out to see the operation at first hand using loco D1893 to do the Ferrybridge 'C' power station discharge loop.

The Knottingley operation was Monday to Friday only so their locos were used on summer Saturday holiday trains, giving them a chance to clear their bronchial tubes of the coal dust with a run to the seaside. My impression was that they were reliable and that maintenance of a small fleet of the same class at a single-business depot worked well – quite the opposite of the railway template at the time. I have discovered a run I made with Knottingley's D1893 on a summer Saturday Llandudno train and 385tons gross. After switching from the fast to slow lines at Gledholt Jct as was then the custom, where an uphill 1-in-96 eases slightly, the Class 47 accelerated its train to 50mph against 1-in-105 which was unusually good for a Type 4 with eleven bogies.

During the operating week Don and I would make adjustments to the plan as necessary. Perhaps a colliery had hit a difficult seam so production might be going to cause a cancellation. Another might be creating a surplus so the train would be switched there and any extra time accommodated in the alterations made, taking account of relief requirements. The wagon sets had to be kept up to the full 30 in length otherwise a tonnage shortage could arise. That 30th wagon was all railway profit, although it was widely believed that if British Rail made any monopoly profits anywhere in its overall operation coal supply to base load new generation power stations was where it happened. There was no real alternative so if we could stay the right side from the electricity board being able to claim we were making unfair profits it worked out well.

As my training scheme came to an end I made the first error of my career moves and probably the second most important. The worst one was probably giving priority to pursuing the unsuccessful process towards a second adoption when I was at Exeter, instead of going back to the Eastern Region and being close to family. The third most important was accepting the Neville Hill job; after all I was happy enough at Bradford and something would have come up. The mistake I now made was not accepting a job in Leeds Control. I had apparently made a good impression on the number 2 in the operating pyramid, a live wire known as Bill Halpin and his freight assistant. I think this had started one day when the freight chief came into the office with an urgent request from the coal board to move some surplus traffic, only to find Don on his lunch break and the 19yr old trainee answering the phone calls, and being taken aback when I had already done what he wanted. This happened a few times.

The training scheme offered nothing more than applying for C.O.2 jobs in competition with other staff members. I thought this was unfair even at the time because if I had taken say a booking clerk's job I would have been promoted within the year and be looking at the next rung on the ladder. It seemed that the training scheme had impeded me. In the end I had the choice of travelling to York every day (home to home time 07.00 to 19.00) for a job on a project team or accepting the job of 'assistant controller' on three shifts. This grade did not seem to feature in my literature and so far as I could see it was short of being even a C.O.2. I had some thoughts about not working the shifts my dad had worked in the police and how I would cope with the shifts as my first train did not get to Leeds until 07.10. Apparently this was covered by reciprocal shift change arrangements but I did not ask and was not told. The deal breaker though was my Saturday afternoon football and cricket which would be impractical to pursue. I was to give up sport a year after I was married anyway. The wedding was only eight months ahead and sporting retirement 20 months away so that would have been not many missed matches. On call and supervisory shifts would have enforced retirement in my mid 20s anyway, but I did not want to miss out on my cricket and football. I also doubted my tea-making skills were up to standard and there seemed precious few other duties except for providing controllers with the train record cards. I had not realised that the assistants sat in for the supervisors when they were called away for meal breaks or other distractions and what no one had told me was that promotion to a well paid Grade 'C' supervisor would have happened very quickly if I had shown any aptitude while sitting in. There was no family advice to call upon and put me in the ways of the world. In the end it was another six years before I made a supervisory grade job. Admittedly, I do not think I would have been selected for post-graduate fast track management training from Control and I might have been stuck indoors with a low pinnacle available in the pyramid in which I was working. Shifts at York Control would probably have followed.

So off I went to my project job at York Headquarters in the old fashioned West Offices, high sash windows, brown lino on the floor and a junior hand in a crew of 'lifers' waiting for dead men's shoes to coincide with their rise to the top of the seniority tree for whatever jobs appeared on the sparse vacancy lists. Most jobs were spoken for even before the vacancy was advertised and if the favourite fell before the finishing line there was usually a stewards' inquiry. Definitely a major tactical error.

8. YORK HEADQUARTERS

It is not my intention to cover each detail of every task performed in a headquarters' organisation of 1970, but just to give a flavour of what work was performed at a junior level behind the serried ranks of desks that were hidden behind endless corridors of closed doors. The scariest place on the railway was outside the H.Q offices at 17.00. How could the railway support all these jobs?

York headquarters comprised three buildings. First was the Main Building, the former North Eastern Railway Headquarters of 1906 which housed the finance and commercial functions. It was here that the general manager resided and where the traditional panelled board room was to be found. Second was Hudson House a brand new building built for the 1967 merger in the yard of the original 1841 station and where all the technical departments had their being. It was named after 'Railway King' George Hudson, despite his dubious reputation for financial fair play as the current football administrators might refer to his business methods. If you had a meeting with the civil engineers, or any other technical department it would likely be here rather than the third block of buildings where the operators were to be found. The West Offices were the original station buildings which had been accommodated by displacing the 'Hospital for Poor Women'. There was a car park and a dock where the platforms used to be, with two wings connected by 'The Bridge'. This was hallowed ground where the timing section clerks presided over large draughtsman-style boards with huge time/distance train graphs pinned to them. Down the corridor were the second group in the pecking order, the 'diagramers' who sent out the programmes of work allocated to each turn of duty. There were diagramers for the train crew, for the diesel units, for carriages and for locomotives. I do not think it unfair to say that these were self contained units that selected from within. There were usually lots of time-servers within each grade queuing up for the next vacancy.

The office in which I worked was formed of two teams of three plus a data clerk who was in charge of the library of standard terminal times. Graham Eccles, who was to become a luminary of the privatisation era was just leaving that job on promotion which I think had resulted in the opening for me after an internal promotion had taken place to his job. My two colleagues were Colin Smith, an extraordinarily gifted diagramer and train planner who helped me a great deal and Les Wilder who, so far as I could, see was aiming for as quiet a life as possible towards his impending retirement. To anyone sitting across from him on his train to work, as I often did, he looked just like every other railway clerk on what was almost a staff train. If really pushed though, he could occasionally be persuaded to mention his time parachuting behind enemy lines at Arnhem.

My first job was to help graph all the locomotive diagrams. Red for spare time, another colour for freight, another for passenger marking the location of the start and finish of train working elements. When this mammoth job was finished a layer of 'chinograph' transparent plastic was placed on the graphs and arrows would be directed where possible to absorb the spare time with productive work in order to squeeze a loco out of the requirements. This could best be done when comparing one depot's diagrams with another because they were often compiled by different people. The way to attack the problem was to shift work out of the peaks. It was no good combining work at 02.00 to find there was no home for the work being done by the now under-utilised loco at 08.00. The graphs showed that the peak of Stratford Class 31 working was during 09.00-16.00 mainly owing to local trip working. The peak for Finsbury Park locos was 22.00 at night with much of the fleet trapped on the buffers at King's Cross having brought in the empty stock of overnight trains and having to await their departure. With what might amount to an extra driver and second man the locos could be transferred westbound in the early evening and back for 09.00. But did this amount to saving money?

Recruitment and training of staff was expensive, as were wages. The cost reduction of saving locomotives could be illusory because the so-called cost of running them included an apportionment of the depot costs. Reduce the number of locos and the remaining ones had to shoulder more overheads. If the remaining locos did more mileage they would need more maintenance and replacement parts which were included in the loco cost savings being claimed. The lessons I carried forward were that cost management by formula was usually not useful and that decisions made using arbitrary allocations of fixed costs to variable cost assets like locos had to consider where those fixed costs went if the variable cost assets were removed. It was also the lesson of branch line reduction where, for instance, the whole costs of the main line junction station would then fall on the main line service and, above all, where the ditching of freight traffic that covered only its marginal costs threw its fixed costs onto the remaining flows and left them to carry the burden.

The next project was examining the options available to move the burgeoning Thames Haven oil traffic through Essex and across London. We took the classic approach of looking at all possibilities, including a new Thames Crossing to avoid Essex, quickly discarding it as it just created a new problem pathing the traffic through North Kent. As the modern vernacular would have it…Doh! We were pursuing false goals because, as is so often the case with headquarters' projects, the oil crisis intervened and traffic levels did not rise as expected. In any case most of it was diverted to new piplines on the basis that if there was enough product to justify an intensive train service there was enough to justify the oil companies building their own fixed means of distribution.

Next came a comprehensive view of the automatic routing codes through marshalling yards. This developed into a close examination of the 'Joint Line' from Doncaster to Whitemoor and on to Temple Mills. It transpired that the substantial number of loaded coal wagons moved from the Yorkshire and Nottinghamshire pits to the London area, for instance to utilities such as Lea Valley power stations Broxbourne and Brimsdown, was exceeded by the routing of empties from the south east as a whole which tended to return via the Joint Line. Large locomotives, including the experimental 4,000h.p. 'Kestrel' working from Mansfield Colliery, taking maximum loads up the Joint Line could bring back no more empties than the length limit would allow and no more than a 1,250h.p. Class 31 could handle. So it seemed that out and back small locos were a better idea. We also identified the inefficient use of Toton Class 44 locos D1-D10 on special coal trains from Toton to Whitemoor that often returned light diesel as there was insufficient traction knowledge for the loco to be retained until a spare load was available as March crews did not know how to drive them if the Toton crews were sent home 'passenger' (or 'on the cushions' as the older generation used to say in the days before cushioned seats were abolished!). That way, Toton did not lose a loco and the crew had a 'Type 4 1Co-Co1' taxi to get them home.

In order to familiarise myself with the geography Colin and I had a long day out, up to London, back across London via Temple Mills, down the Lea Valley and back down the Joint Line with the Colchester-Newcastle train which was a survivor of heavy armed forces' traffic. I had to fill in expenses for breakfast, lunch and dinner and claim overtime which was anathema as I would have paid to do it. I thought the extra expense would result in future similar permission being declined but, I was told, it was the system. I used to keep a close eye on lunch expenses in later years, noting the propensity of Swindon Sector staff in later years to turn up at Exeter mob-handed for middle of the day meetings and even area staff having a quick trip to say Axminster at lunchtime. I would disingenuously suggest they went earlier, came back for lunch doing their paperwork on the train, and set off again after an office lunch. This did little for my popularity of course.

Perhaps here a word about the use of some terms. For a start the Lea Valley seems to be officially known as the Lee Valley but the railway in those days always used 'Lea'. There was a dichotomy between staff who used new terms and old ones even fifty years ago. For instance older staff insisted on using the term 'light engine' and the abbreviation 'LE'. This had been officially altered to 'light diesel' and 'light electric' using 'LD' and 'LE' as appropriate. It had been decreed, probably after several lunchtime meetings all around the network, that steam locomotives could legitimately be called engines but, in the case of modern traction the engine was the bit that whirred round inside it. Eastern Region youngsters who saw their elders use the term 'LE' on their jottings would facetiously ask where electric loco had been obtained and how it could move without a power supply. In a flurry of Americanisation the Eastern also decided that the lists of work that had been called diagrams since time immemorial would now be called 'programmes' After all 'diagram' did not describe what they were in any normal application of the term. Indeed it had confused me when I read about them in my Christmas annuals as a child. So the diagramming section became the programming section and the booklets issued became locomotive programmes. In fact, why not fully embrace the concept and call them 'programs'. That really is American. As a result we had three names for the same documents and the Eastern's new word did not seem to have been adopted elsewhere. When I went to the Western people looked at me as if I did not know what I was talking about if I referred to programmes and if I called them programs they thought I could not spell either. To this day I still hover momentarily before deciding which word to use, in both spoken and written situations.

While I was having fun with words the railway's search for economy was taking shape and the two project teams were abolished saving six posts. No one noticed we had gone. Everyone was reallocated in traditional railway fashion. I took a post in the Freight General section (as opposed to the Freight North, West and South planning sections). My most interesting job was assisting with producing briefs for the head of freight planning (Charles McCarter) or the chief operating manager F.J. (Jimmy) Burge to take to investment meetings.

These briefs used to concentrate on the operating issues at stake, not the overall benefit of the railway. They were strictly departmental briefs showing the benefits and penalties to operations. The big advantage from my point of view was that if the person in charge of the briefings and my boss were unavailable when either of the chiefs wanted to prepare for a forthcoming meeting I was the one who was called upon. This was a huge opportunity, perhaps crucial in the long term, and exemplified what I would not have been able to do had I gone into Leeds Control.

Charles McCarter was considered an eccentric, a mad professor with maverick ideas. He was a tall man with a bushy beard and bald pate, a bit like those sketches where heads look more normal if they are turned upside down. He would think nothing of reclining in his comfy chair with his feet on the table and his eyes closed while I ran through the agenda, occasionally interjecting with a pithy question. On one occasion he picked up a letter from his desk and read it out loud. "Therefore I wonder if you are now in a position to reply." He would scribble on a corner of the paper, speaking as he wrote, "Yes thank you I am lounging in my chair with a cup of tea and my feet on the desk." It amused him. I think he was an Oxbridge management trainee who was considered to be stronger on strategy than operations but he did seem to display some interest in the shunt neck down which I felt I had been placed.

F.J. Burge was perhaps the opposite. If you were in the corridor, say by one of the many pairs of swing doors, and he was coming the other way, then beware. Belying his small stature he would charge head down with a bundle of papers under his arm, expect the door to be opened for him and for you to stand well back. There was never a hint of recognition as he shot past. When I was called into the hallowed ground of his office there was the opposite image. The desk was neatly arranged and calm pervaded. Jimmy Burge had started on the LMS around 1930 as a booking clerk at the Lancashire & Yorkshire Railway's far flung outpost of Snaith on the Goole line. He had been interviewed for promotion to traffic apprentice in the Euston L.M.S Board Room by a panoply of the great and good of senior management, the 'board' being chaired by the legendary Lord Josiah Stamp. He was what I wanted to become. A lesson I absorbed subconsciously was to keep a tidy desk, giving the impression to subordinates and superiors alike that you were on top of the job. The alternative theory was to pile up your desk with files, to strew correspondence randomly around it and claim to be too busy to do anything you wanted to avoid. This was better advice for clerical staff so your boss did not think your job could easily be cut out. I had not been at York very long before ex-paratrooper Les Wilder took me on one side and advised me to take a bundle of files with me under my arm if I went for a chat to a friend in a neighbouring office.

I spent just under a year covering the post that issued authority for 8ft 6in container trains and heavy axle-weight vehicles to use routes of lower route and clearance availability than they were otherwise permitted to use. If the flow was inter-regional I rang up my opposite number for their routing and restrictions. Occasionally I would have a trip out to a divisional office because I was not confident they were keeping their files up to date. There was no fail safe method of ensuring old forms had been destroyed if a new restriction had been imposed or, as was more often the case in the early 1970s, one had been removed and the train was being delayed unnecessarily by observing it. The whole system of expecting a driver to know where the miles and chainage was in the dark, and on routes where mileposts were missing more often than present, was not satisfactory. I wrote occasional memos about it. I remember one trip to Leeds shopping when there was a 'warnpass' displayed that an oil train had been derailed at Garforth and I worried until Monday morning about whether I had missed quoting a restriction. I hadn't. Perhaps the Victorian clerk in the Wellington Street offices was right and I was a worrier. Certainly my anxiety levels were higher than they should have been. Here was a lesson I was not to learn. When I was an area manager I would turn over my biggest problem in my mind even if it were insignificant and everything was otherwise going well and I think this ultimately, along with domestic stress over the adoption procedures, resulted in my succumbing to ulcerative colitis and retiring at 40.

Another round of cuts, which I can see from this distance was due, resulted in my route availability post being taken by a displaced clerk from the 'west' section. I was expected to train him and move on to the 'productivity' section staffed by two small teams of sour old men who resented the aura of entitlement I probably exuded. An exception was someone perhaps five years older than me whom I next encountered signalling preserved trains on the North Yorkshire Moors Railway when I was writing an article about the line in about 2015. One of the more cantankerous individuals was someone who had been promoted quickly and early in his career but had been sidetracked and put out to grass at the next desk to me. His pet project was reviewing the drivers' depot establishments. He would compare the drivers' tickets with the staff available and every now and then throw down his pen, exclaim, "That's another ferry set!" then start scribbling. It was one way to pass time on to retirement. I was given several projects by my boss Vic Lane that involved using drivers' tickets and I used to engineer trips to the accounts offices, often at places like Stevenage or Bush Hill Park to examine them. I could bring them back to York sometimes and insist on taking them back personally because they were far too valuable to consign to the railway post.

In 1972 I had applied for the post-graduate advanced management training scheme as a staff entrant but had not been chosen even to go forward to central selection. This was a huge disappointment. No one told me why. So far as my unbiased opinion went I had every qualification necessary both with experience and academically. Perhaps it was something to do with having nearly chosen a cupboard door to leave the board room after the interview. Perhaps it was something to do with the fact I had been on the Studentship scheme. I looked around me at the prospect of spending a life in York Headquarters taking what few promotion opportunities arose and I did not like the life I saw mapped out. I suppose I noted this for the future - that people whom I might meet along the way who were interested in management training should be given advice and encouragement, also that ex-trainees in my organisation should be counselled, sometimes whether they wanted it or not.

I started looking for jobs outside the industry and came up with a few. I was offered a transport management training programme with Graham's builders' merchants but that would have been a huge mistake. I can scarcely imagine an industry in which I have less interest. I had resolved to continue day release and evening classes to become a full chartered member of the Institute of Transport to see if that helped but, in the meantime, I had seen an MSc course in Transport Planning and Engineering at Salford University. In those days there were very few transport courses around and the engineering elements seemed only distantly related to the planning aspects. Back then Salford was served by just a handful of trains in the peak, there was a dearth of trains even from Huddersfield to Manchester and the university was a real trek from Victoria. Nevertheless I persisted and was given a place. Now for headquarters. I told my boss what I was going to do and was given an interview with the chief personnel manager of the Eastern Region. I informed him that I wanted to do the MSc course but would like to be given leave of absence, the promise of a job after qualification and to retain my travel facilities so I could travel to Salford at no more than minimal expense. Application denied. My courage ebbed away, I did have a mortgage to pay, and I retired to my corner desk in the productivity section.

It was towards the end of 1973 when I applied for a job in the Chief Finance Manager's office of the Eastern Region in investment appraisal, across in the main building. This would draw on my experience of train planning, briefing officers about investment meetings and utilise my transport and business studies' qualifications. The problem was I was 23rd on the seniority list and there was bound to be someone who was senior and suitable above me. But this was not the staid and stodgy operating regime. The regional investment manager officer was called Dai Thomas, an outwardly dapper accountant, but someone who said he was looking for an enquiring mind that was able to process complicated financial criteria. Obviously I said that this was definitely me so I was given the job.

Again we were in two teams of three, the chief in each team being three grades higher than I was and a certified engineer, one in 'civils' and one in signalling but we often worked as individuals. We would be allocated projects as they emerged from the investment meeting minutes. Our brief was to attend all the planning meetings and ensure strict accountancy guidelines were applied to the process of cost estimates and benefits claimed so that the decision whether to proceed was soundly based. If for instance a claimed benefit could have been obtained by only partial investment then it could not be set against the marginal cost increase of a bigger scheme. Naturally the senior staff had the major schemes. The very largest like King's Cross station rebuilding might take two of us. One that I was given concerned car park extensions at a long list of east London stations that required site visits with the council staff who were financing much of it. Chirping up in a cold wind in the car park of some suburban Chingford line station to tell the chairman I could not possibly sanction some projected revenue increase or other being included in the discounted cash flow calculation was not popular but good fun nonetheless. There were no computers in the office or electronic calculators. I did my discounted cash flow analysis on an old fashioned adding machine with a large lever to pull when I wanted to enter a figure. The method of analysis reduced the benefit from future, less certain, revenue streams and gave higher credit for quicker risk free return. The benefit of knowing about it came when dealing with investment managers and sector managers in the future when they tried to play fast and loose with their figures to get their way. Just the mention of discounted cash flow in a confident fashion was usually enough to cause a retreat.

This is what we thought was a lack of variety – four corporate blue Class 47s at the south end of York station at 13.30 on July 25, 1981. Left to right these were: Nos. 47508 working the Edinburgh-Plymouth having replaced 47519 as booked, 47446 on the 13.50 to Liverpool and No. 47239 having run round the 09.00 from Llandudno ready to go empty stock to Neville Hill.

In the meantime I had pursued my application for the 1974 staff management training scheme and was this time sent to central selection. One sunny afternoon I set off for West Hampstead Midland (later 'Thameslink') and settled in for my session of tests and interviews. Much of it is now a blur but I was alongside Peter Maxwell who was also from the Eastern. In the end we both won through and he was an area freight assistant at Tees when I was area operations manager which lent itself to difficulties if I felt something needed to be improved. One of the selection tests was the 'inbox'. It was a pile of documents that you had to imagine that as a senior manager you had encountered with an hour before you went on annual leave. Establishing priorities, delegation and spotting red herrings were all involved. One of the more testing ones was a reminder you had sent yourself to buy a birthday card for your wife. Not sure what was considered right and wrong about dealing with that one or whether political correctness had set in by then. The group discussion was always a tester. Have opinions but not entrenched ones, make a contribution but don't hog it, look to make progress towards an effective inclusive agreement not division or point scoring. There were also the expected verbal reasoning, maths and logic I.Q. tests to be undertaken and three relatively brief individual interviews.

Ten years later and I was back at central selection, although on the other side of the table. I was fully aware just how much the day meant to most of the people in front of me. And if it didn't mean much they were not suitable. I would admit to having a special interest in the potential entrants from the staff. Their disadvantage in terms of assurance was usually palpable. Strangely, if they were at the opposite extreme and too self confident perhaps that meant they weren't actually suitable either. I particularly remember one young woman who had been recommended by Mike Donnelly (operations officer at Newcastle Division) who was then area manager at Brighton. The applicant was well ahead of the running for a place until the written test papers where she scored an abject failure which meant she could no longer be considered. The boffins would not agree with me I suppose but some of the I.Q. tests seemed to give better scores the more you had done beforehand and it seemed to me more of a level playing field was necessary. The other shortcoming was that the main assessors had to agree on an appointment and some of the ones with whom I was paired at what was the then salubrious 'Grove' training centre at Watford (now top class hotel used by the England football team etc) would not have reached agreement with me on very much at all. I described the process in the Area Manager's Diaries quoting a case study in detail for the benefit, or otherwise, of posterity, if posterity were ever to show any interest in the subject.

So I left my 4½years in headquarters behind me. It had been a frustrating time, sometimes a waste of time, sometimes just marking time. On the other hand I had matured considerably, I had learnt train planning to the point that I could always match anyone I met or chose to encounter on the subject. I had an appreciation of finance and I knew how Headquarters operated, or failed to function. I knew that its role was to convert Board policy into deliverable action plans. It should contribute to policy formation but not decide its own. It should create an atmosphere where the areas could function and flourish at delivering the quality specification at an agreed cost. It should not dabble in the detail, it should appraise rather than criticise and its manager should not forget the lessons they had learnt on the way there. If some of the regional officers for whom I was to work in the future had remembered even one item on this list we would have had a better railway.

Every now and then I would try to assess whether my threat to leave for the MSc course helped or hindered my eventual selection. With British Rail it could have been either or neither. As we trainees proceeded along our career path we would sometimes debate whether there was a masterplan that was being applied to our destiny or whether it was a simply random sequence of events. It was the same process that any debate about the existence of Super Power/s in the Universe might take. It is only while writing this that I wonder if the investment appraisal job was actually the idea of Dai Thomas or divine intervention in the manifestation of the regional personnel manager.

9. DONCASTER

It was mid-September 1974 when I set off to Derby for my first week of training, a course that was to double as the inaugural week for the graduate entrants I was to meet, six of them being allocated to the Eastern Region along with Peter and me. I was paired with Mike Hodson and allocated to the Doncaster Division under the mentorship of the divisional manager Cyril Bleasdale who was to become InterCity director in due course and who never forgot your name or even your background when paths crossed in later life, no matter how many years had intervened. The same went for Chris Green who was then area manager at Hull and who became the legendary Network SouthEast director. Mike and I were so lucky to have both these lively and unconventional managers helping with our training.

We had not been there long when emergency budget cuts resurrected the spectre of wholesale rural line closures. On our division it was the Hull to Scarborough line that was the target and had it not been for the Bleasdale/Green factor I am convinced we would have lost it. A publicity campaign was launched featuring Ken Dodd and his Diddymen involving publicity material and logos on the side of rattling Birmingham R.C. & W. and Cravens dmus. It was not to everyone's liking, even mine, and regional disapproval was voiced. Neither am I sure what was the initial reason for choosing the subject as it had no direct link to the route so far as I can see. I could only surmise that Mr Bleasdale knew Ken Dodd from his commercial days at Liverpool, and because the boss hailed from St. Helen's. The revenue-raising exposure given to the line could not do other than gain the backing of local M.Ps., regardless of their affiliation, the end result being that the Transport Minister was clearly too embarrassed to sanction the line's closure. Playing for time had averted the calamity long enough for times to change.

The view of Doncaster station from the Gresley House divisional offices, now a car park. Deltic No. 55003 'Meld' pauses with a down express.

Cyril Bleasdale told us to make an appointment with his secretary for individual interviews on Friday afternoons when we were in Doncaster and he was around. The interviews took the form of rigorous question & answer sessions where he would explore not only what you had learnt but what you thought should be done. He would lead you down a garden path and then looked surprised at whatever you might say at the point near the gate where you had taken yourself before changing the subject. I learnt from him that when I was a mentor for management trainees I too should be available and rigorous. Not sure I managed the former and the latter probably frightened them off. I had however, come to the conclusion that a closed door and an appointment via a secretary were major obstacles to being in the picture about what was going on, regardless of the subject. If I was not in a meeting or in a confidential discussion I would always prop my door open for anyone to come in. An 'open door policy' was a method of management like 'managing by walking around' but an open door in my opinion has to be physically so. You get to know a lot more by adopting both.

Mike Hodson went on to collect an impressive array of appointments ending as managing director of the London Midland franchise in Birmingham having survived the firestorm of privatisation. He and I were neck and neck in the promotion stakes when he was area manager at Doncaster and I was at Exeter but he then surged ahead as I took a few years sabbatical by the seaside for the adoption process to take place. We had become good friends. He helped teach me to drive on his car so I would be ready for a supervisory appointment that required signal box visiting and I was honoured to be his Best Man when he was area manager at Leeds, a time when his area covered what used to be the former Leeds division – too large to know everybody though.

I had asked to be allocated to Leeds so I could travel from my Huddersfield home but the authorities thought I already knew the patch too well. Doncaster was selected and in many ways it was the ideal choice. Travel was not as easy as it is nowadays of course in terms of frequency and speed. My normal way of reaching Doncaster was by TransPennine to Leeds and a 3min connection into the 08.30 Leeds-King's Cross. Going home on a normal day I would catch the 14.20 King's Cross-Leeds that did not leave Doncaster until 17.11 and connect into the highly unreliable 16.10 Newcastle-Liverpool and a bus home.

Besides the normal rounds of offices, I had the usual 'learning' attachments. I was posted to the Hull area for many such periods working in the booking office and enquiry office much as I had done in Huddersfield five years earlier. I also went to the Full Loads department and wrote a report. I examined the shortcomings of the National Carriers' contract in a little more detail and conducted an investigation into the trailer provision that showed the contractual position still had major flaws. An early turn meant the Aberystwyth mail at 01.40 changing into a

03.00 parcel train from Leeds to Hull in which I often had to survive sub-zero temperatures.

National Carriers Limited (NCL) was a subsidiary of the National Freight Corporation the business of which was chiefly trunk freight road haulage. If British Rail lost traffic to other than 'own account' operators NCL would likely as not pick it up. A Code of Practice for hiring what the railway was still calling 'cartage' had been developed. British Rail predicted its requirements over the forthcoming six months but adjustments could be made and extra vehicles hired from external hauliers if NCL could not provide it.

The daily hire charges per 'unit' included a motor vehicle, one trailer, 9 driver-hours and a 40 mile allowance but a shortfall on one day could not be held over to counteract a later surplus. On the week I studied the fleet undershot its maximum full week contract mileage by 44 miles but on two of the days it incurred 217 extra miles, all of which were chargeable. This was subsequently amended in a future Code. I'm not saying I had anything to do with that, just that I had spotted the iniquity.

Excess overtime hours had to be paid in full but there were no set performance targets for the drivers. If they slow timed their deliveries they would most likely earn more money (in much the same way as some British Rail freight drivers were occasionally inclined to do, one might say). Privately hired drivers usually achieved more. It is true that there are many variables that affect driver productivity but that should not have prevented setting running & terminal allowances and monitoring reasons for failure to achieve them.

The most common reason for delays was detention at firms. British Rail believed that NCL drivers often failed to demand their rightful place in the queue, unlike their more forceful private colleagues. They did not have much incentive to turn round quickly after all. Disputes with drivers could not be settled without involving NCL, although some locations gave a rebate to B.R. for acting as supervisors. This was particularly important if a customer complained about misconduct and threatened to move their business to another carrier.

If NCL used one of our contracted trailers when it was not required by British Rail, such as on a night trunk run, they would have to refund only 20% of British Rail's hire charge even though they were probably under-cutting railway rates and stealing the traffic. There was a clause stipulating NCL could compete with British Rail only when rail transport could not offer an equal service. This was plainly nonsense when transferred from the paperwork into actual operations. For instance, all NCL needed to do was to say they could place the traffic at say 05.30 when the B.R. shunt could not be done economically until 06.30 even if the customer's staff did not actually come on duty until 07.30.

If B.R. requested extra vehicles then NCL would charge at the cost of obtaining them or the B.R./NCL contract cost whichever was the higher. Therefore, if NCL obtained a private operator's vehicle for less than their own charge to British Rail, it pocketed the surplus.

If NCL failed to provide the number of contracted vehicles they would not apply the standing charge of course but B.R. still had to pay for any excess overtime caused by the vehicles that had been supplied having to do extra trips. I was astounded when I submitted my report that the Doncaster Divisional Commercial manager thought I was being unreasonable by objecting to this. In fact the report received a defensive hearing altogether.

The Hull terminal was at the opposite side of town from its main customers which resulted in substantial traffic congestion delays. B.R. had surplus land all over Hull which might have been used instead but there was the impression that investment to retain the traffic, as had been suggested for Stourton when I was in Leeds, was not going to be countenanced. The local relationship between the two companies was laissez-faire with charges rarely levied for extra trailers and ones being 'borrowed back' on an informal basis. B.R. would often save time by hiring private transport directly and squaring it with NCL later. In those days British Rail paid its bills at the end of the month which meant it could get road hauliers to work for a discount compared to performing work for less prompt payers. On the other hand the monitoring of private drivers' hours restrictions when carrying our traffic was sub-standard. The Doncaster Commercial manager said this was "NCL's business". I disagreed on both financial and moral grounds.

I also raised the question of the Metal Box company's traffic that was being carried in old fashioned non-Freightliner containers, the condition of which was deteriorating daily. I was told that the traffic was being 'gently discarded'. I could not see the justification for this. If it was profitable we should spend what was necessary to keep it, if not why were we shambling along like this? I guess the answer was probably cash flow. Let them pay us while they were silly enough to do so? Such attitudes provided the shifting sands for sinking morale. TOPS had yet to be used for predicting arrivals and planning the workload so most decisions were ad hoc.

The second part of the project was to assess the trailer position. There were 8 vehicles with their contracted trailers and 15 extra ones, for instance being loaded ready to be picked up when the lorry returned, to be loaded with steel while the lorry was away to prevent double handling by being put to ground thereby allowing a rail vehicle to be released into traffic, or to be left at customers' premises for unloading. The carrying capacity varied from 5 tonnes to 21tonnes, the greatest number being ten 8-tonners. The ratio of contracted vehicles to trailers was one to 2.9, the same as the long-haul company British Road services. B.R. had just surrendered two 8 tonne trailers bringing the ratio down to 2.6. A cynic might have suggested they knew someone was coming to look round so gave up the two they normally kept up their sleeve.

The annual cost of a trailer averaged £442 per year in 1974 equating to a daily charge of £1.75. Paltry as these figures seem in 2020, their inflationary value to day is £4,000 and £16 a day. Against these potential savings had to be weighed the likely idle time of the crane and its gang having no spare trailer available, the additional standing time of an arriving lorry waiting because no spare trailer had been available to be loaded and poor rail vehicle utilisation. The report remarked that it was not practicable to put any manually handled traffic to ground, as it was with cranage traffic, which was itself inefficient. In terms of retaining traffic that might otherwise be lost it was prudent to have some spare trailer capacity at (2020) £16 a day.

A new Western Region form was being touted as best practice and I guess that is why I had been given the project, to enable its rejection on factual rather than tribal grounds. The Western system concluded with a percentage utilisation figure but that was against 100%, which was impossible. You could judge if your utilisation figure was rising or falling but not how many trailers could be given up, or extra ones hired of course. It also made unrealistic assumptions that the trailer capacity available could be used for whatever traffic was on hand. For instance that a 20tonne consignment could be split onto three 8 tonne trailers by a vehicle making three trips. Surely the Eastern could do better!

I suggested that the number of vehicles in the depot, in use or available for use should be listed by capacity and compared to the contract with an explanation of the reason. This would show mismatches such as always needing an extra 8 tonne trailer and needing one fewer 5 tonner. The actual use on the survey days could be graphed (in the way I had done with locomotives in train planning at York) and work reallocated where possible to concentrate spare time on one vehicle rather than it being spread out. On my sample days this showed the work could have been completed with a reduction of 6 trailers totalling 50 tonnes' trailer capacity. However, the traffic on the survey days had included some special loads to the docks that had a large volume to weight ratio so two trailers of 37 tons capacity were required to move 19 tons of goods. This brought the surplus down to four trailers and my reservations about traffic fluctuations would halve that again to a recommended two trailers at an annual saving of just £8,000 at 2020 prices. Of course, such projects are often devised to provide a justification for conclusions already reached. For trainees just two months into the programme, even if they were from the staff, the task provided a challenge.

Introduction of the computerised TOPS system had reached Doncaster by then and one of our jobs was to become expert in how it worked but, more importantly how it was used, through what nowadays looks like a complicated and unfriendly enquiry system. Lots of 'fields' had many possible entries to be made in them. One digit too many or too few and you had to start again. It was relatively easy though to find out which wagons had been in your yard how many days and to set alarm reports for say all wagons at the same location on your area more than two days. Summaries for wagons on hand for a given destination or intermediate yard could be produced at shift changeover, wagons overdue routine maintenance, wagon order fulfilment etc. The loads of approaching trains and destinations of the vehicles were easily found and pinpointing an individual wagon or loco was simple.

Mike Hodson and I were looking at the booklet in detail one afternoon on late turn when Chris Green came in on a regular progress check. He said he was going home for something to eat but he would come back to go through it with us that evening. This was why he had such a loyal following. For every cynic who said he was only in it for himself, there would be two of us who knew differently. He would not tolerate slacking and even less a lack of enthusiasm. If something could not be done then do something to ensure it could be done. Alter procedures, break some bureaucratic (not operating) rules but get the job done. One of the other small but important feature of Chris Green's time as an area manager was that he visited all staffed locations on Christmas Eve, I believe on all shifts. That was a lot of signal boxes and a large number of crossing keepers. He had a driver I believe but it made a statement to staff that was, I think understood. When it became my turn I tried to do the same but compromised and then compromised on the compromise, attempting to visit all staffed locations at least once in Christmas week, but it was a pale imitation. Chris could extract the only dreg of enthusiasm sitting in the souls of the most disillusioned and battle hardened veterans who thought they had seen it all. He would ride with an Exeter-Waterloo driver on a Class 50, few if any of whom I would place in that category, but I might get one who would shrug his shoulders when told to expect the Network SouthEast sector director. If I saw them a few days later though, they would more than likely volunteer how much they had enjoyed his company. The essence was to listen to what the driver had to say and give an intelligent reply then ask pertinent questions and listen to what was said. There were few problems on the railway that most drivers had not considered in depth and about which they had not formed an opinion.

Probably the most important aspect of the management training was to spend some time in signal boxes. You had to put in the hours to absorb the atmosphere, become half-competent at working the box if you were to do really well and stick around for the unusual to happen. On the Hull area I really wanted to spend some time in Staddlethorpe Jct, renamed the no more attractive or less complicated Gilberdyke. It was a classic country junction, where the Leeds and Doncaster to Hull lines met, with enough traffic to make it interesting and test your knowledge of Regulation 4 acceptances. The train service there and back from Huddersfield was not really suitable though so I decided to try Brough East to become comfortable with level crossing work on absolute block. My training officer at Doncaster, the assiduous John Melton, had set up the arrangements and I duly presented myself at the top of the box steps at the appointed time. The signalman said he knew nothing about it and didn't want to be bothered with a trainee anyway. I think this was the only time in my career that I met or even heard about that sort of situation. There was no point arguing of course. Even if he had heard about it he was within his rights. Had I been a bona fide trainee signalman there might have been a point to be made.

Instead I walked along the platform to Brough West and explained to the signalman on duty what had happened. It was a bit like the future Bingley Jct situation was to be at Bradford. The Brough East signalman was not popular and the experienced Brough West signalman had no grudge against management trainees. In fact he probably relished the variety. So I worked the box for my shift, insisting that we worked 'straight up of course' with all call attentions made and answered properly. The Brough West signalman said that his awkward neighbour would be wishing he had welcomed me and spent the shift reading his newspaper instead of being up and down every few minutes.

The other box I worked for a short time at Hull was Paragon which controlled the terminal station. I did not stay long because the only real virtue was the fact it was busy. There was some interest in the fact that it was a between-the-wars art deco layout with power points and signals (pneumatic I think) and huge fist sized switches with which to operate them. I had never worked in a dead-end station box before and I could not break the habit of looking to send 'train out of section' for starting trains or 'train on line' for arriving ones.

John Melton asked where I might like to go for training on an east coast main line absolute block box. I wanted one near a passenger station but not Doncaster where the main boxes were not typical and booking boys were usually on duty. Retford North struck me as interesting with Babworth to the north when it was open or, if not, the curiously named Botany Bay. To the south was Grove Road crossing box and there was the Whisker Hill tightly curved single line round to the old Manchester, Sheffield and Lincolnshire line. This used to cross the east coast main line on a flat junction in the same way as is still done at Newark, the justification for providing a dive-under at Retford in being the coal traffic to West Burton and Cottam base load power stations. Incidentally, I met John Melton in the 1980s on a train when I was at Exeter and had the chance to thank him for my training, taking the minor liberty of saying how Mike Hodson felt the same. His method was to be imaginative and allow us a lot of leeway but to be supportive and ensure proper arrangements were always made.

So here I was walking down the ballast from Retford station to the nearby box one December morning in 1974 for my third appearance. My presence would straddle the morning and afternoon shift and I knew both signalmen who were going to be on duty. I could work the box in terms of levers and bells but found that keeping the train register current caused me to lose concentration and rhythm. This was ridiculous because the east coast main line was not that busy in the mid 1970s. Express frequencies were sparse, local trains were infrequent and daytime freight rare, certainly compared to modern times. In the early 1970s it was normal to go from Wakefield Westgate to King's Cross on the Bradford Executive and not see a moving freight train. What the mid-1970s railway had that the modern railway has forsaken was relief trains. Almost every Newcastle or Scottish train had one on the run up to Christmas, and some Leeds trains too. The box was quite high and as I would reach to send 'train on line' to Grove Road for a Class 40 thrashing south with perhaps nine coaches I would see a red ring of almost molten metal round the roof-mounted exhaust portals.

The one aspect of working Retford North that I never even considered attempting was the single needle telegraph system. That such a primitive form of communication should be the basis of reporting train running amazed me. The dexterity of the signalmen in operating this prehistoric device amazed me. Some could reach the block shelf to ring out a bell code and send the morse-code based single telegraph message with the other. I was dumbfounded when it was explained that the message 1S12 9.31 had to be sent as o-n-e-s-t-w-e-l-v-e etc by moving the needle to the left hand metal contact for long and right hand one for short. Or was it the other way round? It did not need much resolve for me to decide not to even try and learn this anachronism.

The east coast main line in 1974 was beginning to resemble the IC125 railway we were being promised. Speed improvements had been made and the run down of the 3,300h.p. Deltic loco fleet had not begun. If a Class 7 45mph freight wanted to leave Retford for the Newark direction the time margin was such that it would delay a Deltic that was any closer than Selby, 36 miles away. I suppose it was fortunate that there was little cause to exercise such judgements. The same issues are more prevalent nowadays on a 125mph railway pathing 75mph container trains from loop to loop. The alternative of the grade separation at Peterborough and running 'Joint Line' to Doncaster will probably take just as long and no one seems to pause to ponder that March-Peterborough-Spalding takes a lot longer than my Colchester-Newcastle Class 40 on my 1970 Joint Line study trip from York. Would the money being spent on the grade separation not have supported a basic 20 mile March-Spalding railway from its 1982 closure until now? Of course there were more urgent calls on finance when it was closed than could be justified by betting on some resurgence of freight validating its retention.

The 'Joint Line' was viewed as a white elephant linking small rural communities at great expense needing wholesale modernisation, with funds that were not available, to remove the need for manual signalling and the many level crossings that employed 'keepers'. But while we had it Cyril Bleasdale was happy to make marginal improvements such as the 1975 opening of Ruskington and Metheringham. I remember being on an inspection saloon stopping at Ruskington and inviting a young woman with her pram to ride into Sleaford with 'Cyril' enjoying coffee and biscuits in the observation saloon end. Mr

Bleasdale was keen on inspection saloons and I remember another interesting trip joining the Wickham dmu saloon at Wressle via Anlaby Road Curve to Filey and back to Doncaster.

Back in the box that gloomy afternoon with the stove crackling from a shovelful of coal I had fetched from the bunker at the bottom of the box steps, I signalled a local 2-car dmu from the Whisker Hill line to the up platform, a Cravens set I think. There was no rush to clear the up platform for a connecting express to make a call but its next working was becoming due. I cannot remember now whether it was back round the curve or over to the down platform, both moves requiring the set to cross both the up and down fast lines. I asked the signalman whether he wanted the unit shunting now or after the Aberdonian. He said 'yes', as he tended to some other job - probably the single needle telegraph. He must have heard the levers as I set the points and the locking bar before clearing the ground shunting signal. Before the train moved he pirouetted and demanded, "Who said to do that?" "You did" "I said no such thing." I stood back in suppressed indignation and surprise. As I thought for a millisecond what I should do, Grove Road called our attention. The signalman answered and was offered 4 beats, it was the 12.00 from King's Cross, the Aberdonian, a Deltic on 12 coaches. The signalman looked across the tracks. The driver was not in his cab. Against the rules, he put back the ground signal without informing the driver and reversed the points for the through main lines. 2 beats from Grove Road, 'train on line'. Acknowledged, the express offered forward but there was a 2min backlog in the interlocking to prevent signalmen from making hurried, wrong and perhaps dangerous decisions. For instance the dmu driver might not have rechecked his signal and moved off. The block shelf had a series of releases that were covered with a paper seal, dated and signed by the lineman. If you used them you had to call him to replace it and enter the details in the train register book. I discovered that this could be circumvented by a pinhole in the paper as the release would respond to the blunt end of a pin. Later, signalmen thought it one of my annoying traits, when box visiting, to peer at the releases looking for such abuse.

The Deltic would appear soon no doubt emitting that uniquely argumentative horn sound they had which brooked no indignities to its importance. The signalman reached behind the frame and extracted what looked like a long handled broad blade knife, with a rounded end, more like a giant spatula. He rifled this under the interlocking of the down home signal a few times until the lock lifted and he could clear the signal. This was the worst breach of regulations I had ever observed up until that time and, in terms of misuse of equipment, it remains as such. I retired to the signal box window ledge to think about it while the signalman worked his box in silence. Fortunately the afternoon shift was soon to take over and I never met that signalman again. It was so much on my mind I think I must have discussed it in the three hours or so I was to spend with his relief and I wondered if I should report what I had seen. If I was going to, I should do it immediately otherwise I would be complicit as soon as the signalman took duty again. Wisely in terms of my career I filed it under the heading 'experiences to be avoided' and moved on.

Mike and I had done a tour of the Doncaster boxes including the possibly unique Low Ellers box that could be seen line sitting up on the South Yorkshire line that went over the main line at the back of Doncaster Down Decoy sidings. The Decoy name came from the duck lakes nearby that were by then already a nature reserve. Low Ellers was a junction between the line out of the yard and the Worksop to Kirk Sandall line that took coal to Scunthorpe without touching the main line. It worked a single line to three signal boxes using three different single line methods.

Mike and I also had trips to see single line working in operation, including a night visit to Misterton and Beckingham in February 1975, accompanying the pilotman on 6G53 with No. 37018, returning with 8D85 hauled by No. 25212.

My favourite box that I ever worked was Bentley Jct on the two-track Doncaster- Scunthorpe/Hull line where it was joined by another line that kept freight out of the Doncaster area, the two-track Doncaster Avoiding Line from Hexthorpe Jct on the Sheffield-Doncaster line. When one considers these two freight by-pass lines in conjunction with the heavy freight in the station area itself you can imagine the volumes being carried. Bentley Jct should not be confused with Bentley Colliery on the main line between Doncaster and Shaftholme Jct or Bentley Crossing on the Doncaster-Leeds line.

Four lines went forward from Bentley Jct towards Thorne Jct where the Scunthorpe and Hull lines parted ways. Two were main lines signalled by absolute block and two were goods lines signalled by permissive block. It was not unusual to see four trains running towards the next box to the east (Kirk Sandall Jct) one on the main line and three following each other separated by line of sight not signals. I derived huge entertainment with a passenger train on the down main line and a freight on the down goods with another freight accepted from the avoiding line and then to accept a light diesel from Doncaster station and squeeze it between the two freights. At any given time you could easily be dealing with half a dozen trains at once. Eastbound avoiding line freights had a flyover to clear the passenger lines to and from the station.

Mike and I had a number of joint projects between the Derby courses. One concerned the train service at Ancaster, the first station out of Grantham on the Skegness line. At the time it had a token service but house building had taken place without the number of stops having been increased so we were charged with doing market research to gauge the demand for more trains. We spent a few evenings delivering and picking up market research forms. So many railway surveys ask only those who had already discovered the railway what they would like. The problem of 'off rail' surveys is that if you ask people if they want more of something they will say they do. No matter how you frame the questions, the overall message is in danger of remaining the same. Yes we would like a train to get the kids to school, to go shopping, to come back from a night out in the fleshpots of Grantham. But when it comes to it, everyone will still jump in the car which offers an infinite number of potential departure times, especially if it is cold and wet. Drivers tend not to assess the petrol cost of an individual short journey but they have to find the cost of their train ticket immediately. I believe the train service increased but is now down to just four return trips Monday to Friday, three on Saturdays and none on Sundays.

In September 1975 Mike and I were consigned to Scunthorpe to produce a report on the condition of bogie bolster wagons which were losing productive time because the steel works were rejecting too many of them with absent or broken equipment. This could mean missing bolsters (on which the steel would rest), bent and missing stanchions or broken chains and shackles. Until then I had no idea just how much equipment there was on board a steel carrier. The remit specified the need to devise a system of wagon examination and movement tracing which would identify where equipment s being lost or damaged. Although it was the British Steel Corporation's complaints that had triggered the project, Mike and I decided to monitor British Steel Scunthorpe's performance as well. Having overcome the insistence of the Scunthorpe area manager that I should take lodgings in some doss house hostel he recommended, I travelled daily from Huddersfield.

We selected 265 bogie bolster wagons of types C, D, and E, loaded and empty that were in and around Scunthorpe at the time of the survey, excluding wagons that were in booked circuits which were already subject to planned preventive maintenance (PPM). The railway usually used 'preventative' but I refused to do so. Mike and I worked early and late shifts in an attempt to catch 'our' wagons when they returned empty and when they set off loaded, noting anything that was damaged or missing and any extraneous debris. The first job was to identify exactly what equipment each type of wagon should have because there was a range of opinions to consider. Then there were individual quirks such as some bogie bolster D (BBD) wagons having 18 fixing rings mounted externally on the wagon frame as opposed to the normal 12 on the wagon floor.

BBC and BBE wagons should have had 4 bolsters, 8 stanchions, 14 fixing rings, 4 securing chains four planks and no rubbish. A BBD would have 5/10/12/5/4/0 respectively. Damage was closely defined such as the amount of displacement tolerated. A securing chain for instance was considered damaged if it was not complete with hook and screw and securely fixed to the wagon floor.

The individual wagon numbers were recorded on the punch cards then in use by TOPS and a wagon location inquiry print out was done twice a day. Catching the wagons between arrival and being wolfed by the works was difficult because there were many locations to be covered and two or three trains could be heading inwards at any given time. Entrances A and B, Normanby Park and West Yard were easy but some using Anchor Exchange (Entrance C) were missed. Some wagons came and went more than once in the survey because the trains that delivered the wagons to the steel users and stockists usually came back to Scunthorpe. Exceptions included wagons sent to Skinningrove (on Teesside), Weaverthorpe (Scarborough branch and surprisingly busy back then), Eastleigh and Newport Alexandra Dock, the first and last on this list rarely returning as the unloading points were near to steel works. Our 265 listed wagons visited 77 different destinations in the four week survey.

When the wagons were inspected against the damage definition, penalty points were incurred for damage to specific items such as 1 point for a damaged fixing ring to 5 for a missing securing chain. In theory, if every item on the wagon was marked as damaged the wagon would receive a 100 point penalty. This enabled qualitative judgements to be converted to numerical conclusions, something I have used throughout my time on the railway. The damage recorded was split between steel works and unloading points with destinations that appeared more than five times being shown separately for comparison purposes.

Goole was the best of the unloading points with 0.92 penalty points per trip and Grimsby Docks the worst at 3.2. Within the Scunthorpe complex Entrance B actually managed a 0.28 improvement and the worst was Normanby Park at 1.9 penalty points. We were comforted to know that wagons going in and out of the Scunthorpe carriage shops registered an average 6 point improvement per visit.

The initial examination showed that only 12% of vehicles were undamaged but 57% were under 10 points (for instance, two damaged stanchions and littered with rubbish) 88% were below 20 points and 5% were over 30 points. The average deterioration per wagon was 1.72 points per trip, or less than one bent stanchion. The net penalty per visit to B.S.C. Scunthorpe was 1.15 points but that was made up of damage amounting to 2.38 points per visit and an improvement on others of 1.23 implying some cannibalisation of poor wagons to make good ones.

It was recommended that similar surveys could be done occasionally, or a blitz organised on terminals thought to be causing most damage. An allocation of the duties was suggested for which the area manager said he had no budget. This disturbed Mike and me at the time but I see it now as a bargaining stance with headquarters. A national means of assessment was also suggested using the Central Wagon Authority.

Taking the position that a 30 point deficit was unacceptable, each round trip incurred 3.44 points (2x1.72) and the average number of days per round trip (leaving the steel works to the next time it was released) was 10.52 days then preventive maintenance could be scheduled every 91.7 days – three months. Although this would be expensive, the cost of lost traffic from a proportion of the fleet being defective would be saved. We also considered that it would take a long time for a wagon to deteriorate from 20 points to 30 points compared with say 0 to 10 and that might mean the service periods could be extended. The alternative of better training for crane drivers was also suggested as this was thought to be the cause of most damage, especially bent stanchions.

I have run through the detail of this task to show the kind of thing management trainees had to do to get to grips with and to demonstrate the physical state of the freight rolling stock in the mid-1970s. Mike Hodson and I had spent a lot of time and effort on this project only to achieve little change but I was to learn that the majority of consultancy reports suffer the same fate.

There were more entertaining days to be had on other visits here – sampling the Santon ore trans, working the panel signal box and a trip to the bottom of Gunhouse bank at the foot of the limestone escarpment on which Scunthorpe was situated, to bank freight trains in the cab of Class 20 No. 20053.

If the Scunthorpe project had needed some dedication, the opposite end of the spectrum was encountered when we had our week with a traction inspector and a footplate pass. I have looked up my notebook from the time and it bears examination to give a flavour of those times to younger readers.

Linda and I had been to Dawlish for the Easter weekend and returned north on the Devonian with Class 45 No. 45056 on the usual 12 coaches. I did not bother to time it though. The following morning, April 2, 1975 I caught the 07.30 stopping train from Huddersfield to Leeds and went to Sheffield with D30 on the four coach portion of the Poole train that joined the Newcastle main train at Sheffield, 3min late following a signal stop at Rotherham. It was routed via the former Midland main line through Cudworth booked 14½min from Normanton Goose Hill Jct to Wath Rd Jct with a top speed of 82mph at

Houghton Colliery Sidings. This is contrary evidence to the normal view of this route. The routing did not, however, permit the traffic centre of Wakefield to be served.

Arrival at Sheffield was at 09.13 and I caught a dmu to Worksop at 09.27. My normal way of getting there was via Retford and the loco-hauled newspaper empties but this meant a rather late morning arrival so a correspondingly late arrival home. I went home via the 16.27 Worksop-Retford dmu and 47419 on the 14.20 Kings-Cross Leeds booked 16.49 from Retford, arriving at Leeds ½min late on its booked time of 18.00. My connection was the 18.02 to Huddersfield, the 16.10 Newcastle-Liverpool which I missed on only one or two occasions despite the unlikelihood of the timetable. Yes, the King's Cross train was a good runner but the Liverpool was far from being so. It was indeed an unfortunate coincidence if a late arrival from London found a punctual Liverpool leaving Leeds.

On this occasion the Liverpool was in the far from capable hands of Class 40 No. 40148 with 9 coaches running 7½min late on a 25min gross and net booking for the 17miles to Huddersfield based on D350 timings. The otherwise underpowered loco with only 315tonnes pulled back 46sec despite not exceeding 46mph to Morley, mainly by letting the train run up to 73mph on the 60mph limit from Morley Tunnel to Dewsbury before taking the precipitous Dewsbury viaduct at a restrained 62mph. As I have shown in some Railway Magazine articles, Class 40s ran faster on this stretch than Class 47s, I suspect because the track seemed further away from the driver and the extra axle on each bogie gave a better ride. I arrived at Huddersfield at 18.33.34. My bus home went from about a quarter of a mile away at 18.35.

The following day I set off for Worksop on the 3 coach Halifax-Wakefield Westgate portion of the 09.30 Leeds-Kings Cross. As described in the Neville Hill chapter, this train came via the Greetland and Bradley curves that were mothballed for decades before being re-opened. The Halifax portion could not survive HST introduction, coal from Clayton West and Skelmanthorpe pits to Elland ceased and the summer Saturday holiday train portions could not support retention of the two curves. At Huddersfield, Class 31 No. 31417 ran round its train and went past Healey Mills yard to Wakefield Kirkgate, where it ran round again. It then waited in the through road at Wakefield Westgate for the Leeds portion, booked a Class 47 but sometimes a Deltic, and propelled its three coaches onto the rear of the London train. The run round at Kirkgate was booked 09.29-09.40 and arrival at Westgate to departure for King's Cross was allowed 14min. On this occasion arrival at Westgate was 4½min late, 2½min of which had been caused by severe temporary (the West Riding permanent variety of temporary) speed restrictions between Horbury Jct and Wakefield Kirkgate. The main train was waiting in the platform behind Class 47 No. 47520 when we arrived in the middle road at 09.47.30, we started to reverse at 09.48.17. No change of ends by the driver? Perhaps the second man was in the rear cab. And perhaps not. We stopped for the buckeye coupling to be raised into position from 09.50.22 to 09.50.47 and coupled up at 09.51.05 which left 5min 55sec for the brake continuity test prior to a departure smack on time at 09.57. No surprise then that this arrangement did not survive HST introduction. It was to be 2020 before Huddersfield was to see another timetabled through train to London under the IET timetable, although the launch of this service was interrupted by the coronavirus pandemic emergency arrangements.

Normally a Class 40, the passenger and newspaper empties head west through Retford Low Level.

Back in 1975, No. 47520 arrived at Retford 2min late owing to a 3mph check at Bawtry but completed its station stop in just 44sec, departing ½min late. I had 28min before my Cleethorpes-Manchester with two empty newspaper and four passenger coaches behind Class 40 No. 40029, named after the Cunard liner 'Saxonia'. Maximum speed was 65mph at Manton Wood. I joined 6T65 11.50 Worksop-Whitwell, an empty merry-go-round (mgr) service hauled by Class 37s Nos. 37019 and 37166, returning with the 13.15 loaded train to Worksop West a round trip of only 10miles or so. I then joined the driver of Class 47 No. 47305 on 6F49 14.05 Worksop West to Cottam Power station on a fully laden mgr via the Retford low level underpass. The newly emptied wagons were destined to Kiveton Park Colliery, six miles east of Worksop, where I abandoned my Class 47 and caught the 16.15 dmu to Retford, No. 47524 on the 14.20 King's Cross Leeds arriving 15sec early and then waited for No. 40148 to roll up, as the previous night but with an extra coach ,18min late, a little more restrained downhill with a 68mph maximum but a good run up from Heaton Lodge to Huddersfield balancing at 49mph on the 1-in-147 gradient and beating the previous night's time by 44sec.

Being trained in a progressive environment meant that Mike Hodson and I sometimes experienced aspects of training others did not. Cyril Bleasdale had mentioned to his opposite number in the Coal Board that their management trainees should have a trip on a mgr train to see the whole process and the way in which the train acted as an efficient conveyor belt style of transporting their products. A reciprocal invitation ended up one morning with Mike Hodson and I standing on top of the massive Frickley coal bunker and then being kitted up with overalls to make a journey to the coal face. This was no Sunday tourist trip. The mine was in full production as we squeezed on board the lift with miners taking their shift. We plunged into the depths of the earth on a conveyance that amounted to little more than a hotel dumb waiter and then boarded the 'man rider' that was the name for the miniscule train that took us through inky tunnels punctuated by occasional lights on the helmets of people manhandling coal trucks down adits from our main thoroughfare. Keep your hands in. Keep your feet up. Keep your helmet on, no matter it might be two sizes too big. Lip read if you could not hear, it might be vital.

When we reached the coal face we found men in 2ft seams, narrowing to 18in, lying on their sides while machinery ripped coal from in front of their noses as they cleared it to the avaricious awaiting transport. With each passage of the equipment the pit props would groan. With every hard won foot of coal more props would be shoved into place to keep the next rock ceiling from caving in. This was not like Hell on Earth, or even Hell in Earth. It was simply like Hell. Try to move and your helmet clonked against the top of the seam. Roll on your side to get away and the wall stared back at you, black, glistening, daring you to attack it and threatening your life just for the temerity of being there. I learnt a lot that day. Not much about railways, perhaps not much about the economics of government energy policies but a lot about humanity. During the coal strikes and closures, on hearing of coal mining communities robbed of their livelihood, when Arthur Scargill came on television telling us of how his members were worth more pay, I was torn: trapped in the equivalent of a 2ft seam between admiration for men who could do this every day of their working lives and puzzlement that they might even consider wanting to perpetuate this way of life for their children. And Frickley was a modern pit. Were there parallels in the railway industry? Not much that I could see. Working underneath trains attaching locomotives perhaps but not really and not on the same scale.

The following day I went to Retford the same way with No. 31417, its load made up to 4, 47414 on the London train, 5min late at Retford caused by being held at Doncaster then No. 40029 again 1min early at Worksop. This time I joined Class 20s Nos. 20204 and 20132, light locos and van to Dinnington. The colliery is on a one mile branch off South Yorkshire Joint line that leaves the Retford-Sheffield line at Brancliffe East Jct and rejoins the Doncaster-Hull/Cleethorpes line at Kirk Sandall Jct, a distance of about 21miles. We picked up a load of Scunthorpe Entrance 'E' coal. At Gunhouse we stopped for banker No. 20031 but my notes imply it was not quick enough off the mark to catch us up. That seems as if it was enough for me so I caught the 17.20 dmu to Doncaster and the 18.13 express to Leeds which was the 16.05 King's Cross- Bradford Interchange that ran via the Wortley South Jct to Wortley West Jct chord. I alighted at Wakefield Westgate 3min late for a booked 11min connection to Huddersfield. The following day I went briefly to Doncaster and came back from there to Westgate in the cab of No. 47524 on the 11.30 from King's Cross. On April 7, 1975 I travelled to Doncaster on the 08.30 from Leeds with No. 47402 to meet the traction inspector who had been saddled with a week of seeing to management trainees

A Deltic passes Cowton with the northbound Plymouth-Edinburgh.

The opportunities were manifold but I am not sure we made the best of it. First we went down to Darlington with Deltic No. 55019 on the 10.14 ex-Doncaster Cross. We started 15min late with slight slipping on 12 coaches. The sound proofing, that had to be added to the Deltic cabs after production, numbed the senses to the full power of the locomotive so it was a loud hum rather than the signature whoop that characterised the application of power at high speeds. The Deltic cab was so high compared to most other locomotives that I remember my reflexes telling me to duck when the first overbridge appeared. Delays at Selby caused the loss of another 5min but we were soon well into our stride down the Vale of York at 99mph. By now, I was sitting in the second man's seat so the driver told me I was responsible for sounding the horn but I was told off twice for dereliction of duties, once for thinking a track gang was so far away from the running line a warning was unnecessary and the second time for not noticing a 'whistle' board over in the bushes. I think the driver was waiting for that one to have some fun. By Darlington the 3min recovery allowance had been claimed and an extra 2min on top. We came back with No. 46017 on the Edinburgh-Plymouth hauling twelve coaches and running 10min late.

Our instructions had been deliberately vague. Something to the effect that we could not use the passes without the traction inspector but drivers would not know that. This seemed like an open invitation but I would rather be told 'you may' or 'you must not'. It struck me that a half an hour's tuition on what you must avoid doing in the cab would have sufficed. No. 40035 'Apapa' working the 16.10 Newcastle-Liverpool proved to be just the temptation I needed to flash my footplate pass to its driver. I always thought the name 'Apapa' was unattractive compared to Cunarders such as 'Samaria' and 'Carinthia' but No. 40035 was named after two Elder Dempster Lines' vessels on the West African run that were both sunk in world wars so more respect would have been justified. As was so regularly the case the 10-coach Class 40 was running 13½min late and, after a ½mile 20mph temporary speed restriction it was 17min late at Church Fenton and 18½min late passing Cross Gates at 82mph. There were 3min of recovery time to come but, as was also a regular occurrence, we skated round Neville Hill curve, like a Pendolino might now do, and made up an extra minute. The driver had requested attention to the train heating boiler at Leeds so our stay was extended from 3min to 6½min resulting in a signal check at Leeds West Jct but a good 23min 4sec run ensued, 70sec better than the 73mph No. 40148 on nine coaches the week before.

The following day took me to Scunthorpe on the 08.30 from Leeds with Class 47 No. 47434 and the 09.18 from Doncaster. Here I picked up light diesel Class 31 No. 31133 heading for Entrance 'E' for empties to Maltby Colliery on the Kirk Sandall end of the South Yorkshire Joint line running as 8T54 and returning to Scunthorpe as 9T54. Home with a dmu and No. 47485 on the 13.10 from King's Cross.

Deltics at King's Cross, No. 55021 'Argyll and Sutherland Highlander' in filthy external condition.

Next came No. 47414 on the 08.30 from Leeds to meet the traction inspector with No. 55002 with 11 coaches on the 10.14 express from Doncaster to King's Cross. We left Doncaster on time but were stopped at Sutton and cautioned to Botany Bay following 'stop and examine' having been sent for a ballast train. That made us 17min late but there were 14min recovery time (normal for a Deltic on this load) and 2min pathing in the timetable. Could we scrape in to King's Cross on time? No. 55002 would have managed it but of course all that recovery time was there for a purpose. Each divisional civil engineer could impose a standard 20mph 60 chain restriction following engineering work. A 30mph restriction for 4chains at Retford cost us 1min but our Deltic was now flying. I am not sure what we might have done without a traction inspector as we held back to 103mph down Stoke Bank picking up a 6min recovery allowance that made our deficit just 7min. However, a short 20mph restriction cost us another 2½min a 20mph signal check hindered our getaway. A 30mph signal check at Huntingdon put us back to 12min late. Is it any wonder some drivers are grumpy? They put all their effort into time recovery and others throw it away at signals and stations? 2min recovery made it 10min late at Hitchin. 3min recovery, 2min pathing and a bit extra from the loco made it 4min late at Potter's Bar but there was a 20mph temporary speed restriction and a 15mph signal check to offset the final 3min recovery allowance resulting in a 5min late arrival.

We were waiting for the 14.20 Class 47 for our return trip to show more starting and stopping techniques and a Class of loco we had not seen from the cab except on the short Doncaster-Wakefield section. The 14.20 King's Cross-Leeds was booked to call at all major stations and a couple, such as Huntingdon, that weren't. Long station times were included for mail traffic and the 156miles were allowed 168min. The sensation of speed was greater on a Class 47 because the track blurred beneath the flat front of the loco compared to the focus being some five yards or more ahead over the nose of a Deltic. Three TSRs and three signal checks could not daunt the Class 47 with one of the latter being a wait for the platform at Doncaster, arriving 1½min early and similarly early at Leeds. What of the Newcastle-Liverpool? Another Class 40 No. 40050 turned up on only eight coaches, 18min late and stopped for 9min before Whitehall Jct after a problem on the 18.18 Leeds-Ilkley. Arrival at Huddersfield was 24min late which was an excellent effort after the delay and equated to a 22½min net run. I recorded 75mph at Batley.

We also went from Doncaster to March with a dmu but explanations were sparse and I had little more idea of how to drive a dmu when we finished than when I started out. The highlight of the week was not the Deltics though. The traction inspector had recently transferred from the Sheffield Division so I asked if there was any chance of a ride with a Class 76 d.c. electric through Woodhead tunnel. After I had caught the 07.38 Huddersfield-Sheffield dmu via Penisitone, Deepcar and

Nunnery No. 4 (reverse), we assembled at Rotherwood sidings to take a trip to Dewsnap near Guide Bridge. The rough wooden floorboards on Loco No. 76043 were a surprise compared to most modern traction but, despite this first impression, the locos had a sophistication way before their time. Speed was usually down to 15mph with regenerative electric braking before the brake blocks touched the wheels , the inspector claiming it cost 'five bob' (say £2.28 at current prices or £5 to allow for disproportionate energy price rises perhaps) on the electricity bill to take 500 tonnes of coal across the Pennines. This assumed that the frequency of trains was sufficient to make use of regenerated power though, which might have been the case when I used to sit on a Penistone station platform bench in the early 1960s but was less so now. We were towed into Dewsnap sidings by pilot loco No. 08604. On the way back I think our train was destined for Deepcar but somehow I alighted there and caught the 15.34 passenger train from Sheffield to Huddersfield at this closed station, the circumstances of which evade me.

The last days of the Woodhead route. Two Class 76 electric locos head eastwards past Huddersfield Jct signalbox at

Penistone with a train of empty hoppers. Double-headed electrics were needed for westbound merry-go-round trains.

There are many crocodile tears shed for the Woodhead route but they tend to flow from theory rather than reality. It would have needed re-electrifying by now, considerable work would have been needed in Sheffield to reach the former Midland station rather than Victoria, Stockport area-Sheffield would not have been served, the Dore Valley route would still have been required although it is granted that journey times would have been much quicker from modernisation of Woodhead. My major disagreement with those who lobbied for the retention of Woodhead was that, even during the 1960s, traffic was artificially routed that way instead of via Diggle, mainly from pits in the south of the West Riding. The Fidler's Ferry (the second 'd' is often gratuitously added as well as an apostrophe planted randomly or not at all) was a case in point which needed two changes of traction with consequent idle time. Two electric locos were needed instead of one Type 5 on the Pennine section although if you had experienced a diesel slipping to a stand between Huddersfield and Marsden your preference might have favoured the traction change en route.

This week of cab trips was mainly one for absorption of the atmosphere, observance of how drivers worked and, in some cases, why. I was forming opinions of what worked and what did not, such as Class 40s trying to keep time on Newcastle-Liverpool trains if anything at all went wrong. The terrible performance on the weeks we have looked at in detail here were chiefly as a result for waiting connection of the perennially late running up Aberdonian at Newcastle where the trains had to follow each other through the same platform. It did not work, but nobody made it work. Get some inspectors out on the Aberdonian, identify the chief reasons and take action to eliminate those causes. Exert better control on the connections. Make the connection at York instead. A lot could be done that wasn't. On the day after my Rotherwood electric trip though Haymarket Class 40 No. 40068 brought the

Newcastle-Liverpool into Leeds just 1min late, my notebook stating 'Aberdonian 38L connection broken'. If it was made in such circumstances, the lost path and lower powered locos meant scant chance of time recovery, that is until the Liverpool drivers pointed their noses back home and were given a clear run.

I think perhaps I missed an opportunity to have longer days and more freight train rides but the difficulty of getting to and from Huddersfield by a relatively infrequent train service should not be underestimated. I had a few other memorable runs such as Immingham to Hunslet East oil terminal on a loaded fuel oil train and two Class 31s Nos. 31200/31235 from Scunthorpe to Orgreave, near Rotherham with a rake of empty coke hoppers. The inspector took me to Worksop via a cab ride on No. 40117 from Retford to Worksop aiming for a merry-go-round trip to High Marnham or West Burton with No. 47304 but we were diverted at the last minute from Clarborough Jct to Cottam again.

As I have said previously, if the message about the cab pass use had been less non-committal it would have made a difference Talking of the mixed messages I was given, it reminded me of regular instructions about signal box training. I naively asked the Mirfield station master back in 1968 whether I was actually allowed to work Mirfield No. 2 only to receive the sentence, "Th'official answer 's No," which passed for a full explanation in Yorkshire.

The cab riding dichotomy did not sit well with me. Looking back at it now, I experienced similar situations later in my career and indeed after retirement when someone in authority would say "it will be alright." Did 'alright' cover a coroner's enquiry if someone jumped in front of the train and it was claimed the driver might have sounded the horn earlier had he not suffered a distraction from an unauthorised person? The Colwich head on collision was partly blamed on a footplate man from a foreign depot having an illegal ride. On other occasions I might be told the trip was authorised but the bits of paper were not available. Perhaps the best illustration of this was some years ago doing a Railway Magazine article involving a cab ride from Dublin to Cork on one of their 'River; Class diesels with a nervous and relatively inexperienced young driver when the driver manager arrived, introduced me, said to the two of us that we would be alright and disappeared.

Management trainees were often used to boost staffing at special events such as the annual Spalding Flower Festival which saw an intensive service of special trains from unusual places, often with curious motive power. I used to like special events like this with large crowds and an intensive train service that required stabling and servicing to work efficiently. Mike and I were expected to attend the planning meetings and then assist the local manager on the day. We also had another trip to Manchester where the divisional parcel manager was keen to show us the carousel used at Manchester Mayfield mail order handling depot (adjacent to Piccadilly station) that was used to sort parcels. It was indeed impressive but I never saw it used elsewhere, including the Peterborough depot on our division.

In between our Doncaster training we spent about 12 weeks at Derby, usually with Thursday nights 'off' which I sometimes used to go home, returning on the 01.40 Aberystwyth mail and the back cab of the 03.00 parcels to Derby, walking up the drive for breakfast with the morning paper tucked under my arm as if I had been out to the corner shop. The only catch would have been if there was a fire drill so it was necessary to identify who had been designated fire warden and make sure they knew not to dive back into the flames to save you if it was more than a drill.

I have described a project that indicated the position of the steel railfreight business in the mid 1970s so it is worth taking the opportunity to cover another report on the working of Doncaster passenger station on May 13, 1975, which had been designated a special 'quality day' with all available area staff out on the ground and the inspectorate riding trains all day. Mike Hodson and I were charged with examining the performance of Doncaster station from 05.45 to 22.10.

Note the use of the word 'quality' not simply 'punctuality'. It was to be another ten years before the concept of quality management was imported from Scandanavia, and adapted from America, then relabelled for British Rail's purposes 'Organisation for Quality' and 'Leadership 500'.

Many operators did not have a good word to say about quality days or as they would more likely be termed 'punctuality purges'. They would sit in the mess room espousing their opinion that all days should be punctuality days while, a cynic might say, an express to which they should have been attending was approaching their platform. So far as I was concerned I liked the concept of giving every train detailed attention. When I chaired the Exeter-Waterloo line of route operations group, formed of operators and engineers at the request of Chris Green, I used to hold four such days a year a couple of weeks before our meetings. It fitted with my view that if you had shown that you cared what was going on and could achieve high standards when being monitored, any slippage would be from a good position. The detailed report on the day's performance gave something concrete to discuss.

There were 95 arrivals and 103 departures from Doncaster station on our 1975 'Quality Day', a calling King's Cross-Leeds train, for instance, counting as one of each. The 2020 equivalent of this 198 total is approaching 500. The punctuality categories chosen were 'on time or early', ½-4½min late, 5-9½min late and 10/+min late. This coincides neatly with the modern criteria with two exceptions. 0-59sec late is now counted as on time. I was taught that if a train is not on time or early it must be late. Statistically, we classified a long distance train was late if it was five or more minutes late, not ten or more as now. The 1975 logic had some merit as the tolerance of 'within 5' coincided with likely recovery time 'boxes' to bring the train back to schedule if it had, for instance, been delayed by track work but not yet received a recovery allowance for it.

The monitoring day was nine days into the new timetable, just long enough for it to have settled down but not too long for problems to have become tolerated.

Deltic No. 55021 'Argyll and Sutherland Highlander at Doncaster on June 17, 1979
Credit: C.J. Marsden

On our May 1975 day 85% of trains were less than 5min late but only 50% were precisely on time or early. Absolute time figures nowadays have a certain imprecision massaged into them but they are no better. In fact they are remarkably similar which perhaps says something about the timetable structure, running times, terminal times and provision for adverse factors. 8% of trains were 10min/+ late. The only incident occurred at 19.30 when a severe electrical storm affected signalling equipment at Shaftholme Jct. Apparently no one had told the elements it was quality day. This accounted for two of the 'over 10min' delays to expresses.

The average lateness of trains leaving Doncaster was 3min14sec but that includes a lot of starting trains that left on time. 2min14sec of this was imported from late arrivals to which Doncaster added 6sec of staff inattention per train, 2sec waiting signals for conflicting ostensibly lower priority movements, then 23sec waiting connections and a disappointing 27 sec waiting crew, that had typically caused a late departure from the sidings to the station. Yes, there was 2sec in the category 'other'. No credits were given for early departures by the advertised time, of which there were seven, caused by the old-fashioned clocks running fast on three out of the four platforms, including number 8 which was 1½min fast. I well remember going to Switzerland and France around this time and being jealous of their red sweep second hands that paused momentarily on the full minute as if to emphasise the train should be moving. The regulating delays came from crossing trains at the north end across to the South Yorkshire Goods line at the west side of the station.

An up Deltic accelerates through Doncaster. This 'Deltic on 8' is probably the 12.20 departure from Leeds.

There was some time lost when two departures coincided waiting for the chargeman to cross to the second train and a little extra lost to parcel traffic but, and I had to pause to re-read this, there was only ½min in the whole day debited to the Post Office. When I went to Exeter eight years later almost every train incurred station overtime, most of which was down to the Post Office. It was eventually eliminated – I had the standard allowance increased from 2min to 3min!

We also had the temerity to analyse the time lost by each chargeman, the overall total being approx.1minute per hour on the down side and 22sec per hour on the up side. We concluded that the last 4hrs of a 12hr shift resulted in a greater incidence of station overtime, supporting the theory I formulated that 12hr turns were counterproductive because people tended to do the same amount of work as they did in 8hrs because their stamina weakened. I felt this was the case when I worked 12hr shifts anyway.

Although the waiting connections category formed 12% of the delay incurred by Doncaster, it concerned just five trains. 1A08 arrived 3min late and the 09.18 to Cleethorpes departed 1½min late. I remarked that there should have been a 'sweeping up' of the last passengers to hurry them along and assure the dispatch staff no stragglers had been left behind. One such unfortunate lady with a pram missed the held connection by a minute or so. 1A11 departed 11½min late connecting into 1A14 that departed 6½min late but only 1½min behind 1A11. It was noted that 1A11 incurred ½min overtime as well so that was doubled by its effect on 1A14. This was again one of my hobby horses that minor delays were multiplied by the number of trains affected when congestion occurred. Equally, smart work that saved say a minute could easily reach five minutes when trains were queued waiting platform for instance on the down main line in the 1980s at Reading.

1S21 was 12min late with a 5min holding margin on the 13.16 Hull connection but Control authorised it to be held 11min also delaying the 13.25 to Cleethorpes. The T.V. screens had predicted a 13.21 arrival for 1S21 which was optimistic. The final connectional episode resulted from the electrical storm where the 20.36 to Scunthorpe was held 18½min and still left 14min before the delayed main line train arrived. The lack of information in a failure situation was a complication but another policy I always tried to enforce was that there was no bigger calumny in applying a connectional policy than initially holding a train and then breaking the connection.

But the worst piece of customer care came after the failure of 1N08 at Peterborough which was reported 48min late and arrived at 11.55 severing the Selby connection into the 11.23 local to York with the next train not scheduled until 14.55, a three hour wait. No taxi was offered but it was discovered that the three passengers could save 10min on that by catching the 13.16 to Brough and coming back to Selby from there. The late running 1N08 left Doncaster only 3½min ahead of the Flying Scotsman (1S17) delaying it at Doncaster North. The best solution might have been to give 1N08 a special Selby stop and let the Scotsman pass it there. I suppose there would have been some York connections between the two trains broken that way though.

Delays experienced 'waiting crew' could have been diagram problems from the new working although this was not specified. The 06.22 to Sheffield and the 06.30 to York accounted for two thirds of the delay under this heading, probably from the same single staff problem, and the 16.50 to Cleethorpes was 9min late waiting for the crew to shunt the unit across from an up side arrival, after which only 9min was allowed. Another delay concerned the 07.38 local to York, waiting the tight working of the inward crew off the 07.00 from York that did not arrive until 07.40, 8min late.

Quality day was not just about punctuality though, so further observations included station tidiness, carriage window labelling, signage, announcements and c.c.t.v. screens. The latter were in their infancy and depended on manual reporting from locations as far away as Selby and presumably Retford, possibly from information provided by bush telegraph. Sorry, single needle telegraph. For instance, out of 15 trains that arrived 5min or more late six were shown on time. One might conclude that nothing much changes but at least trains did not appear to leapfrog each other as nowadays when the first train in a batch is delayed but the one following it has not yet caught it up and therefore remains as predicted to arrive before the delayed one until it too meets the delay cause....and a host of other annoying inconsistencies.

Back in 1975 the announcer, I think I am right in saying, was located in the North box and could see the trains. We judged that the minimum yardstick was one announcement in advance of the arrival, one as it arrived and one just prior to departure. The achievement of this standard was inconsistent and there was a marked difference in clarity between one shift and another, the poorer announcer seeming to make the arrival announcement exactly when the diesel loco was passing the bulk of the passengers.

It was thought that the minimum InterCity carriage labelling standard should be at least one per coach, facing the platform, brakes and catering vehicles excepted but only 57% met this low target. Some had just final destination labels instead of intermediate calls and we were absolutely horrified that the up Tees-Tyne Pullman carried only ordinary labels and not 'named train' ones. Our report was scathing about station untidiness from BRUTE cages and platform barrows partially blocking station stairways and battery charging equipment in transit preventing the use of platform telephones. All these contraptions have since disappeared from the scene as has the activity of regularly sweeping away cigarette ends and matches, some of which were actually dropped by the staff. Some aspects of life have improved.

A final word was left for safety, which would have been first on the list nowadays if only for cosmetic purposes. The main lines were often crossed by train crews, and even the platform chargeman, taking a short cut instead of the subway, the report noting that speed through the station was shortly to be raised from 60mph to 105mph and the practice must be stopped before that happened. It was also noted that the statutory requirement to whiten platform edges no longer applied but the grubby remains let down the appearance of the station.

As a corollary to detailed operating it is worth taking a quick look at another project, which Cyril Bleasdale himself asked us to complete, aimed at increasing our business awareness and also fulfilling a practical function. The 'Green Book' draft timetable for the forthcoming High Speed Train introduction proposed a drastic reduction in the number of Anglo-Scottish trains calling at Doncaster that, it was felt, would undermine the recent growth that had been achieved over recent years.

There were some factors at play which would reduce the influence of Doncaster such as the planned improvement of Hull-York services in 1977 taking that business away from Doncaster and the Humber Bridge opening, enticing some North Lincolnshire passengers to railhead to Hull for York. On the other hand a proposed improvement in frequency to half-hourly from Sheffield, Rotherham and Mexborough was expected to funnel passengers into Doncaster. There was only one Scottish train from Sheffield at the time and none from the others. It was not intended to provide HSTs on Cross Country for a good few years.

We pointed out that redundancies within the Scottish coal industry had split families and there would be an increasing demand for 'friends & family' travel between the South Yorks/North Notts coalfield and Scotland. Rossington, on the main line near Doncaster had particularly strong Scottish connections. The same applied to the steel industry and at that time British Steel's headquarters were still in Glasgow.....apparently!

The railway also recognised the oil industry in Aberdeen both with oil company connections and through firms connected with pipes and pipelines. This was pre-EC fisheries' policies coming to fruition so we were even able to claim Grimsby-Scottish ties from Ross and Findus. Captain Bird's Eye did not

221

get a mention but Alan Pegler did through a firm called Hattersley-Pegler.

Even in the mid-1970s, competition from road was felt to have stalled. The A1 trunk road was dual carriageway from Doncaster to Morpeth and the M1 extension to join the A1 near Ripon was expected. On the other hand building the M18 and M180 were expected to increase the accessibility of Doncaster from its catchment area whereas York station was predicted to become increasingly difficult to reach by car. Further expansion was not planned at that time and the cost of car travel had risen with the oil crisis.

It was argued that coach companies had already seen the potential family travel opportunities with Western S.M.T. operating a daily service all year. A new operator Barton Transport had opened a Corby to Scotland service calling at Worksop with connections from Scunthorpe and Dearneways operated a Warsop/Worksop to Fife service specifically for the market described. British Steel and Christian Salvesen were known to be investing in facilities for their light aircraft and Kirmington airport near Grimsby (now known as Humberside Airport) had been granted operating licences to Scotland with a daily flight to Edinburgh, extended to Aberdeen twice a week. Humberside was offering three flights a day to Aberdeen in 2019, although precious few to other destinations, so perhaps we had identified a market for rail.

Looked at from this distance in time the fares being charged were interesting. I have converted them to 2020 inflationary equivalents:
Doncaster-Edinburgh rail economy return £48
Worksop-Edinburgh coach return £35
Scunthorpe-Edinburgh first class open single £83
Kirmington-Edinburgh air single £103

Against this background the Green Book proposed that Doncaster's four daytime Scottish through trains should be reduced to just one. It was based on standard clockface patterns and, as ever with such timetables, they had a tendency either to over-provide or fail to provide on any given flow. To cut a stop out or put one in meant either pathing time to maintain the regular timetable at the next stop or an off-pattern variation. Although I recognise the attraction of clockface timetables they are not without drawbacks. A letter of support by the then Sheffield divisional manager, and future BRB operations officer, Geoff Myers stated that the current business departure from Sheffield to Edinburgh was 07.42 changing at Leeds and arriving in Edinburgh at 12.44. The Green Book meant waiting in Doncaster for an hour and changing additionally at Newcastle. Reading this report for the first time for some 40 or more years, even I am becoming convinced that the stops in four through trains should have been retained!

These reports give a snapshot view of life on British Rail in the 1970s. It was not as primitive as the exponents of 1980s sector management might have led us to believe.

Mike went off to be traffic manager at March, including his end of the Joint Line and I went to Healey Mills to await the Bradford job becoming available.

10. TEES YARD AND MIDDLESBROUGH

Bradford and Neville Hill appointments have been covered earlier in the book as have some of the features at Tees and Middlesbrough. I have covered the operation of a marshalling yard in my description of Healey Mills but Tees was different. It had two control towers, two humps, 85 primary sidings, adding the two yards together, and two of almost everything else. There were 12 up departure and staging sidings and 14 in the down yard plus 10 secondary sorting sidings also in the down yard.

The total track mileage, including main lines, goods lines and loco transfer roads was 66 and there were 95 parallel tracks at the yard's widest point. This massive investment had a life of just 30 years from 1963 when the chairman of Dorman Long Steel Company had performed the opening ceremony. The combined capacity of the humps was said to be 7,500 wagons a day but the practical limit was about 6,000, with allowances for shift changeovers and meal breaks, but this down time could be reduced by having four-shifted pilots doubled up on each on hump. Eat your heart out Dollands Moor!

When a train was approaching from the west the yard planner would look at its TOPS consist and decide the predominant split of destinations. Often this would be as one might guess – terminals west of Middlesbrough but there could be traffic to Haverton Hill which went back east, or the Urlay Nook 'Covhops' (covered hoppers) carrying soda ash from Northwich that had tight connections for the flow-process chemical industry. So the choice of up or down receptions could depend on urgency as well as volume. The soda ash traffic was lost during my time on Teesside, not because of an unsatisfactory service but owing to the fact the hoppers were life expired and there was no money to finance a replacement. The remaining traffic therefore had to shoulder the burden of the overheads. A voracious Tees Yard could not make proportionate savings to the loss of ten to fifteen wagons or so a day.

Each hump had one primary siding designated for transfer traffic to the other yard, which could be a source of delay, but the pilot engine from the opposite yard's departure sidings could nip across the 'through goods' lines and fetch it. If there were many wagons, nothing too urgent and a lot of destinations, they could be taken to the opposite yard's receptions to be hump shunted again which could actually save time for the transferred wagons and release the pilot for other work such as preparing a departure. If a train from the west required to reach the up receptions it had to reverse into them from the Newport (i.e. Middlesbrough) end but trains from the east could run onto one of the two reception roads that could be reached without reversal. Clumsy as the up yard reversal procedure was, it did not result in any mishaps during my time at the yard.

The variety of traffic on offer was fascinating. Much of it did not ever see Tees Yard, for instance the Skinningrove to Tees Dock export traffic to destinations such as the Great Lakes, of which there was far more than popular belief might have it. The ships would sometimes be docked before the steel had been produced so there was a mad dash to get it down from Skinningrove, sometimes with 15 round trips a day on the single line branch including the Boulby potash trains. This traffic also went to Tees Dock where it disappointingly usually went forward by road, having cleared the national park boundary by rail as per the planning permission. The greater use of 80 tonne BDA wagons and the 100 tonne air brake fleet had made inroads on the hump traffic, both of which were too heavy for the retarders. The 100-tonners went direct from Lackenby to Corby or Workington in block trains, sailing past the yard with an air of disdain, along with Teesport oil trains.

Shildon Works was still in full swing usually taking around three trains of wagons for repair which were inappropriately termed 'cripples' and worked by the declining Darlington depot. I never did understand the complicated system of classification used to call forward what they wanted but the return repaired vehicles helped the humping figures. We used to liaise with the steel works each shift to hear the priorities they needed and occasionally moans about the earlier shift. The shift area freight managers covered Lackenby TOPS office as well as the one at Tees so the middle of the night often provided an opportunity to visit and sometimes to have a tour of the rolling mills and observe the way the molten metal illuminated the night sky, huge steel coils being placed on the 100-tonners often when still scalding to the touch.

Among the other traffic not to be hump shunted were dangerous goods including substantial methanol traffic from Haverton Hill I.C.I. This was supposed to be marshalled on the locomotive to be transferred to the yard without being humped but it was said that the yard would grind to a halt if this instruction were to be obeyed. It was impossible to shunt out the dangerous goods at the I.C.I end for a start, I was told. I presume the area operations manager knew this, first the experienced Bill Lake and then Peter Fearnhead whom I had followed into my post. He must have known. I was uneasy, windy if you like, about this but did not feel as though I could rock the boat as the new boy or impose the regulation on just my shift. I did alter it in the first week that I became area operations manager with a threat of something dire if I found it being done. If there had been a serious accident I could not have said that the staff at Tees were to blame because they knew they should not have been hump shunting dangerous goods, since we all knew it was happening. There were the expected howls of protest from the area freight centre that the instruction was impractical and could not be observed but I was ready. I could say I knew it was neither of those things and I could tell them how to do it. It could be said I should have stopped it while I was part of the Tees team and I suppose that was right but I might not have received my promotion if I had rocked the boat and said I knew better than my boss.

Another item of rolling stock that had not to pass over the hump was a Class 46 locomotive, presumably owing to its long 1Co-Co1 wheelbase although I do not recall Class 40s, which had the same wheel arrangement, being similarly restricted. One day my yard planner became confused about which loco was on which road and authorised the Gateshead Class 46 'Peak' loco to go down into the yard from the hump top. I was on the phone and suddenly recognised there was a hub of consternation. We called the maintenance foreman to have a look at it as we were afraid it would have broken its back, so to speak. It went back into service though.

By far the most dangerous commodity we handled was the hydrocyanic acid from the Seal Sands branch. The line itself was an extension from Haverton Hill and Port Clarence. The further east you went the more it resembled a sandspit. A succession of automatic barrier crossings on a deserted road led past giant golf balls that no one really knew what went on inside. Something to do with radioactivity we thought. The dystopian plant itself looked as though it were at the end of the Universe. I rarely saw anyone come or go when I visited but presumably there was a shift changeover time. Security was either minimal or covert. From here we hauled the hydrocyanic tanks through Stockton-on-Tees and via Stillington to the east coast main line at Ferryhill where the Tees area freight staff wished them on their way. However, that was not the end of them so far as the area manager Middlesbrough was concerned because Tees guards worked the trains.

No. 40192 works a discharged anhydrous ammonia tank train bound for Haverton Hill over Yarm viaduct, between Eaglescliffe and Northallerton.

Credit:

C.J. Marsden

Before leaving the depot, guards picked up a batch of medication including syringes that had to be used if anyone had so much as the slightest whiff of gas from the tanks. Perhaps it was an exaggeration that no one really wanted to know and even fewer wanted to test but it was said that the syringes did not contain an antidote but it would stop your body from disintegrating. It was over the working of these trains that area manager Arnold Wane achieved one of the agreements for which he was infamous. The guards' staff representatives said that some of their colleagues were unwilling to work the hydrocyanic trains despite the assurances given by management, and the medical provisions having been agreed regionally. Arnold said that he could not countenance guards being allowed to pick and choose what traffic they wanted to work and what they did not. He could also not be party to guards not working their fair share of unpopular jobs, placing a greater onus on the remaining individuals. So the roster had to stand but if the guards' representatives could guarantee coverage by arranging mutual swaps he would allow it in the way these were always allowed – that there would be no reduction in competence or route knowledge as a result. Problem solved. Another lesson learnt. Incidentally there were special working instructions that said in the event of a derailment when the driver and guard should normally meet on the off side of the train the guard should instead go back to protect immediately and, of course, the driver forward.

The manipulation of the freight service to infinite variations in the traffic patterns was an absorbing job. Resources were in short supply if demand was at its peak. If we wanted a single manned control orders driver to go light diesel to Skinningrove he might well refuse to go because it was further than the single manning agreement allowed to be run 'light loco' on the first leg. From memory I think the limit was ten miles and Skinningrove was twenty. I seem to remember it was O.K. on the second leg but not the first. These agreements were arcane. No problem to an experienced trip planner though. "Alterations to orders then driver, light to the down yard and pick up a brake van." An loco and van ceased to be 'light' and was therefore not in breach of the single-manning agreement. The normal response was a fortunately inaudible mutter and a light loco setting off to Skinningrove.

Our Healey Mills traffic was of great interest to me of course. On one of my first shifts at Tees I saw the TOPS consist for a Healey Mills departure showing it right up to the length limit of 65 standard wagon lengths (SLUs). The loads book said the limit was 55 but 65 'by prior arrangement'. I dared to ask the yard planner, a crusty former guard who waxed lyrical about only one subject, the electrification scheme from Shildon to Newport yard that had come and gone in his time. "Have we made a special arrangement for this one," I asked naively waving my TOPS list. He said that he had and I asked how. His withering response was, "The special arrangement is that they always keep their longest reception available for our trains." I had not heard about this when I worked there but I guess it just happened without my realising it.

There was always a chance to score a friendly point or two back though. One day we were ordered to send a full train of minfits (MCV vacuum brake-fitted 16-tonne four-wheelers) to Tinsley. We had a surplus from inbound coal and scrap so the yard planner told the west end train preparers to get 65 of them together. 'Make that 69", I corrected him, explaining that 65 SLUs of 21ft compared to 65 minfits that were 20ft gave us 65ft to play with so that was three more minfits and all length limits included a brake van so our fully fitted class 6 could take another one. Pity the poor shunters who had to couple all those brake pipes though instead of around ten for a fitted head by running it partially-fitted with a brake van off the 'kip'.

A wagon order was compiled daily and entered into the TOPS system. This then calculated the transit times and automatically ordered any released or spare wagons to the point of demand. This was all well and good if there were no delays but the result could easily be a shortage. There were ways round this and for large firms like British steel the pattern was more one of a pipleline supply anyway. The most vocal were the scrap merchants in the Stockton area such as T.J. Thompson. We used to circumvent this problem by anticipating orders and entering them a day early, The merchants were particularly generous with Christmas gifts which I always declined as any perceived favour was actually a management decision for the benefit of the railway. Although it pre-supposed relative inefficiency, it was not an abuse of the system.

Around this time the area operations manager, Peter Fearnhead, approached me with a problem he had. It had been decreed that all areas should have a monitoring system for measuring the productivity of their local trip working. Did I have any ideas how it could be done? It so happened that I did, mainly because the rumour machine had told me this was in the offing. Every booked leg could potentially take either the maximum tonnage or maximum length. What was actually taken depended on traffic availability, empty supplies or timing. So if a train of empties that could take 65 SLUs departed with just 40 that was 62% productive. For instance, waiting for another 25 SLUs of empties on the receptions to be hump shunted could have made it 100% but cost a loaded leg of the diagram. If a trip from Lackenby to Hartlepool ran with say 40 SLU but 850tonnes and that was the maximum load then 100% had been achieved. If a trip diagram managed only five loaded journeys, as was often the case, instead of six, it could score only 500 out of 600 (83%) even if the other five legs were full weight or length. Absolute decisions could be made on capacity to be provided and trends would be evident. Peter went away pleased. My fellow shift colleagues were less happy with me as instead of a 2.a.m. fry up they had to wait until 02.30 after coding the previous day's trip sheets and adding it up. It was not a big job as the ones achieving full load or length were the greatest in number and easily spotted and I actually found it an interesting diversion. It was even cheat-proof in many ways. If a trip controller preferred to leave say 5 bogie bolsters in Lackenby to make a full load on his next departure the light loco that came back instead scored nothing.

This was the dawn of the admittedly brief Speedlink age which was designed to convey fully air braked traffic at faster speeds giving better transits. We had a regular flow of steel from Lackenby to Fogarty's, a steel stockist in Blackburn. The Speedlink train was 6M64 22.30 Tees Yard to Warrington and then a Speedlink feeder to Blackburn. It was probably these feeders that sunk the economics, that, plus the compulsory rate of return applied by the Freight Sector prior to privatisation. The load was based on the trans-Pennine section and was higher to Healey Mills so we often put our Blackburn via Warrington section in the Healey Mills portion and arranged for them to run their 03.00 Healey Mills Blackburn with an air-braked fitted head of Tees traffic, arriving before the Warrington Speedlink trip.

One of the more annoying features of working at Tees was the store placed by Newcastle Divisional office on vehicles 'on hand' at shift changeovers. At the end of each shift we had to report a 'leave-over' figure to each destination – 32 Healey Mills, 50 Tinsley etc. In normal circumstances our figures were always low and sometimes clear. Control seemed to think that meant we were quiet but the aim of a marshalling yard was to keep wagons moving and a low leave-over in our case indicated efficient matching of the train service to the traffic on offer. Any fool could create a large leave-over.

Special freights might arrive at Tees down receptions with a crew that said they were going home light loco because their diagram had not specified a return trip, someone had neglected to add 'work as required' to their diagram or they judged working a train would result in unplanned overtime. The response to this was not to argue, simply to say, "Light to shed, home passenger." If they relented and asked for a loaded train back all well and good. If they did not they might well in those days get home later than working back and be more co-operative next time. And, if not, we made ourselves an extra loco. If control insisted the loco went back light it was always too late, the crew was just catching their dmu at Thornaby station.

No. 37259 heads a Class 8 freight from the Northallerton line through Eaglescliffe towards Tees Down Yard receptions on May 18, 1982.

Credit C.J. Marsden

If some of these situations constituted a win for the yard over the drivers, they were often quick to reverse the tables. The Redmire and Thrislington turns were a perennial problem. The day would start with a train of empty stone hoppers from the up staging sidings to Northallerton, a complicated move to get onto the Redmire branch and return with a loaded train. The timings were tight and the last thing that was required was the discovery of a green-carded repair vehicle that the previous day's late shift had not spotted. Then there was the problem of crossing the main line at Northallerton with, I think, a propelling move. As for Redmire, anything could happen from waiting the wagons being loaded to a trip to a few extra cups of tea. The loaded train was supposed to pass nonstop through Tees and discharge its stone at Redcar Mineral Terminal. There always seemed to be vehicles to knock out of the set for repair there before returning to Tees. If there was the slightest excuse for not going through it would be taken. If it was touch and go we would wait with bated breath to hear whether the train had stopped to ask the signalman for the down stagings. If it went through there would be great joy in the TOPS office. If the crew did bail out we would probably have to cancel a control order full turn to cover it and even that did not help if the train was late back for the afternoon Thrislington leg. This required any shortfall in length to be made up to the full 30 PGA wagons with ones newly off repair. The train then had to go to Ferryhill, load in the adjacent stone terminal and then come back through Tees to Redcar with the same difficulties as the morning train. It rarely went in accordance with the tight plan but the reason was clear to me then and it stayed with me. Do not book train crews to run past their depot after five hours on duty. From what I have seen it is different now with drivers having a greater conception of the direct link between customer satisfaction and retaining their now well paid jobs.

There was one particular driver who used to fail every engine he was ever given. Sometimes a fit one could not be found for him. On good days he might take the third or fourth by which time he had forfeited one of the return trips to Lackenby on which we had been relying. When I was area operations manager we engineered early retirement for him, jumping the queue with the compliance, I seem to think, of the Thornaby drivers' LDC who shared our exasperation. The next we heard he had secured a job driving the Shell Teesport and not giving them the slightest difficulty.

Some turns were recognised as the turns that crews manoeuvred themselves to cover as frequently as possible. The most popular one at Tees looked on paper an unpromising candidate. 7P61 Tees to Whitemoor as far as Doncaster, home passenger. Staple traffic for the train was Haverton Hill urea and methanol traffic for the likes of Great Chesterford. Travelling home passenger from Doncaster in the early hours of the morning was not much fun so crews used to volunteer to cover any back working Control needed to be covered. I suspect certain trains were deliberately left uncovered for the Tees crews to work but the diagrams would have been too long for it to be a booked working. A typical job would be to relieve a Follingsby freightliner from Doncaster to Tyneside, then volunteer to work light diesel to Tyne Yard for a spare load to Tees. The trick was to sign off as close as possible to the theoretical maximum twelve hour turn which meant you did not miss your twelve hour rest period before the following night's turn.

Not everyone wanted a long turn though. One supervisor used to tell the tale, from when he had been a guard ,of a certain Thornaby driver who was once paired with a notorious second man who used to bully his elderly drivers. Once coupled to the train at Tees the second man would roll out a blanket on the cab floor and sleep. This wily old driver though had his measure. As the Class 37 purred its way up the slow line to York with the reflection of the successive green colour light signals lighting the cab roof at relatively frequent intervals and the soporific rhythm of clear automatic warning system bells and vigilance device beeps took hold, the driver caught sight of the second man awake for a few seconds. He then feigned drowsiness and pretended to shake himself awake at which point the secondman leapt into his proper seat and sat on the edge of it for the rest of his shift. Or so the story went. Personally I have never been aware of a situation where a secondman could have exercised aggressive behaviour to drivers and got away with it without informal and effective peer group intervention.

Our world was shortly to end though. A prolonged and damaging steel strike in the early months of 1980 destroyed the livelihoods of steelworkers and its suppliers alike. It was not long before peripheral locations with high unit costs were closed, Consett being the prime example on a steeply graded branch line from Ouston Jct near Chester-le-Street. Middlesbrough installations lasted longer but the damage had already set in there too. Perhaps it was inevitable regardless of the strike but it certainly seemed to hasten the decline.

Keith Marquis, who usually worked the shift ahead of me, and I were seconded to special duties to achieve economies. This meant the closure of one of the yards. The concept was not new. Combined humping figures were down to an average of 6,624 per week, still over 1,000 a day but still only 25% or so of the capacity of a single hump. The change in traffic flows to trainload operation, the use of heavier wagons, the loss of traditional industry had all contributed but the absence of the steel traffic exposed the problem. It had always been assumed that it was the down yard that would close first but I was not happy about the reversing onto the up receptions of all down trains. It seemed a recipe for congestion and unreliability. There were six up receptions available to reversing down trains and on the down receptions only two available to up trains, although this was without reversing.

A survey of the retarders revealed a need for much higher maintenance expenditure on the up hump than the down because the majority of up yard traffic had been loaded and the preponderance in the down yard was empty wagons for the steel works. Making an extra two down receptions available for up trains would mean the more sensible decision would be to retain the down hump. I favoured the conversion of the down secondaries to become up departures but the suggestion was beaten at a consultation meeting I did not attend, having moved on twice by the time this stage was eventually reached. When examining the performance of this megalith whose days had come and gone in just 30 years, within the compass of an individual's career, it should be noted that the staff cost savings from closure of one yard were not great. Totting this up now I think it would be about eight posts plus relief per shift on each of the early and late turns, say 21 including relief cover. I think the night shift used to do half a turn in each hump top cabin towards the end.

With the valuable encouragement of Colin Marsden, I wrote my first full length feature article for the Railway Magazine, after a few in Railway World, for the June 1994 edition under the title 'Into The Abyss – The rise and fall of Tees Yard' The abyss was looming before us back in 1980 and when I re-visited in early 1994 I wrote the following. "Today the scene is one of desolation. As I stand among the rusting rails my mind drifts back to those cold nights when it was my custom to take a walk round the yard in the early hours. The clank of buffers rings more clearly in the still night air. The floodlights, punctuating the darkness, seem to intensify the sense of endeavour. Away to the east the growl of a Class 37 can be heard accelerating a Teesport oil train through Middlesbrough. It grows steadily louder, its headlights now visible as it rounds the curve. It shoots past, the rattle of the wagons eventually drowning out the sound of the engine, until the din subsides and all that remains is the wink of the battery tail lamp in the far distance. Only the night shift allowed time for reflection, a time to absorb the atmosphere, to wonder how long the scene would last. Few of us would have guessed how near the end was to be." I did love my marshalling yards! So concluded a history of shifts conducted in the teeth of a biting easterly gale, of trying to keep the yard working despite snow clogging the hundreds of points and the overtime – sometimes welcome to pay that bill behind the mantelpiece clock, and sometimes reluctantly just to keep the job going.

Peter Fearnhead moved to the Newcastle Divisional passenger operations job, after Martin Best went to York and I was interviewed for his Middlesbrough area operations manager job a week before the others. Not because I had mistaken the date - I was going to be away on holiday on the appointed day. I failed to answer only one question to my own satisfaction (although it might have been many more to the interviewing panel). The divisional manager was John Thompson a large bluff engineer who had a reputation of being unreasonable, out of touch with operating, shouting to get his own way and shouting even louder if he did not get it. Some will remember him banning the use of paperclips in the divisional offices after some important documents were misfiled after their paperclip had attached itself to another batch of papers.

It seemed to be understood that there was some connection with the public relations officer that was an unspoken undercurrent to everything that was said and done. It was believed everything was somehow relaid to the boss. She was always unfailingly pleasant with me. She used to come and sit next to me on the train to and from work and occasionally stop for a talk in the corridor but I always felt uneasy about telling her anything the operating department did not want communicating elsewhere. That interview question problem concerned whom I should tell about a major incident when I was on call. I reeled off the usual operating contacts and a few engineers, most of which were control's responsibility but I suppose I needed to check. I ran out of ideas and he asked me repetitively if there was someone else. I shook my head a few times before he bellowed, "ME!" This failed to change my mind though. I still don't think I would have told him. I would have left that decision with the divisional operating manager Derek Jenkinson with whom I had worked at Doncaster. I went on holiday disconsolately thinking I had blown it for reasons with which I still did not agree but came back to find a letter of appointment behind the door.

Much of the routine of being area operations manager has already been covered. I have not previously said that we had excellent relationships with the steel and chemical sales force which most sector thinking did not believe existed. I would often be consulted about transits that could be promised. I would know if priority connections could be offered at Tees or whether booked trips could be nominated. Sometimes I would be taken along to customer meetings to give some 'street cred' to the sales' promises. We had regular liaison meetings with major customers of course. We even secured some traffic from Port Clarence by loading during the closed period with a possession. It was not strictly by the book I suppose but if the engineer had wanted to load some scrap metal onto a wagon while he had possession he would have been perfectly within his rights, so why could it not be done, at least on an irregular basis, for paying traffic? I have heard of this being done after the Port Clarence situation and I supposed it was done before but this was the first time I had encountered it and I thought I was being original.

I chaired my first Joint Inquiry while I was at Middlesbrough after a collision between a Class 40 locomotive and a loaded steel carrying vehicle at Lackenby. I have forgotten the loco number but it was perhaps 40193 or similar. The driver was conducting a run round move on what he thought was an empty road behind some tank wagons, clearly at too high a speed to stop short of any obstruction, but in the leading cab when he encountered a bogie bolster in his way. The nose of the Class 40 took the brunt of the collision but the driver had been hurt. It seemed like his fault, although I cannot now remember what the shunting staff had told him. The employment inspector was impressed, as was Arnold Wane, and I was invited to join the inspectorate but the pyramid would have been small compared with the operating structure of British Rail.

Arnold had given me a lesson on taking Joint Inquiries, showing me first how it should not be done - an interminable length of pointless questions and semi-evasive answers. He said that the way was to get the witnesses on your side and say you were going to summarise their evidence. So, as Inquiry chairman, I took hurried notes and at the end dictated to the secretary a decisive question and the answer I had been given. So something on the lines of - Question: "At any time did you exhibit a green hand signal from your signal box?" Answer "No I did not but I was using a green tea towel to do the washing up." This would be instead of 'did you didn't you' leading to a reluctant admission. I used to describe what was intended to the witnesses and their trade union observers saying that if the words attributed to them were not to their liking or the tone was wrong they should feel free to intervene. They would be able to alter anything they wanted before signing the record. I rarely had any trouble at all, perhaps a couple of requests to make minor alterations over all the Inquiries I took and, surprisingly if you believe railway trade union reputations, nothing whatsoever from the observers.

We avoided a Joint Inquiry after a derailment of an oil train leaving Teesport siding, climbing up the steep gradient to the main line when its Class 47 locomotive derailed. As was common practice representatives of the carriage & wagon, civil engineers, signalling & telecomms and operating organisations turned up as quickly as possible to survey the scene. My memory is that because the oil tanks were involved the emergency services were called but soon lost interest. It was around lunchtime on a freezingly cold day as a gale whipped into the Tees estuary off the North Sea. We hopped from foot to foot, pulled our black mac collars closer to our necks and shivered. The permanent way ganger initially said the track was fine and the cause must have been excessive speed. I could scarcely conceal my scorn, as Class 47s had all on to get the train up to the main line at all let alone at an excessive speed. We all looked again at the ganger. He picked up the hostility directed through those piercing gazes. "Alright," he conceded, "this one's ours." There was still rerailing to be done but at least that involved doing something and not standing around.

No. 37167 passes Cowton with a Teesport-Jarrow oil train.

At this point it is worth fast forwarding to January 19, 1983 when I was in my Newcastle job sitting in a room with the area civil engineer Middlesbrough, on one side of me, the estimable divisional traction & rolling stock engineer Derek Reeves and Mike McLoughlin from Derby research on the other. My task was to chair a Joint Inquiry into the derailment a week earlier of an oil train, once again, on the branch from Tees Refinery to the main line at Shell Jct, Grangetown. The maximum permissible speed was 20mph and the line was worked under track circuit block for single lines regulations.

At 12.10 train 6K76 Teesport-Jarrow, formed of 8x100 tonne oil tanks came to grief on plain line after leaving the terminal. Two of the tanks derailed one wheel but the track damage caused two further tanks also to derail and roll down the bankside causing a spillage. The emergency services attended but there were neither injuries nor a fire.

The Shell chargeman noted nothing unusual about the departure but the Thornaby driver said he felt a sharp jerk before he reached the signal onto the main line and stopped his train. The Tees guard testified that he was travelling in the front cab at the time of the derailment so saw nothing of the derailment but was certain that the brake test and inspection had not revealed any potential problems. The signalman became aware of the incident and alerted control and the emergency services.

Back in the area manager's offices, the station manager Middlesbrough went immediately to the site and concluded the derailment had been caused by bank slippage and the track being wide to gauge. It had not proved possible to agree a cause. The weather was clear and dry. Perhaps it was easier to obtain agreement in a howling gale and therefore perhaps the original follow up had therefore been less thorough? At this inquiry I knew the chargemen, signalman and station manager well.

The trackman said he walked the line three times per week and had already inspected it on the day of the derailment, finding no fault. No one had ever complained to him about the condition of the track! The sub-section permanent way inspector had last walked the track in November and was unaware of any problems other than the fact that frequent track key replacements were needed to maintain the gauge. The section supervisor said re-sleepering, re-gauging, ballasting, and the fitting of gauge stops had been undertaken in April 1982 but the curvature meant there was heavy side-wear to the outer rail and the nature of the dangerous goods traffic meant more than average detailed attention was given. The carriage & wagon supervisor said that his examination of the wagons had not revealed anything to explain the derailment.

As ever, a number of irregularities not directly related to the derailment were unveiled during questioning which showed a lax approach all round. In my experience this was not unusual on Tees-side and I paused to wonder if I had failed to effect any improvement while I had been there. From this evidence, probably so. The driver was unaware the speed limit had been raised from 15mph to 20mph in the supplementary operating instruction of August 1981, he started his train before the driver's slip was completed, allowed the guard to ride in the front cab and failed to carry out detonator protection in accordance with Rule Book section M. The guard was complicit in a couple of these failings. Had he been in the back cab he might have noticed the first derailment and stopped the train before the worst of the repercussions happened. The driver also said that there was a well known kick at one point on the track but it transpired that no drivers had ever troubled to report it.

The signalman was slow to apply reminder appliances and check on full protection having been carried out and the station manager failed to check this. The first job to be done on taking charge of an incident is to ensure protection is in place. The sub-section supervisor admitted to signing a track report only a month earlier concerning gauge problems. In fact admin changes two weeks before he signed it meant that this track had been transferred to someone else and he therefore had no authority to have signed it off. I also criticised the permanent way supervisor's lack of both initiative and interest in the investigation procedure/track plots.

The panel members attended the site within 24hrs of the derailment. Mike McLoughlin of Derby research found clear evidence that the 1st wheel on the right hand side of the trailing bogie on the 5th wagon was derailed first. This wheel dropped inside the low rail, bursting the track. The downward weight of the loaded vehicles prevented the left hand wheel flange riding upwards and over the rail head. The leading bogie of the 6th vehicle performed similarly but the 7th and 8th vehicles reached track so badly damaged they were pitched down the embankment. A train division therefore occurred and the automatic air brake pipes parted, causing an immediate brake application. The distance travelled was consistent with the 20mph limit not having been exceeded.

There was clear evidence that the track was wide to gauge. Indeed it was intended to be ½in wide to accommodate the forces of the curvature but it was actually over three times this amount after the derailment but not under load. The vehicles towards the front of the train were judged to have spread the track sufficiently for the rear vehicles to become derailed.

Mike calculated that the first wheelset to derail would have done so with a track gauge of 1520mm compared to the standard 1435mm and measurements taken, not under load, had shown 1485mm. The tank bogies were fitted with Avon sidebearer rubbers which were known to be less rotationally stiff than other types so would not have caused extra track stresses. In contrast wear on the high rail and a rolled lip on the low rail, indicate stress being regularly exerted. At the point of derailment the chain radius curve was as low as 8 compared with the average branch figure of 13. The cause of the derailment was the track being excessively wide to gauge

If this had been agreed on site we would then have not had the expertise of Mike McLoughlin, the lessons of his investigation or the certainty of the conclusion. However, the protocol for dealing with a spillage of dangerous goods would have resulted in a full Inquiry being ordered. I paused to reflect that if my Teesport derailment in the howling gale had involved a spillage, or if the cause had been disputed, then this second incident might have been avoided.

Another inquiry had to be held into an incident at Hartburn Jct where the line from Middlesbrough to Stockton met the Northallerton to Newcastle via the Coast line south of Stockton station. Trains crossed from the Middlesbrough branch to the down main by way of 'switch diamond' crossings but one day the driver of a Middlesbrough-Newcastle via Stockton dmu passed the signal controlling Hartburn Jct at danger. An up Hartlepool-Darlington train was about to leave Stockton station so the Hartburn switch diamonds were set for a move straight up the main line. The Newcastle dmu hit the diamonds and somehow managed to negotiate them without becoming derailed and came to rest on the up main instead of the down main looking at the Darlington-bound dmu that was fortunately still a mile away in Stockton station.

While I was at Middlesbrough two tragedies struck. The first was when my Tees Yard trip planner George did not turn in for work one afternoon. This was most unlike him. George could be grumpy and self contained but he was conscientious. I believe he lived near Bishop Auckland so he had a long car journey to work each day and he lived alone.

The shift area freight assistant had covered his job but thought he had better tell the office who then told me. I think the B.T. Police were the ones who called round to check he was alright but found him in his garage with the car with the windows closed and the engine running. He had been there since late the previous night after finishing late shift and there was nothing that could be done. We speculated whether he had just fallen asleep on arrival home because he could nod off at work occasionally but we could not get over the garage doors being closed. Perhaps the wind had closed them? We had to accept the worst. His was the first funeral I had attended since the death of my father in 1967 and I am sure I was not the only one there who was wondering if we could have done something differently to prevent this.

The second incident occurred early one morning at South Bank. There were a few female 'number takers' employed at locations around the area. Even in the post-TOPS era they continued to be known by their old title although the job had changed. I wondered just how necessary these jobs were, in the light of TOPS and simplified operations, but they were the responsibility of the area terminals manager Bill Wood who later retired to manage the North Yorkshire Moors Railway. Bill had twice been passed over for my Operations job but he never showed any rancour; in fact he could not have been more helpful.

Female yard staff had taken the jobs during the war and remained in post through the 50s and 60s and were now approaching retirement. The first Saltburn train had reported seeing a body on the up main line and it turned out to be that of the late turn South Bank 'number taker'. It was my job to ensure normal working could be resumed as soon as possible. Fortunately it was possible to convert the permissive block goods line into passenger use to keep traffic moving which was just as well because the B.T. Police were treating the incident as a crime scene. The traffic supervisors had needed no help from me over the incident but this was a new turn of events so I made my way to the scene.

It transpired that the lady concerned had made it clear to her colleagues that she had been receiving threats that she would be killed on her way home from work. The police had been to her house earlier that day and found notes to that effect on her dressing table. So often the police will treat a body on the line as a potential crime scene just to make sure they do not miss anything but I had to agree they were right in this instance. The delay to trains was not too great with three miles of double track goods line running so there was no pressure to get the main lines back in traffic. Later that day I had a visit from the police to say they were satisfied that there was no threat made and the context was a carefully prepared subterfuge. The human torment behind these two deaths did not bear being further dwelt upon. There were trains out there to be run.

One dark Teesside afternoon, perhaps in November 1981, I was doing some paperwork in the area manager's offices in Middlesbrough. The office lights had been on all day as a thick smog settled over the town. Middlesbrough fogs were all contaminated with chemicals in the atmosphere, a sort of fug from I.C.I at Haverton Hill's urea plant. Or so it seemed. This was in contrast to the many clear blue, if cold, days which were far more frequent than in the Pennines. Mind you, York was always an overcoat colder than the West Riding and Middlesbrough was a cap and scarf colder than that, more if an easterly gale was blowing. I thought that the chemicals in the air burned off the water vapour on decent days so there were no clouds left but I do not think my theories had any meteorological merit.

The phone rang. It was Teesside Airport. Very few planes used the airport even then but there are fewer now. There was a London business service and a few holiday charters back in the early 1980s but not much more, from memory. A small insubstantially built halt had been opened to encourage access by rail from airline passengers and staff but it did very little business. It now has just a 'parliamentary' minimum legal level to prevent the need for following the expensive and damaging closure procedures that apply. But here we were with the airport manager on the phone. They were about to receive a Transatlantic Jumbo jet diverted from Heathrow. There would be 300 or so passengers landing who required to get to London. Coaches would not be easily obtained, especially at school time, and the journey times were unattractive. "Could you do anything?" I was asked in a plaintiff tone that expected a negative answer from the nationalised inefficient bureaucracy known as British Rail.

My mind went directly to strengthening local trains to get the passengers to Darlington then I suddenly realised the time. It was about 15.00 and in an hour or so there would be an HST passing Teesside Airport on its way empty from Newcastle to Middlesbrough to form the 16.40 to King's Cross. It had always puzzled me why it did not run via the Coast, or from Ferryhill to Stockton via Stillington to keep diversionary road knowledge for the crews at no additional cost, but the actual routing that I had queried would be to our advantage today. When I replied I could have an empty high speed train at his station within the hour it took him some time to gain his composure. I am not sure how we organised ticketing but a few words with Control to tip off the driver and guard before the train got there and the problem was solved.

No. 31236 at Teesside Airport on May 21, 1982. The train had become divided and the loco was propelling the front portion of the train back to recouple to the rear portion.
Credit: C.J. Marsden

One day I had a visit from a Dr Youell, a physics lecturer at Leeds University and one of the RCTS luminaries who was also a leading light in the Middleton Railway. He told me he had come from Darlington in the back cab of a dmu that had exceeded the speed limit at most locations on the way. What was I going to do about it? Well, I was not going to discipline the driver on the basis of what one person had said, reading speeds from the rear speedometer. However, I did not really doubt him. He went away threatening that this was not the end to the matter but I think it was. All that can really be done is to have a quiet word in the driver's ear, a job for the train crew manager who knew the drivers far better than I did.

Some time later I was on a Saturday afternoon Saltburn-Darlington dmu in charge of a Darlington driver when we took a 20mph speed restriction at 60mph. This was as bad as it sounds of course but the reason for the restriction was not evident and it rode well at say 30mph when some drivers took liberties with it. In fact I found it did not ride badly at 60mph either. This was not on my area so I introduced myself to the Darlington station supervisor and got nowhere at all. In fact I was treated more as a nuisance, worse than I had treated Mr. Youell in fact. A B.T. Police officer who had been on the train came into the office during the discussion, which was becoming quite heated. I asked him to confirm the approximate speed of the train and whether there had been any brake application for the restriction at Teesside airport. He replied he did not know. Lesson learnt about the B.T. Police and operational matters. I could not work in the current environment when they issue press releases about railway operational matters that verge on business issues and take charge of accident scenes above operators. On reflection I should have spoken to the Darlington area manager Bill Lake if necessary and at least whoever was on call instead of two junior-graded albeit elderly supervisors. That was a lesson I had not quite yet learnt though. The only previous similar incident I had experienced was when I was at Bradford and I rode from Huddersfield to Stalybridge on a dmu over a line that had semaphore signalling and no automatic warning system behind a dmu driver who was listening to the radio and checking his football pool coupon. 'Beware Saturday afternoon syndrome' was one of the lessons.

11. NEWCASTLE

Around Christmas of 1981 alterations in the divisional office had resulted in Peter Fearnhead moving sideways from the passenger assistant to the divisional operating manager to the equivalent freight job so I followed his tracks for the third time. Many people would have made the move only if they could have been exempted from moving house but I went on the proviso that full removal allowances would be met. I had done enough long-distance commuting when I was at York and the prospect of a call out so say Wetheral or Berwick from a house south of Middlesbrough made no sense at all. We were happy to move for the fourth time in six years and take on our second six-month rental also within that time. After nearly making the mistake of moving to a new house in Cramlington, where part-exchange was on offer, we took a rental in a modern detached house in the former mining village of Bowburn, a ten minute drive from the station and a 15min train ride into Newcastle, handy for trips to parents in Huddersfield and only two minutes from the A1 (M) to attend those potential emergency calls. In fact we rented it for a year until our house was sold and then bought next door at Bowburn which our rental landlord was selling. We moved in on 23rd December and by April the boxes that we had managed to unpack were refilled prior to our move to Devon. Bob Poynter, my regional operating manager boss on the Western, said he had moved, was it, fifteen times for his work. It did not sound much of a prospect.

A Class 40 enters Durham station with a Liverpool Newcastle train in 1982.

The weekend I transferred to Newcastle there was a severe snowstorm on top of freezing ground conditions. Many locomotives on Gateshead were iced up and we took a trip to Huddersfield on the Sunday morning with a Class 40 via an engineering diversion and a run round movement at Bradford (by then) Interchange. We returned on a Class 25-hauled relief with no heat that reached 90mph down Micklefield bank but the driver had whistled for a fresh engine at York where we had to sit half an hour in freezing conditions before a Class 31 appeared, which did not produce enough steam heat to register even in the first coach before we reached our Darlington changing point.

251

Deltic No. 55015 'Tulyar on Gateshead shed March 12, 1977

Credit: C.J. Marsden

On my first day I rolled in at about 08.40 to be told in no uncertain terms that they started before 08.00 by meeting in Control to assess events and prepare for the morning conference. My train to work therefore became the 07.25 dmu from Durham, a Darlington starter. A conference call took place every morning chaired by a senior York operating manager to discuss what had happened in the previous 24hrs. Newcastle's representative was the operating manager on call, so that was me every third week. You were expected to know just what had happened, why, and what you were going to do about it. Not to know the answer was a definite black mark against both you and your colleagues so it was necessary to have read the log carefully and probably to have rung one of the area operation teams to get some background. You also had to know the freight traffic position and what was intended to shift any surplus that was building up.

One of the main jobs of the assistants to the divisional operating manager was to chair sectional council meetings. This could be quite a tough, even confrontational job, at least it could get that way when I was in the chair. It was considered good tactics to demand more savings than were reasonable to let the staff side seem to claim some pyrrhic victories and make management appear open to compromise. I usually had a minimum figure in mind that I could concede and still meet the budgetary savings I had promised. This tactic was frowned upon under later regimes, usually by those who had never chaired so much as a tea party. The task was eventually devolved to area managers after the Divisions had been abolished and the Regions decided they were too distant from the action to know the answers demanded so I landed for a double dose of chairmanship when I moved to area management at that juncture. The problem with some divisional schemes was that they sometimes involved trying to force through badly prepared area schemes. We always had a detailed sentence by sentence analysis of the consultation document and a management side meeting the day before the joint session in case extra information was needed.

Nevertheless, on my first day at Newcastle the divisional operating manager Derek Jenkinson handed me a file of papers for the withdrawal of supervisors from Berwick-on-Tweed. Since the scheme had been prepared there had been a change of policy stating that all train crews had to be seen by a supervisor as they signed on duty. This was subsequently watered down to non-supervisory staff judging fitness to take duty and nowadays signing on by telephone is normal, perhaps until another major accident from this cause.

I decided to hold the meeting at Berwick because I considered it an insult to fetch staff to divisional office to cut their jobs from under them. This was a mistake on a number of grounds. First, in football terms, in conceded home advantage and, second I came to think the staff wanted a day out, their lunch expenses and, in this case, probable overtime.

Berwick had a sparse train service in 1982, occasional main line trains and minimal locals. The rump of its train crew depot was used to re-crew the few remaining east coast main line freights and, of these, the only ones that were not able to run from Tyne to Millerhill (Edinburgh) fast enough for crews from either main marshalling yards to do a round trip. It was policy to run the depot down by attrition (or as Mr Malaprop once famously termed it at a consultation meeting 'closure by nutrition') to save redundancies and associated displacement costs. The staff side helpfully suggested the supervisors could perhaps be considered for withdrawal only if and when the train crew depot actually closed. And if the supervisors were withdrawn then who would attend to operational incidents at, say, Goswick level crossing (where an express had been derailed in 1947 with 28 deaths, which some of the 1982 supervisors still remembered well), 44miles away from the nearest alternative supervisor at Morpeth. Management reserved the right to manage at consultation meetings and implement the proposals but this applied only if the management side chairman felt he had satisfactorily addressed the staff side objections. I often did this in the face of what I considered obstructionism but not over this.

So here I was, new to the job and having failed to deliver a consultation scheme which would adversely affect the Division's budget, sitting in front my boss, a wiry, stony-faced Yorkshireman whose chief railway interest was running as many coal trains as possible. With this in mind, he had recently designed the operational layout at the new Doncaster panel box, which, even in the years following the death of King Coal, I used to quote as the reason why my express passenger train was being held outside the station.

As I made my excuses I thought I saw a sardonic smile twitch at the corner of his mouth. He interrupted. "If you had delivered this you'd have been a bloody world-beater," was all he said. He later told me that he never criticised the management side chairman of a sectional council meeting. "If I wanted it done better I should have gone myself," summed it up. This was a lesson I tried to take forward with me when analysing my own performance at meetings, many of which were relatively antagonistic, but also in local meetings which I thought I could delegate. Once or twice the chairperson would come back semi-apologetically having compromised a little further than I might have felt inclined to have done but I would like to think I adopted the 'Jenkinson Principle'.

When not on call most of my discussions in the Newcastle control office were held with the passenger controller who was responsible for the dmu position. I would check that there were no short formations or that the contingency plans had been implemented. Perhaps Heaton or Darlington depots were running up a backlog of repairs that needed some pressure to clear. The depot manager at Heaton at that time was Pete Edwards with whom I had worked at Neville Hill so we had a good relationship. This was perhaps just as well because I used to inadvertently open mail addressed to D.M. Heaton and he would get letters to J. Heaton.

On at least a couple of mornings each week the boss, divisional operating manager Derek Jenkinson would barge into the office and deliver a list of cleaning shortfalls on the unit which he had caught from his home on the Hexham line and occasionally some errant piece of material he had found. I continued this habit when I was at Exeter and used to take a perverse delight in picking up some oily rag from under a table on my morning Exeter-Waterloo stock on its feeder run from Dawlish to Exeter and putting it in a large manila envelope addressed to Laira.

Newcastle Control was behind the times compared to where one might expect it to have been at the turn of the 1980s. It had not converted to the card record system I had disliked at Leeds, almost ten years before, but still used graphs. The section controllers used to sit hunched over a desk with a large train graph rolled out in front of them. This was overlaid with a chinograph transparent covering as I had used at York to graph loco diagrams. The controller wore an earpiece through which he received train running information from reporting points which he would then graph onto the chinograph in a selection of colours depending on the type of train. If something came to a stand its graphed line would of course become horizontal and the colour was changed to red. If there was a long hold-up a succession of trains would be shown in red one behind the other. If you wanted to start single line working or send an assistant engine you knew exactly what was where. Controllers could give accurate advice to signalmen concerning train regulation against a tight budget of tolerated delay. Our allowance between Tyne and Ferryhill was no more than one passenger train delay per week caused by a freight, despite the large number of partially fitted trains to be accommodated.

A Sunday Leamside diversion by-passing Durham as an HST strolls through Shincliffe on the original route to Newcastle.

If there was a major delay between Newcastle and Ferryhill the deputy chief controller (shift manager) would stand up from behind his desk and make a one word announcement, "Leamside" and the word would go out to signalmen, traincrew and station staff that diversions via the original route into Newcastle avoiding Durham were to take place. It was not unusual during these alterations for diverted up trains to follow each other over the border to the Leeds division, south of Northallerton, under 10min late. Admittedly we had a 4min recovery allowance that we jealously guarded to keep our handover figures looking good.

Derek Jenkinson believed in keeping everyone on their toes. If something happened that could have been handled better, or for which no reason was known, he might order an inquiry. I never knew him take one himself but the team had no doubt he would have done had it been an incident with loss of life for instance.

One cause for an ad hoc inquiry happened in the Ferryhill area in the early hours of Wednesday December 1, 1982. Headquarters were obviously unhappy with the explanations offered and Derek Jenkinson wanted word to get round depots and the Control that what had happened was not acceptable. I held a formal inquiry with the assistance of Gerry Frank a Newcastle traction inspector with observers Andy McFadden of the N.U.R. and Bill Ronkesley of A.S.L.E.F. both of whom had fearsome reputations. The area concerned was controlled by the small old-fashioned panel box at Ferryhill under track circuit block regulations. Signal F.451 was the last signal on the down main line before Ferryhill itself and protected the lead at, what we would now term, Ferryhill South Jct to the up and down Stockton-Leamside pair of tracks.

In dense freezing fog at 01.30 No. 47411 working 1S70 21.00 King's Cross-Aberdeen failed and coasted to F.451. It was decided to assist it in rear with 1S37 19.01 King's Cross-Aberdeen premium parcel train which was standing at the signal in rear, F.455. The plan was to propel the failure to Durham where No. 47426 would be waiting, having been dispatched from Gateshead depot. At 02.40 it was reported that the 1S70 and 1S37 had been coupled but it was proving impossible to raise sufficient air pressure to release the brakes. It was therefore decided to send No. 47426 from Durham to F.451 to assist from the front.

As luck would have it the down line was in the possession of the engineers and single line working was in force on the up line. The pilotman was at Tursdale Jct ready to work 1S70 in the wrong direction over the up line so he had to be sent to Durham to authorise 1E41 19.20 Aberdeen-King's Cross to proceed, followed by light diesel No. 47426. The assistant class 47 arrived at Ferryhill at 03.30 and the failed 1S70 was on the move at 04.02.

The passenger train was single manned, the parcel train double manned and the assistant loco was, correctly, also double-manned. The relief driver in charge of No. 47426 stated that when he reached the front of 1S70 he found that the driver's safety device (dsd) had been isolated incorrectly. He put this right and rendered assistance as required.

The responsible officer for the single line working was at Ferryhill box. When he became aware of the failure he asked Control whether he should take his pilotman from Ferryhill to Durham but he was advised not to do so. Later, this was reversed. On return to Ferryhill the build up of traffic was so great that Control asked him to contact the engineering person in charge to give up his possession early but it was 05.15 before this was done.

Observations on the evidence offered reflected no credit on anyone involved. The responsible officer failed to seize the initiative and act as the person in charge of the incident although he was in the best position to do so. He should have given better advice to Control and had taken only a narrow view of his role until late in the proceedings. He should have exerted pressure to have the single line working abandoned as soon as the situation escalated and when he returned to Ferryhill signal box he failed to sign the train register book which contained discrepancies. As for asking where his pilotman should go, his single line working title was the 'Responsible Officer'. The pilotman was his to command.

The Ferryhill signalman (a railwayman since 1940) had sustained a severe leg injury on his way to work which was no doubt a distraction to him and hindered his mobility. While his dedication in taking duty is unquestionable, and demands on his time were considerable, there were omissions from the train register book. He failed to obtain an assurance that 1S70 would not be moved when he authorised the assistant loco to proceed to the front of the train and did not tell the driver of 1S70 personally that this was going to happen. He did not recall and had not recorded the cautioning of the next train through the section after the failure had been cleared, as required by Signalling Regulation 14.

The York driver of 1S70 (joined the railway in 1945) frankly admitted that the failure to create air pressure after the attachment of the assisting train was because he had mistakenly isolated the radiator shutter cock instead of the driver's safety device. He did not protect his train in advance until shortly before the arrival of the assistant loco. The guard of 1S70 (a newcomer with a mere 9yrs service) was uncertain about how his train should be protected and despite testifying that visibility was only 20yds he placed just one detonator as protection, only 100yds from his train. He failed to conduct the assisting train on foot for the last 100yds as he was required to do and then committed the same error when later conducting the assistant loco to the failure.

The Doncaster driver (joined 1941) of the assistant train is believed to have driven with extreme caution from F.455 signal to the rear of the failure but it was concluded that he had not brought his train to a stand when exploding the only detonator and had continued to move until 3-4yds from the failed train without setting down the guard. Although it was not his responsibility, he failed to notice the d.s.d cock had not been isolated when he had chance to do so. His secondman (joined 1962) also failed in that respect.

What of the Gateshead driver who salvaged the situation when he eventually arrived with No. 47426 to assist from the front? This relief driver (or 'passed man' in traditional terms) was less experienced than his fellow drivers (joined 1964) but spotted the error and rectified it. Should he be commended for doing so? Well, yes, but he had also failed to obtain the signalman's personal authority to proceed in the wrong direction to the failed train and to ensure he would find it properly protected. His secondman (another relief driver, joined 1978) condoned this irregularity.

We did not interview the deputy chief controller but considered his written report. The conclusion was: "that he failed to institute, or attempt to institute, a number of alternative strategies to minimise delays including diversions, abandoning single line working, use of locos from freight trains and calling out extra staff. Furthermore the strategy of ordering the assistant locomotive to Durham failed to register the potential seriousness of the delays and the General Appendix instruction to give absolute priority to the clearance of main lines which could have been effected by using the more direct Leamside line unhindered by single line working.

Why was he not called to give evidence? His retirement took place the following day. Born 1926, joined the railway in 1941 and became a deputy chief controller exactly two years before the incident. One might perhaps pause to consider if the appointment had been wise.

The delays were listed in the report in terms of minutes lost between Northallerton and Berwick (on and off the Newcastle Division) or terminating at Newcastle.

1S37 19.10 KX-Aberdeen 181
1S70 21.00 KX-Aberdeen 161
1S79 22.15 KX-Aberdeen 150
1S42 22.05 KX-Aberdeen 144
1N12 22.45 KX-Newcastle 108
1S72 22.30 KX-Edinburgh 120
1E49 00.35 Manchester-Newcastle 91
1E38 19.35 Bristol-Newcastle 82
1S77 23.55 KX-Edinburgh 105
1S38 23.00 KX-Edinburgh 110
1N20 00.05 KX-Newcastle 40
1E41 19.20 Aberdeen-KX 59
1E42 23.20 Edinburgh-KX 70
1E48 22.00 Aberdeen-KX 8

4S86 Nottingham-Coatbridge 140
4S80 Felixstowe-Coatbridge 240
4S85 KX-Edinburgh 209
Total delay: 1918=32hrs

There were a lot of horizontal red lines on the Control graph that night.

No. 31275 passes Ferryhill signal box with a northbound freight on May 19, 1982.
Credit: C.J. Marsden

The report concluded that the delay occurred owing to the failure of loco No. 47411 compounded by the driver of 1S70 failing to isolate the d.s.d. equipment, exacerbated by the lack of action by Control." In addition reference was made to the wholesale breaches of train protection rules. I would be one of the first to admit that an Inquiry chairman sitting in his centrally heated office with a pen poised over his writing pad, coffee mug steaming on the coaster next to his green signalling book and red rule book is in a privileged position compared to ground staff frustrated by defective equipment as delay builds during the early hours enveloped by freezing fog but the irregularities highlighted here amounted to more than misinterpretation or forgetting a detail. Drivers would sometimes say that people who worked in offices, such as their roster clerks, could rub out their errors but they could not do so and I had to agree with them. At least I had some experience of what it was like out on the ground and could appreciate that the thick fog would inhibit normal thought processes. A month later I conducted the Teesport Inquiry and met similar ignorance of Rule Book Section M and raised the need for better tuition and examination on a regional basis but I do not think any steps to rectify the problem were taken.

When I was on the Western conducting rules' exams, for instance, for on call managers, I ensured section M was covered in exhaustive detail. I think the understanding was better from train crews on the Western though but I did not pause at the time to consider why. Another lesson I took away with me from this inquiry was to pursue parallel solutions to failures. If one was then not needed, it could be stood down easily enough. One of the phrases that made my blood run cold if I heard it when walking into an incident control room was "fitters are on their way" especially if expressed with a note of relief in the voice. This did not mean they had the right tools or parts or that they could diagnose a problem and it was always better to send an assisting engine, or whatever was needed, than rely on one solution.

It was not long before I had my own direct involvement in what could have been a long delay. My wife and I were travelling back from Huddersfield to Durham with our cat-in-a-basket, a bit like chicken in a basket and about as edible, when we ground to a halt between Croxdale and Relly Mill, just short of Durham station. We were told that a freight train had failed ahead of us and we would be some time. The prospect of repercussions if it was discovered you were in the vicinity of disruption and had done nothing about it was always uppermost in my mind. If you were on the railway you were a heartbeat away from being on duty. The guard confided that it was a 100-tonne steel wagon train ahead and the brakes were locked on the loco but a fixed pipe breakage made the maintenance controller suspect it could be assisted neither in front nor rear. If fitters came to free the brakes it might be different but the driver said that even if his loco brake was isolated assistance from the front would not be able to free the wagon brakes. No mobile phones then of course so I spoke to the signalman on the signal post telephone and the driver of my Class 46. I seem to think I also spoke to Control in great detail, presumably the signalman linked me through somehow.

I arranged to go up to the rear of the protected steel train and release the wagon brakes using the assistant train. The driver of the steel train and I would then isolate the loco brake and propel the train into the middle road at Durham station. My passenger train could then reverse and drop into the platform and controllers could sort out the failure at their leisure. Having an unbraked vehicle ahead of a train like this was irregular to say the least. The gradient fell steeply into Durham station but then there was a mile or two of level/uphill track through Newton Hall then downhill past Tyne Yard to Low Fell. If a coupling broke between the freight vehicles and the failed loco on the descent to Durham it could be catastrophic. I sought to mitigate the effect by ensuring we had a clear run to Tyne Yard. I reckoned a loco would stop well before then but at least it could be diverted into a dead end in the yard. With this assurance we dropped the train into the middle road at Durham and the Newcastle passenger train went on its way. Yes, if something had gone wrong an Inquiry would have held me responsible and, yes, it was against the rules but in a strictly controlled manner and with an awareness of the consequences.

I suppose one of the other rules I encouraged to be bent concerned the provision of brake vans on passenger trains. There was one occasion that the guard on a Newcastle-Liverpool train failed to unscrew the hand brake in the Bogie Gangwayed (BG) vehicle that was the only brake vehicle on the train. The train entered the station with a loud banging noise from the wheelflat. Presumably the guard had been sitting in a first class compartment for the trip. The train was busy but faced cancellation or a huge delay replacing the brake vehicle. It was decided that the brake was fit to travel but if the guard had any doubts en route he should stop and have the vehicle detached. A nod was as good as a wink to a guilty guard so this was done on the High level Bridge. After all the rule said that a train should have a brake van starting its journey but could proceed if it was detached en route. Word had to be sent to Edge Hill to try to find a replacement of course for the trip back the following day.

Naming ceremony for HST power car No. 43113 'City of Newcastle upon Tyne at Newcastle Central on April 26, 1983. Of the characters mentioned in the book, first on the left is divisional maintenance engineer Phil Crosby, then divisional manager John Thompson and Derek Reeves who assisted on many of my Joint Inquiries, 5th from left is depot manager at Heaton Pete Edwards then operations officer Mike Donnelly. First left in the right hand group is the author looking a little

more sprightly than nowadays then Michael Woods, assistant to the divisional passenger commercial manager.

Durham used to be a regular source of controversial decisions. Every two hours or so a King's Cross Newcastle semi-fast HST was closely followed into Newcastle by a Scottish express HST making a comfortable and convenient connection at Newcastle. It was by no means unusual for the semi-fast to arrive at Durham late with the express on the block behind it. Should we put perhaps ten minutes into the express from signals and then waiting for transferring passengers making their way across or should we break the connection and make passengers wait, two hours normally, for the next train? The answer depended on the likely transfer which varied on the time of day and year. Late afternoon trains were often last services to Northern Scotland for instance. It was usually guesswork because the guard would not have done a call over and we had no phone connection. Telling him at Darlington to let us know at Durham was too late. The connection was often broken, an easy decision for Control but one that made life difficult for platform staff. I used to tell controllers regularly that they did not have to face passengers and convey spurious reasons that had led to their making their remote decisions. Nevertheless that does not mean that all trains should wait around for ever but a rational decision in the light of prevailing circumstances should be made. In my Exeter days Control seemed to be intent on engineering the cancellation of an Exeter-Waterloo train of two-hourly frequency as some kind of political point scoring between the regions and Network SouthEast over how many dedicated locomotives the sector had underwritten. That's the kind of spurious reason I would not like to have to convey to a passenger.

These semi-fast HSTs had an annoying, although irregular, habit of setting off the hot axle box detector alarm adjacent to Tyne Yard box on the approach to Newcastle. It did not happen every day or perhaps even every week then we would get two or three together. The train had to be stopped and examined, often with the Scottish express behind it. No reason was evident. I was discussing this with a guard who was once a catering steward when he said he knew why it was happening. I treated this remark with a degree of circumspection but he explained that the catering crews on terminating trains often drained the kitchen hot water off before arrival at Newcastle and sometimes this must be being done near the detector. It all sounded improbable and readers who know about these things might say it would not trigger the equipment but it was better than any other deduction we had managed to make. We put the word around when we travelled and spoke to the catering managers and the problem disappeared, at least during my time.

We also had a period when I noticed regular slight signal checks near Chester-le-Street. It did not amount to anything that showed up anywhere and probably caused only a ½min delay even to a labouring Class 40 on a Liverpool train. The first once or twice I let it pass but the third time was with No. 40012 'Aureol' on June 18, 1982 which lost a full minute. I searched on the graphs for anything that could have caused it. There was no reason why a signal should have been late being cleared as it was in an automatic section. I noted the number and that it was a yellow aspect clearing up on the approach of the train if I remember correctly. The signal engineers were told and came back saying they had found a fault and rectified it. No delay is too small to be addressed.

Class 40s on Liverpool trains had long been a target of mine. I enjoyed the spectacle they provided and the unequal struggle that occurred if they had more than 'load 8' to keep the Class 46 load 11 schedules but it was not unusual for even an eight coach train to stick at 83mph, or even less, heading south from Darlington. The Newcastle power controllers were a special bunch, each one a character. One was David Tyreman who knew more about North Eastern steam locos than most people who had worked with them for a lifetime, writing some of the detailed histories for the RCTS. Another worked part time for undertakers as a pall bearer and used to work early turn in his funeral gear if he had an afternoon rendezvous to undertake. Occasionally he would break out into song. Perhaps 'The Lord Is My Shepherd' or 'Abide with Me' or even 'Nearer my God to Thee'. All three tunes provided sobering reminders of our mortality.

Each locomotive on the division had a card in a slot. It might be in the bank of 'on repair Gateshead' or 'Tyne Yard' and perhaps it would have a little metal tab on the corner to signify its train heating boiler was not working. It was not unusual for two or three Class 46s to be standing spare at lunchtime prior to an evening job. Neither was it unusual for a Class 46 to have been sent out on a Newcastle-Liverpool job and for a Class 40 to be sent back. The production of a lower power loco in such circumstances was not commonplace because other regions, and for that matter Eastern Divisions, would often snaffle a "good 'un" and send you their rubbish. This was not the case with Class 46s and the London Midland though because most of their depots were not passed to drive the class. Between verses of a depressing hymn the controller might switch some tatty Wigan Class 40 from the inward train to its booked return working and that was that.

In the time I was there I would encourage them to dispatch a spare Class 46 from Gateshead to Heaton depot, where the stock was cleaned prior to return, and take the Class 40 back to Gateshead. The retort would be to the effect of "They sent it us, they can have it back," or "We sent them a perfectly good Class 46 yesterday," or "What can I do with a spare Class 40?" If no one intervened the same wrong loco could work for a full week; 08.05 Liverpool-Newcastle, 13.22 Newcastle Liverpool. On winter mid week days it did not matter too much but in summer and at weekends when 9-11 coaches were the norm it did affect punctuality. Perhaps I was over-influenced by the number of late evening meals I had suffered at the hands of the underpowered locos when I worked at York. I would persist and get my own way because I was responsible for passenger operation on the Division. The reaction of haulage enthusiasts waiting for their favourite Class 40 to bring the stock in from the depot is better imagined than observed. As for the now spare Class 40, there was a fast, light express parcel job to Edinburgh overnight.

When I worked at Headquarters one of my projects was to write a report about the attempts made to rectify wrong loco class and depot allocations. I would review the records in a control office and mark them up. 1 point for right loco class and depot in and out, 2 for wrong loco class in and right loco class out and 3 for wrong loco and depot in and right loco and depot out.....or something on those lines. If someone had been doing the same exercise on those Liverpool trains I would have scored a few bonus points.

There were many occasions at Newcastle, as elsewhere, when you simply used what locos you had, regardless of either class or depot. It was Sunday January 2, 1983 when I was on call and worried about the lack of relief trains from Scotland the day after the New Year holiday. Normally most trains at that time of year would have a relief scheduled but this year some genius or budget-minded boffin (expenditure budget only, never mind future lost revenue) had decided there were to be no reliefs. My mind went back to my training days and the smooth process of booking extra trains at holiday periods.

I went into control, sat at the desk where we did the morning conferences and waited for developments. It was not long before we had our first message from Scotland that an up HST had just left Edinburgh full and standing. We knew we would have a full platform waiting to join it when it reached Newcastle in 1½hrs or so. Just like Neville Hill we had a yard full of Mark 1 stock for the likes of the summer Yarmouth holiday train and football excursions. It was the New Year break so we had a shed full of locos at Gateshead due to the low requirement for holiday period freight. Crews could be a problem because of holidays and perhaps York Headquarters Control would be as difficult as their office-based planning colleagues.

Crews proved not to be the problem we had feared. Perhaps there were spare drivers from the freight working or extra shed & ferry sets that my York colleague had moaned about ten years ago. We ordered a loco to Heaton for a set, announced it as having the same stops as the main train and set it off 10min in front as a Control special. I have forgotten how many times we did that but I would guess at about five. We went out onto the platform advising people to buy their refreshments, where to change if they wanted somewhere odd, scared them to death that their reserved seats might have been occupied on the parent train, even added extra stops if there were a few people wanting somewhere like Stevenage that was not on the schedule of the main train. Gateshead ran out of spare Cass 46s that day. Goodness where the spare crews came from. Perhaps the mileage payments were sufficient incentive to call out drivers to cover. Goodness knows where King's Cross platformed the spare trains or shunted them to the carriage sidings. I suspect one or two trains might in the end have made it no further than Finsbury Park but we kept people moving and we avoided what I believe might have been a public order situation followed by bad publicity about overcrowding and, it would have been construed by the media, safety.

The other major event where overcrowding was feared was the visit of Pope John Paul II to York on May 31, 1982. Vast crowds were anticipated and a comprehensive programme of frequent special trains was planned to run all night. I was on call that week so took the night shift in Control so we could react appropriately to emergencies. I cannot remember the exact train plan but I seem to remember multiple departures every hour with train sets shuttling backwards and forwards. In the end hardly anyone travelled and the trains ran empty making it a lot of wasted work and a missed night's sleep for me.

One morning on my way to work on the dmu I noticed a traction trainee driving and an older driver supervising him.

This was not strictly correct but the normal way of learning and sometimes, as I have said previously, the divisional traction and rolling stock engineer drove the train. The booked route in the case of this train was to cross King Edward Bridge South Jct and enter Newcastle Central's east end bays via the High Level Bridge. King Edward Bridge South Jct was subject to a 20mph permanent speed restriction. Braking was often late because 40mph to 20mph in a dmu could be quickly achieved. But this morning there was no brake application and we bounced across the junction at all of 40mph with the train feeling to take off and land a couple of times. On arrival at Newcastle I challenged the driver (not the trainee) with exceeding the speed limit at King Edward Bridge South Jct, asking him what speed he had been doing. He replied with a non-committal 20mph. I looked incredulous and said something to the effect of "Come on just admit it and save a lot of trouble." He replied, "I was doing 20" and walked off.

I went up to Control as usual and reported the incident, expecting the driver to be relieved of duty before his return working but the divisional maintenance engineer, to whom drivers reported at that time, took hold of the matter. An hour later I was called in by Derek Jenkinson, the divisional operating manager, who was in the process of clearing his desk of all books and phones. He was about to take a disciplinary appeal hearing and he had once had the desk phone thrown at him by an indignant appellant. He also used to hold the hearing as early as possible in the morning considering where the person worked so they did not get a lie-in by making a frivolous appeal

I was asked to sit down and tell him what had happened on my way to work. I related the events. He said ASLEF had registered a complaint that one of their members had been threatened that if he did not admit to something he had not done he would have a lot of trouble. And he wanted an apology. I replied that he was mud-slinging and I would certainly not apologise. Instead, he should be suspended pending discipline if he thought 40mph was 20mph. Derek

Jenkinson said he agreed there was no question of an apology but had I learned my lesson? I was not sure I had but I tried a few platitudes to satisfy him. "Be precise when challenging a driver?" "No." I tried again, "Ensure your facts are accurate before speaking?" "No." I had hardly half finished a third attempt when he interrupted. "No. Hit the buggers before they hit you." The interview was over but I was more than annoyed all day. In fact I still am.

One of the issues which was being pursued when I was at Newcastle was the extension of through working from the likes of Bishop Auckland to Saltburn and Sunderland to Carlisle. In many cases there was no through market to be had and the aim was simply to save diesel units by having fewer turnround margins. In the absolute peak at somewhere like Newcastle this could just save a dmu set with the doubtful savings I have discussed earlier if the depot overheads remained the same and the dmu's overheads had to be redistributed among the rest of the fleet. With the constraints of only three through platforms at Newcastle and two at Darlington the chances of delay were increased compared to slipping into a bay unmolested by main line trains. The process also imported delay from one part of the network to another. My job requirements included maintaining local passenger train punctuality at '90% within 5min' and improving it to 95% so it would counteract my objectives. The only case I could really see was from the Durham Coast to the new Metro Centre being built on the Carlisle line. The direct line from Newcastle to Blaydon Jct via Scotswood Jct had been closed causing more congestion via the Norwood Jct alternative so even the case favouring the development of this market was likely to be to the disadvantage of Newcastle-Sunderland returning commuters.

We also saw the first HSTs on Cross Country and I arranged for the 2+7s to use the west end bay platforms instead of blocking one of the few through ones. I did not measure it though and I was lucky they could just squeeze in. Derek Jenkinson had one day asked if I was sure they could. I had

271

said yes but then anxiously gone out to check. The 16.15 Newcastle Bristol used to be a loco hauled passenger train that conveyed an extra 3 or 4 parcel-carrying vehicles. With the change to an HST the train became two separate ones; a passenger train and a parcel train. There is no need to investigate much further into the question of how rising parcel sector costs outpaced revenue resulting in losing the business.

This is perhaps a suitable point to draw these memories to a close in the same way as they started, with a Joint Inquiry into a plain line derailment this time at Butterwell Opencast site. My views and, I would admit in certain aspects, prejudices about privatisation started to form as early as May 7, 1982 when I chaired an investigation concerning an incident that had occurred on April 23. Butterwell Jct led in the facing direction from the east coast down main line via a crossover onto a single line from the up main line towards the Butterwell Opencast site, some four miles north of Morpeth. My inquiry panel colleagues were Dave Doggett (area civil engineer at Morpeth and future assistant engineer at Exeter), Bill Gilpin (assistant to Derek Reeves on traction and rolling stock) and a Mr. Cook (manager of the Butterwell Opencast Mining Site). In attendance were the usual N.U.R. representative, the general manager of the Opencast Executive track maintenance contractor and the regional works engineer of the Opencast Executive. To be as clear as possible: the track was owned by the National Coal Board (N.C.B.) administered by the opencast executive and managed by the Butterwell site management with a private contractor maintaining the track.

A passing loop for inbound and outbound trains was controlled by the N.C.B. Ashington No. 1 signalman who forwarded empty trains needing the bunker to its operator. At 09.50 Loco No. 37030 entered the Butterwell single line hauling a train of 22 empty unbraked hoppers (TOPS code HTO), forming 9B08 05.15 West Blyth to Butterwell Open Cast, when the Blyth Cambois depot relief driver felt a snatch. He said that train was brought gently to a stand in about 30yds only for him to find the 15th and 16th wagons had become derailed and had run around 550yds in a derailed state. The train's maximum permissible speed at the point of derailment was 15mph but the driver said he was doing only 8mph. I might normally view such a low figure with some scepticism but it was given credence by the guard successfully jumping off to apply handbrakes on the rear hoppers. The driver had been in the footplate grades for 35years but was still graded as a relief driver ('passed man') such was the wait for promotion following closures, dieselisation and single manning.

The traffic manager who attended the site was W. Hunter of Blyth who had joined the railway in 1940. It is worth a moment to reflect that at the time of writing in 2020 his grand-daughter Anna-jane Hunter is director North of England Rail for Network Rail. Bill Hunter checked protection was properly in place, examined the cause of the accident and called for a complete track plot to be made when it was evident the opencast executive was going to claim damages from British Rail for wrecking its track. This was exemplary.

There was no doubt among the British Rail manager's or witnesses about what had happened and why. The key factor was the track plot. The B.R. permanent way supervisor stated that the derailment was caused by flange climbing caused by serious cant deficiencies as steep as 1-in-122 when not even under load. The Warden derailment in the first chapter had a 1-in-239 cross level gradient.

The Butterwell manager was determined not to accept responsibility. If he did so, his firm would have had to pay for the damage to our rolling stock, no doubt a big bill for overtime and lost utilisation as well as foregoing any compensation for his damaged track. He tried every avenue of investigation into potential wagon faults – that the missing axle box had caused the derailment, that the HTO had a scratched side implying an earlier collision, that its springs were broken. All the damage was a result of the accident not its cause. We even traced the wagon movements (with the help of traffic manager Chris

Dickinson who had followed me into my Bradford job). The engineer on site spelt Timken roller bearings as Timpken and I perpetuated the error in my report. Shame on me.

Supervisor Hunter had initiated a search of the line right back to the Blyth coal staiths and found no wagon debris. There had been no collision or damage either. The derailed HTO had left Ashington for West Blyth yard at 16.00 the previous day. The morning of the derailment it had been taken to the staiths and emptied before being taken to Butterwell and derailing at 09.50. The reputation of British Rail was that wagon utilisation was poor but not at Blyth that April morning. When it was suggested the handle damage on the derailed HTO had come from a collision prior to being sent to Butterwell supervisor Hunter said that if it had happened before reaching the staiths the doors could not have been opened and if it had happened during the unloading they could not have been closed. Questioned by Mr. Heaton, "How many years' experience have you had in the Blyth area, supervisor Hunter?" Answer "42½"

I was unable to secure an agreement from the mining manager to the majority's conclusion whatever was said and done. This was followed up in writing and became legally entangled. I consulted Derby Research for as independent an opinion as I could muster, again dealing with the estimable Mike McLoughlin. He believed the train had not been mishandled. There was no evidence of jerking and the buffer-locking was caused by the derailment. There was no evidence of excessive speed, although, I was surprised to hear him say that a vehicle is just as likely to derail on bad track at low speeds as at permitted high speeds. There was no evidence of prior damage to the HTO and both wheel and flange gauges were within tolerances. HTOs are torsionally stiff and susceptible to derail on steep defective cant gradients rounding curves. The track was grossly over-canted and, if on B.R. the track would have been classified as in need of urgent repair. Maintenance procedures were being undertaken that did not correspond with B.R. standards. Staggered rail joints exacerbated the cant deficiency and the change, measured at 12ft apart, from 1-in-122 to 1-in-182 on this curve would produce a clockwise twist which unloaded the front right hand wheel of this vehicle. I suggest it does not get much clearer than that.

The findings were put to the Opencast Executive once again and they continued to refuse to endorse the conclusion. By mid-August it was necessary to leave negotiations to the courts and I signed off the conclusion as "The B.R. members of the panel agreed the cause of the derailment was the track faults which existed." At the time, this was highly irregular. When I heard of the Railtrack organisation to be set up by John Edmonds under privatisation with safety maintenance done entirely by contract, and with many disparate voices capable of denying responsibility, I feared the worst. It happened at Hatfield on October 17, 2000 when a Class 91-hauled express displaced a rail that should have been repaired with the paperwork lost in the system between companies.

12. WESTERN INVADER

I was by now applying for area manager jobs, which I thought was my next logical step. There were a few headquarters' jobs around but nothing that would give me my own patch. One of the unsatisfactory aspects to the promotional process was that a Division could give only one recommendation to an appointing panel. Peter Fearnhead was in front of me in the queue for the exit but he fortunately seemed to have had different priorities. I had done myself no favours by declining to go to Darlington on a lateral move to shut the area down and combine it with Newcastle. I did not get on all that well with the Newcastle area manager Neil Clarke, although I recognised his considerable strengths and later tried to emulate many of them, and I knew I did not get on with most Darlington staff I had met. I really did not want to spend another year closing something down and making myself redundant and did not waste time on thinking what job Darlington might lead me towards. In quick succession, I think on the same vacancy list, I applied for Norwich. Saltley, Shenfield and Exeter. I went to Norwich for interview with the Newcastle Division's recommendation, travelling home with Phillip Benham from the Leeds division. Feedback said I had given a good interview (it rarely said one had done badly though) but the job had gone to Graham Eccles. Graham was the one who left my York office as I arrived there and went on to reach eminence in privatisation. At the time of the interview he was area manager Ipswich and the Ipswich and Norwich jobs were being combined. Not much surprise not to get that then.

Nos. 25239 and 25228 passing Cowley Bridge Jct with a bitumen train from Ellesmere Port to Exeter Riverside on July 21, 1983.   Credit P. Medley

Something similar happened at Saltley where the incumbent local applicant got the job. Too heavily involved with train crew. Specialist needed. Neither was too big a disappointment. Linda did not like the housing scene at Norwich and getting back to Huddersfield to visit relatives could scarcely have been harder. We looked at Solihull and liked it but not the prices. Interviewees at Bristol Divisional office for Exeter ran to double figures from something like 40 odd applicants. The front runner was the now late Charles Nicholls who was area manager at Plymouth with a pedigree of Great Western senior manager relatives. I was told he had visited the area manager's office and listed what improvements would be necessary to make it comfortable. I got the job and made no alterations.

A rare shot at Aller Jct, not only because of the Devon snow but also because these clayhood wagons were unusual outside Cornwall by the time this photo was taken on January 19, 1985. Loco Nos. 37230 and 37207 are hauling ball clay from the Heathfield branch bound for Fowey.   *Credit P. Medley*

The word was that they had appointed someone who would go in, make a clean sweep and get out. As for this 'wise man from the east' (heavy sarcasm) there was no chance of such an ambitious young man succumbing to the 'graveyard of ambition' tag. I had been drafted in to replace Derek Lewis who was much loved by his staff but who had, I think it fair to say, allowed some standards to drop. There had just been a national scandal over a delay owing to a Tiverton Jct signalman being sound asleep under the affluence of incohol and that was only the tip of the iceberg. The operations manager had been moved out to a job of lesser responsibility at Newton Abbot, on my patch, and the budget was in a mess. No change there then?

I am not going to diverge into a long narrative about events at Exeter before my diary started except to mention a couple of points. I had been told by my boss to hit drivers before they hit me. I had no intention of even trying to do that because I had already discovered they could punch harder than I could. I was determined on two counts though. I knew I was going to be able to recognise all 145 drivers very soon in my tenure. I could not bear to walk along the platform wondering if the person coming the other way was an Old Oak, Plymouth, or Exeter driver. And I was determined to ensure I communicated with drivers directly and not rely on the local staff representatives to interpret my words for me. I made my first meeting with them a week after I had started instead of the day after. I ate my sandwiches in the supervisors' office and wandered in and out of the lobby. I rode home in the cab of a Class 33 on my local service to Dawlish. I travelled everywhere on the area by train, except remote signalboxes such as Somerton, half way from Taunton to Castle Cary, and often in the cab as I went back and forth. Exeter had a surprisingly high proportion of London work because Plymouth drivers at that time did not work through.

Hastings line narrow-bodied No. 33206 at Barnstaple with the 15.26 from Exeter St. David's on July 28, 1984, before signalling rationalisation took place.
Credit: P. Medley

After a week I met the drivers' LDC and discovered the most professional and pleasant group of staff representatives with whom I ever worked. They were no pushovers but they had the depot's health at heart rather than individual drivers. If an Exeter driver put a foot out of line they would get a rocket from the LDC before one from my train crew assistant, Vic Bragg who had crewed ambulance trains after the Dunkirk evacuation. My deputy was operations manager Bernard Price who had worked the Shrewsbury boxes in his youth and who would take no lip from anyone even at the legendary Exeter West signal box.

The sectional council reps at Exeter were more than suspicious of me and had me marked down as someone who would cut, burn and run. I had not been there long when we were given no choice but to make a 10 percent budget cut even if it impacted on the basics of the railway. Most of my costs were in a way fixed. You could not cut out 10% of drivers' jobs without cutting a lot of train services. I cut some night shift signalboxes out where the costs were disproportionate and would not work rest days at the likes of Somerton where relief staff costs and the infamous Spanish custom of 'walking time payments' were eye-watering.

The first passenger train at Okehampton since June 3, 1972. A special train ran on May 25, 1985 formed of Class 118 dmu Nos. 51309/59476/51324. Thirty-five years later permanent reopening was still under consideration. Credit: P. Medley

There was delay to overnight summer Saturday down trains and reliefs from Paddington on the B&H but I had structured my response to the budget cuts into three columns. Cuts I would make immediately, cuts I would make unless instructed not to do so and cuts that I would not make unless specifically instructed to do so. The first ones were existing inefficiencies, the second ones would hurt the railway more than they would save it money and the latter group would cause permanent damage but were the only way of reaching the target. I was told this was the best submission ever sent to Western H.Q. from an area. Wise men from the east indeed! I overcame a misrepresentation programme from the N.U.R. and sought to re-establish operating discipline. I charged a driver with abandoning his train on a running line without detonator protection when he left his Speedlink train at Taunton and caught the 'sleepers' home when he had been refused a run in front of the overnight express. I was advised not to do it because it would be seen as a flexible rostering dispute but I stuck to the rule book for justification. Abandonment of his train within a block section without protection I had picked on one of the most conscientious drivers on the depot and one of the most pleasant. He still sends me a Christmas card though.

I had been there less than 18months when I was invited to go to Paddington as a 34yr old area manager. The reasons are in the 'Area Manager's Diary books' but I was told by the regional personnel manager that 'No-one has ever refused Paddington." When I related this to a former Western deputy general manager well after both our retirements he laughed heartily. I asked him what had amused him. He replied, "We could never get anyone to go there."

On April 11, 1984 a special train was run to Exeter City Basin to mark the acquisition of the bitumen plant by Colas Roads Ltd. using the Rail Ambassador set hauled by No. 33014, seen here on the stub of the former Heathfield line.
Credit: P. Medley

The aim of this book has been to show the defeats and a few victories learnt during an admittedly foreshortened railway career. The process was incessant. On the railway, as in life generally, only a fool stops learning.

BY THE SAME AUTHOR

A series of diaries written at the time showing how the railway was run in the 1980s; the incidents, the personalities, the successes and the failures.

THE AREA MANAGER'S DIARY VOLUME 1 1986/7

THE AREA MANAGER'S DIARY VOLUME 2 1987/8

THE AREA MANAGER'S DIARY VOLUME 3 1988/9

THE AREA MANAGER'S DIARY VOLUME 4 1989/90

And a historical novel set in the Victorian era with frequent flash backs to the 1745 Jacobite campaign.

FASSIFERN

A Highland Railway ship is hi-jacked on its voyage from Strome Ferry to the Isle of Skye. The hostages find they have much in common, but widely different views of their forebears in the Jacobite Rebellion. Heroic or perfidious? Many generations later in Victorian Scotland will there be a price to be paid?

All titles available on Amazon in paperback or e-book format
Prices include free post and packaging

Printed in Great Britain
by Amazon

33954736R00159